Microsoft® PowerPoint® 2002

Illustrated Introductory

David W. Beskeen

COURSE TECHNOLOGY
THOMSON LEARNING™

Australia • Canada • Mexico • Singapore • Spain • United Kingdom • United States

COURSE TECHNOLOGY
THOMSON LEARNING™

Microsoft® PowerPoint® 2002 - Illustrated Introductory

David W. Beskeen

Managing Editor:
Nicole Jones Pinard

Product Manager:
Emily Heberlein

Associate Product Manager:
Emeline Elliott

Production Editor:
Jennifer Goguen

Developmental Editor:
Katherine T. Pinard

Editorial Assistant:
Christina Kling Garrett

QA Manuscript Reviewers:
John Freitas, Ashlee Welz, Alex White, Harris Bierhoff, Serge Palladino, Holly Schabowski, Jeff Schwartz

Text Designer:
Joseph Lee, Black Fish Design

Composition House:
GEX Publishing Services

Illustrated Series Vision

Teaching and writing about computer applications can be extremely rewarding and challenging. How do we engage students and keep their interest? How do we teach them skills that they can easily apply on the job? As we set out to write this book, our goals were to develop a textbook that:

▶ works for a beginning student

▶ provides varied, flexible, and meaningful exercises and projects to reinforce the skills

▶ serves as a reference tool

▶ makes your job as an educator easier, by providing resources above and beyond the textbook to help you teach your course

Our popular, streamlined format is based on advice from instructional designers and customers. This flexible design presents each lesson on a two-page spread, with step-by-step instructions on the left, and screen illustrations on the right. This signature style, coupled with high-caliber content, provides a comprehensive yet manageable introduction to Microsoft PowerPoint 2002—it is a teaching package for the instructor and a learning experience for the student.

ACKNOWLEDGMENTS

It has, once again, been a pleasure working with all the talented people at Course Technology. I would like to especially thank Katherine Pinard who has worked hard on my chapters to make them better and easier to understand. I would also like to thank my family, Karen and the three J's, for being so understanding during the long hours of writing.

Thanks also to the reviewers who provided feedback and ideas to us: Brenda Jacobsen and Rick Sheridan.

David W. Beskeen
and the Illustrated Team

Preface

Welcome to *Microsoft PowerPoint 2002–Illustrated Introductory*. Each lesson in the book contains elements pictured to the right in the sample two-page spread.

► How is the book organized?
The book is organized into eight units on PowerPoint, covering creating, modifying, and enhancing a presentation, as well as creating charts, embedding and linking objects, and using advanced features.

► What kinds of assignments are included in the book? At what level of difficulty?
The lesson assignments use MediaLoft, a fictional chain of bookstore cafés, as the case study. The assignments on the blue pages at the end of each unit increase in difficulty. Project files and case studies, with many international examples, provide a great variety of interesting and relevant business applications for skills. Assignments include:

● **Concepts Reviews** include multiple choice, matching, and screen identification questions.

● **Skills Reviews** provide additional hands-on, step-by-step reinforcement.

● **Independent Challenges** are case projects requiring critical thinking and application of the skills learned in the unit. The Independent Challenges increase in difficulty, with the first Independent Challenge in each unit being the easiest (most step-by-step with detailed instructions). Independent Challenges 2 and 3 become increasingly open-ended, requiring more independent thinking and problem solving.

● **E-Quest Independent Challenges** are case projects with a Web focus. E-Quests require the use of the World Wide Web to conduct research to complete the project.

● **Visual Workshops** show a completed file and require that the file be created without any step-by-step guidance, involving problem solving and an independent application of the unit skills.

Each 2-page spread focuses on a single skill.

Concise text that introduces the basic principles in the lesson and intergrates the brief case study (indicated by the paintbrush icon).

Unit C
PowerPoint 2002

Adding and Arranging Text

Using the advanced text-editing capabilities of PowerPoint, you can easily add, insert, or rearrange text. The PowerPoint slide layouts allow you to enter text in prearranged text placeholders. If these text placeholders don't provide the flexibility you need, you can use the Text Box button on the Drawing toolbar to create your own text objects. With the Text Box button, you can create two types of text objects: a text label, used for a small phrase where text doesn't automatically wrap to the next line inside the box; and a word-processing box, used for a sentence or paragraph where the text wraps inside the boundaries of the box. Maria has a slide that contains information on the typical cycle of a product. Now, she uses the Text Box button to create a word-processing box to enter a label for the information on the slide.

Steps

1. In the Slides tab, click the **Slide 4 thumbnail**

2. Click the **Text Box button** 📰 on the Drawing toolbar
   The pointer changes to ↓.

QuickTip
To create a text label in which text doesn't wrap, click 📰, position ↓ where you want to place the text, then click once and enter the text.

3. Position ↓ about 1" from the left side of the slide, above the top of the chart on the slide, then drag toward the right side of the slide to create a word-processing box
   Your screen should look similar to Figure C-12. When you begin dragging, an outline of the box appears, indicating how wide a text object you are drawing. After you release the mouse button, an insertion point appears inside the text object, ready to accept text.

4. Type **Market, players, shifts and competition**
   Notice that the word-processing box increases in size as your text wraps inside the object. There is a mistake in the text. It should read "Market shifts."

5. Double-click the word **shifts** to select it

QuickTip
You also can use the Cut and Paste buttons on the Standard toolbar and the Cut and Paste commands on the Edit menu to move a word.

6. Position the pointer on top of the selected word and press and hold the mouse button
   The pointer changes to ⬚.

7. Drag the word **shifts** to the right of the word **Market** in the text box, then release the mouse button
   A dotted insertion line appears as you drag, indicating where PowerPoint will place the word when you release the mouse button. The word "shifts" moves next to the word "Market."

TABLE C-1: Color scheme elements

scheme element	description
Background color	Color of the slide's canvas, or background
Text and lines color	Used for text and drawn lines; contrasts with the background color
Shadows color	Color of the shadow of the text or other object; generally a darker shade of the background color
Title text color	Used for slide title; like the text and line colors, contrasts with the background color
Fills color	Contrasts with both the background and the text and line colors
Accent colors	Colors used for other objects on slides, such as bullets
Accent and hyperlink colors	Colors used for accent objects and for hyperlinks you insert
Accent and followed hyperlink color	Color used for accent objects and for hyperlinks after they have been clicked

► POWERPOINT C-10 **MODIFYING A PRESENTATION**

Hints as well as troubleshooting advice, right where you need it – next to the step itself.

Quickly accessible summaries of key terms, toolbar buttons, or keyboard alternatives connected with the lesson material. Students can refer easily to this information when working on their own projects at a later time.

Every lesson features large, full-color representations of what the screen should look like as students complete the numbered steps.

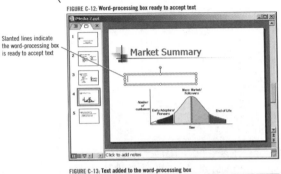

FIGURE C-12: Word-processing box ready to accept text

Slanted lines indicate the word-processing box is ready to accept text

Market Summary

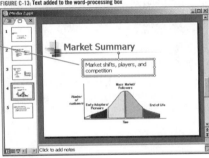

FIGURE C-13: Text added to the word-processing box

Your text might wrap differently depending on the size of your word-processing box

Market Summary

Market shifts, players, and competition

Revising a Presentation

You can send a copy of a presentation over the Internet to others for them to review, edit, and add comments. To send your presentation out for review, you can use Microsoft Outlook, which automatically tracks changes made by reviewers, or you can use any other compatible e-mail program. To send a presentation to reviewers using Outlook, click File on the menu bar, point to Send To, then click Mail Recipient (for Review). Outlook opens and a "Review Request" e-mail with the PowerPoint presentation attached to it is automatically created for you to send to reviewers. Reviewers can use any version of PowerPoint to review, edit, and comment on their copy of your presentation. Once a reviewer is finished with the presentation and sends it back to you, you can combine their changes and comments with your original presentation using PowerPoint's Compare and Merge Presentations feature. When you do this, the Revisions task pane opens with commands that allow you to accept or reject reviewers' changes.

Clues to Use boxes provide concise information that either expands on the major lesson skill or describes an independent task that in some way relates to the major lesson skill.

The pages are numbered according to unit. C indicates the unit, 11 indicates the page.

▶ Is this book MOUS Certified?

Microsoft PowerPoint 2002 – Illustrated Introductory covers the Comprehensive objectives for PowerPoint and has received certification approval as courseware for the MOUS program. See the inside front cover for more information on other Illustrated titles meeting MOUS certification.

The first page of each unit includes ⌐MOUS⌐ symbols to indicate which skills covered in the unit are MOUS skills. A grid in the back of the book lists all the exam objectives and cross-references them with the lessons and exercises.

▶ What online content solutions are available to accompany this book?

Visit www.course.com for more information on our online content for Illustrated titles. Options include:

MyCourse.com

Need a quick, simple tool to help you manage your course? Try MyCourse.com, the easiest to use, most flexible syllabus and content management tool available. MyCourse.com offers you brand new content, including Topic Reviews, Extra Case Projects, and Quizzes, to accompany this book.

WebCT

Course Technology and WebCT have partnered to provide you with the highest quality online resources and Web-based tools for your class. Course Technology offers content for this book to help you create your WebCT class, such as a suggested Syllabus, Lecture Notes, Practice Test questions, and more.

Blackboard

Course Technology and Blackboard have also partnered to provide you with the highest quality online resources and Web-based tools for your class. Course Technology offers content for this book to help you create your Blackboard class, such as a suggested Syllabus, Lecture Notes, Practice Test questions, and more.

PowerPoint 2002

Instructor Resources

The Instructor's Resource Kit (IRK) CD is Course Technology's way of putting the resources and information needed to teach and learn effectively into your hands. All the components are available on the IRK, (pictured below), and many of the resources can be downloaded from www.course.com.

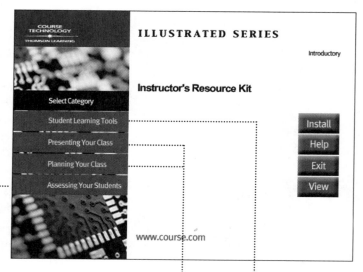

ASSESSING YOUR STUDENTS

Solution Files
Solution Files are Project Files completed with comprehensive sample answers. Use these files to evaluate your students' work. Or distribute them electronically or in hard copy so students can verify their own work.

ExamView
ExamView is a powerful testing software package that allows you to create and administer printed, computer (LAN-based), and Internet exams. ExamView includes hundreds of questions that correspond to the topics covered in this text, enabling students to generate detailed study guides that include page references for further review. The computer-based and Internet testing components allow students to take exams at their computers, and also save you time by grading each exam automatically.

PRESENTING YOUR CLASS

Figure Files
Figure Files contain all the figures from the book in .jpg format. Use the figure files to create transparency masters or in a PowerPoint presentation.

STUDENT TOOLS

Project Files and Project Files List
To complete most of the units in this book, your students will need **Project Files**. Put them on a file server for students to copy. The Project Files are available on the Instructor's Resource Kit CD-ROM, the Review Pack, and can also be downloaded from www.course.com.

Instruct students to use the **Project Files List** at the end of the book. This list gives instructions on copying and organizing files.

PLANNING YOUR CLASS

Instructor's Manual
Available as an electronic file, the Instructor's Manual is quality-assurance tested and includes unit overviews, detailed lecture topics for each unit with teaching tips, comprehensive sample solutions to all lessons and end-of-unit material, and extra Independent Challenges. The Instructor's Manual is available on the Instructor's Resource Kit CD-ROM, or you can download it from www.course.com.

Sample Syllabus
Prepare and customize your course easily using this sample course outline (available on the Instructor's Resource Kit CD-ROM).

SAM, Skills Assessment Manager for Microsoft Office XP
SAM is the most powerful Office XP assessment and reporting tool that will help you gain a true understanding of your students' proficiency in Microsoft Word, Excel, Access, and PowerPoint 2002. (Available separately from the IRK CD.)

TOM, Training Online Manager for Microsoft Office XP
TOM is Course Technology's MOUS-approved training tool for Microsoft Office XP. Available via the World Wide Web and CD-ROM, TOM allows students to actively learn Office XP concepts and skills by delivering realistic practice through both guided and self-directed simulated instruction.

Brief Contents

Contents

PowerPoint 2002

Contents

Creating a Presentation   B-1

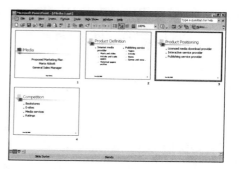

Modifying a Presentation   C-1

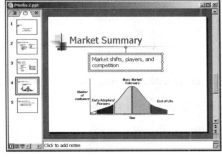

Enhancing a Presentation   D-1

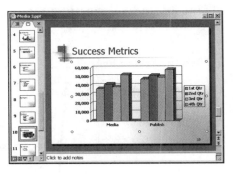

Contents

Customizing Your Presentation   E-1

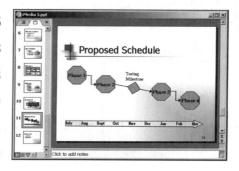

Enhancing Charts   F-1

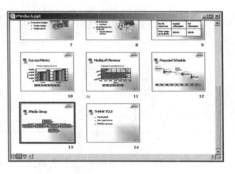

Working with Embedded and Linked Objects and Hyperlinks   G-1

Contents

Using Advanced Features   H-1

Read This Before You Begin

Software Information and Required Installation

This book was written and tested using Microsoft Office XP - Professional Edition, with a typical installation on Microsoft Windows 2000, with Internet Explorer 5.0 or higher. There are several instances where, in order to cover a software feature clearly, an additional feature not part of the typical installation is referenced. To insure that all the steps and exercises can be completed as written, make sure the following features are available before beginning these units:

- PowerPoint Unit A (page A-9): Using AutoContent Wizards (Clues to Use)
- PowerPoint Unit B (page B-5): Using Speech Recognition (Clues to Use)
- PowerPoint Unit C (page C-14): Converter feature to import text from Word into PowerPoint

What are Project Files?

To complete many of the units in this book, you need to use Project Files. You use a Project File, which contains a partially completed document used in an exercise, so you don't have to type in all the information you need in the document. Your instructor will either provide you with a copy of the Project Files or ask you to make your own copy. Detailed instructions on how to organize your files, as well as a complete listing of all the files you'll need and will create, can be found in the back of the book (look for the yellow pages) in the Project Files List.

If you are using floppy disks to organize your files, you will need one floppy disk for each unit for Units A-F. Because the files created in Unit G can be very large, you will need to organize the files onto 7 floppy disks if you are completing all the exercises. In Unit H, you will need to have access to a hard drive in order to save the files created in the lessons. You can organize all your completed files onto floppy disks. Please see the Project Files List for more information.

Why is my screen different from the book?

1. Your Desktop components and some dialog box options might be different if you are using an operating system other than Windows 2000

2. Depending on your computer hardware capabilities and the Windows Display settings on your computer, you may notice the following differences:
- Your screen may look larger or smaller because of your screen resolution (the height and width of your screen)
- The colors of the title bar in your screen may be a solid blue

3. Depending on your Office settings, your toolbars may display on a single row and your menus may display with a shortened list of frequently used commands. Office menus and toolbars can modify themselves to your working style by displaying only the most frequently used buttons and menu commands.

Toolbars on one row

To view buttons not currently displayed, click a Toolbar Options button  at the end of either the Standard or Formatting toolbar. To view the full list of menu commands, click the double arrow at the bottom of the menu.

In order to have your toolbars display on two rows, showing all buttons, and to have the full menus display, you must turn off the personalized menus and toolbars feature. Click Tools on the menu bar, Click Customize, select the show Standard and Formatting toolbars on two rows and Always show full menus check boxes on the Options tab, then click Close. This book assumes you are displaying toolbars on two rows and full menus.

Toolbars on two rows

Getting
Started with PowerPoint 2002

Objectives

► **Define presentation software**
► **Start PowerPoint 2002**
► **View the PowerPoint window**
ᴸᴹᴼᵁˢ⌐ ► **Use the AutoContent Wizard**
ᴸᴹᴼᵁˢ⌐ ► **View a presentation**
ᴸᴹᴼᵁˢ⌐ ► **Save a presentation**
► **Get Help**
ᴸᴹᴼᵁˢ⌐ ► **Print and close the file, and exit PowerPoint**

Microsoft PowerPoint 2002 is a presentation program that transforms your ideas into professional, compelling presentations. With PowerPoint, you can create individual slides and display them as an electronic slide show on your computer, video projector, or even via the Internet. ✐ Maria Abbott is the general sales manager at MediaLoft, a nationwide chain of bookstore cafés that sells books, CDs, and videos. Maria needs to familiarize herself with the basics of PowerPoint and learn how to use PowerPoint to create professional presentations.

Defining Presentation Software

Presentation software is a computer program you can use to organize and present information. Whether you are giving a sales pitch or explaining your company's goals and accomplishments, presentation software can help make your presentation effective and professional. You can use PowerPoint to create presentations, as well as notes for the presenter and handouts for the audience. Table A-1 explains the items you can create using PowerPoint. ◆━━━ Maria wants to create a presentation that explains a new advertising campaign that MediaLoft is developing. She is not familiar with PowerPoint, so she gets right to work exploring its capabilities. Figure A-1 shows a handout she created using a word processor for a recent presentation. Figure A-2 shows how the same handout might look in PowerPoint.

Maria can easily complete the following tasks using PowerPoint:

▶ **Present information in a variety of ways**
With PowerPoint, you can present information using a variety of methods. For example, you can print handout pages or an outline of your presentation for your audience, or you can display your presentation as an electronic slide show on your computer, using either a projection machine or the Internet.

▶ **Enter and edit data easily**
Using PowerPoint, you can enter and edit data quickly and efficiently. When you need to change a part of your presentation, you can use the advanced word-processing and outlining capabilities of PowerPoint to edit your content rather than re-create it.

▶ **Change the appearance of information**
PowerPoint has many features that can transform the way text, graphics, and slides look. By exploring these capabilities, you will discover how easy it is to change the appearance of your presentation.

▶ **Organize and arrange information**
Once you start using PowerPoint, you won't have to spend much time making sure your information is correct and in the right order because, with PowerPoint you can quickly and easily rearrange and modify any piece of information in your presentation.

▶ **Incorporate information from other sources**
Often, when you create presentations, you use information from other sources. With PowerPoint, you can import information from spreadsheet, database, and word-processing files prepared in programs such as Microsoft Excel, Microsoft Access, Microsoft Word, and Corel WordPerfect, as well as graphics from a variety of sources.

▶ **Show a presentation on any computer running Windows 2000 or Windows 98**
PowerPoint has a powerful feature called the PowerPoint Viewer, which you can use to show your presentation on computers running Windows 2000 or Windows 98 that do not have PowerPoint installed. The PowerPoint Viewer displays a presentation as an on-screen slide show.

FIGURE A-1: Traditional handout

- Marketing 2003
  - Maria Abbott

- Marketing Summary
  - Market: past, present, and future
    - Review changes in market share
    - Leadership
    - Market Shifts
    - Costs
    - Pricing and competition

- Product Definition
  - Personal ad space in e-commerce market

- Competition
  - The competitive landscape
    - The players
    - Strengths and weaknesses
    - Product ratings

FIGURE A-2: PowerPoint handout

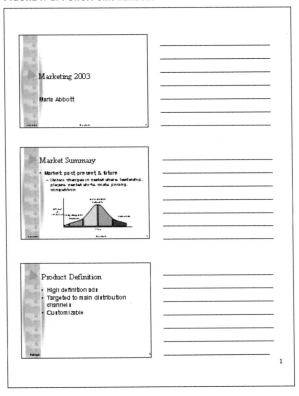

TABLE A-1: Ways to present information using PowerPoint

item	use
On-screen presentations	Run a slide show directly from your computer
Web presentations	Broadcast a presentation on the Web or on an intranet that others can view, complete with video and audio
Online meetings	View or work on a presentation with your colleagues in real time
Color overheads	Print PowerPoint slides directly to transparencies on your color printer
Black-and-white overheads	Print PowerPoint slides directly to transparencies on your black-and-white printer
Notes	Print notes that help you remember points about each slide when you speak to a group
Audience handouts	Print handouts with two, three, or six slides on a page
Outline pages	Print the outline of your presentation to show the main points

Starting PowerPoint 2002

To start PowerPoint, you must first start Windows, and then click the Start button on the taskbar and point to the Programs folder, which usually contains the Microsoft PowerPoint program icon. If the Microsoft PowerPoint icon is not in the Programs folder, it might be in a different location on your computer. If you are using a computer on a network, you might need to use a different starting procedure. ◆━━━ Maria starts PowerPoint to familiarize herself with the program.

Steps

1. **Make sure your computer is on and the Windows desktop is visible**
   If any program windows are open, close or minimize them.

2. **Click the Start button on the taskbar, then point to Programs**
   The Programs menu opens, showing a list of icons and names for all your programs, as shown in Figure A-3. Your screen might look different, depending on which programs are installed on your computer.

Trouble?

If you have trouble finding Microsoft PowerPoint on the Programs menu, check with your instructor or technical support person.

3. **Click Microsoft PowerPoint on the Programs menu**
   PowerPoint starts, and the PowerPoint window opens, as shown in Figure A-4.

Creating a PowerPoint shortcut icon on the desktop

You can make it easier to start PowerPoint by placing a shortcut on the desktop. To create the shortcut, click the Start button, then point to Programs. On the Programs menu, point to Microsoft PowerPoint, then right-click Microsoft PowerPoint. In the shortcut menu that appears, point to Send To, then click Desktop (create shortcut). Windows places a shortcut icon named Microsoft PowerPoint on your desktop. In the future, you can start PowerPoint by simply double-clicking this icon, instead of using the Start menu. You can edit or change the name of the shortcut by right-clicking the shortcut icon, clicking Rename on the shortcut menu, and then editing as you would any item name in Windows. If you are working in a computer lab, you may not be allowed to place shortcuts on the desktop. Check with your instructor or network administrator before attempting to add a shortcut.

FIGURE A-3: Programs menu

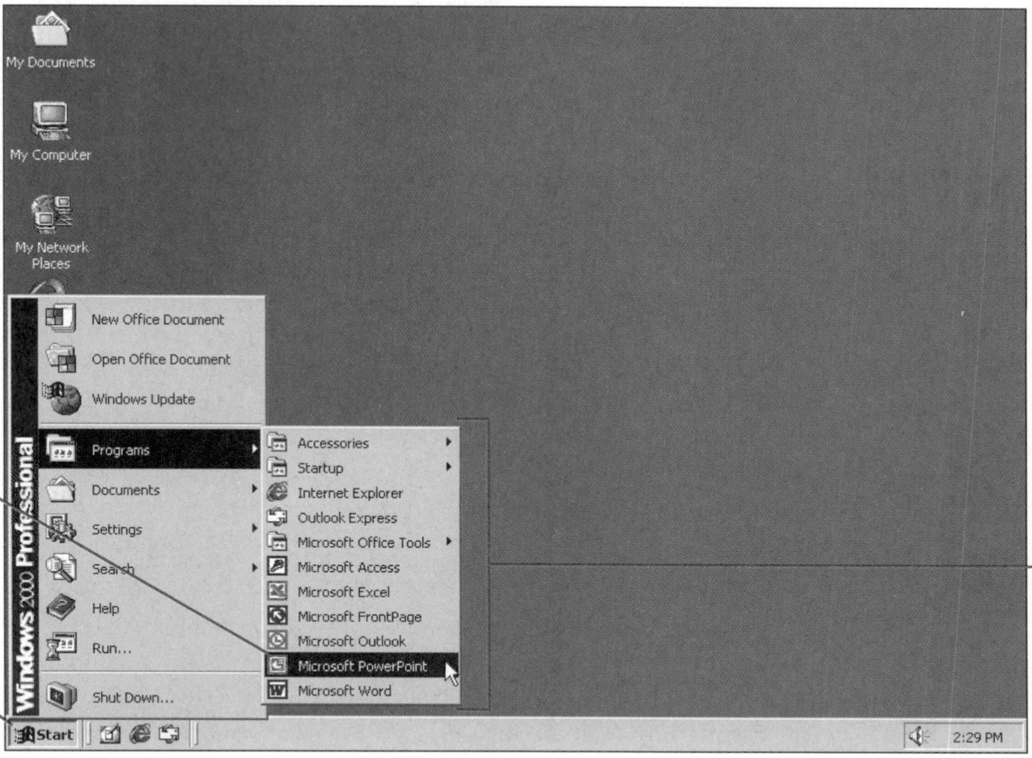

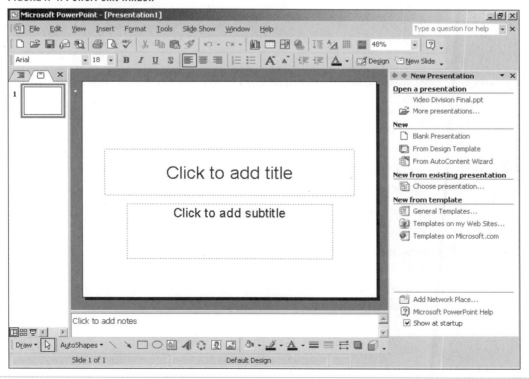

Microsoft
PowerPoint
program

Your list of
programs may
be different

Start button

FIGURE A-4: PowerPoint window

Viewing the PowerPoint Window

When you first open PowerPoint, a blank slide appears in the PowerPoint window. PowerPoint has different **views** that allow you to see your presentation in different forms. By default, the PowerPoint window opens in **Normal view**, which is the primary view that you use to write, edit, and design your presentation. Normal view is divided into three areas called **panes**: the pane on the left containing the Outline and Slide tabs, the slide pane, and the notes pane. You move around in each pane by using its scroll bars. The PowerPoint window and the specific parts of Normal view are described below. 　　　　Maria examines the elements of the PowerPoint window. Find and compare the elements described below, using Figure A-5 as a guide.

Details

▶ The **title bar** contains the program name, the title of the presentation, a program Control Menu button, resizing buttons, and the program Close button.

▶ The **menu bar** contains the names of the menus you use to choose PowerPoint commands, as well as the Ask a Question box and the Close Window button.

▶ The **Standard toolbar** contains buttons for commonly used commands, such as copying and pasting. The **Formatting toolbar** contains buttons for the most frequently used formatting commands, such as changing font type and size. The toolbars on your screen may be displayed on one line instead if two. See the Clues to Use for more information on how toolbars are displayed.

▶ The **Outline tab** displays your presentation text in the form of an outline, without graphics. In this tab, it is easy to move text on or among slides by dragging text to reorder the information.

▶ The **Slides tab** displays the slides of your presentation as small images, called **thumbnails**. You can quickly navigate through the slides in your presentation using this tab. You can also add, delete, or rearrange slides on this tab.

▶ The **slide pane** contains the current slide in your presentation, including all text and graphics.

▶ The **notes pane** is used to type notes that reference a slide's content. You can print these notes and refer to them when you make a presentation or print them as handouts and give them to your audience. The notes pane is not visible to the audience when you give a slide presentation.

▶ The **task pane** contains sets of hyperlinks for commonly used commands. The commands are grouped into 10 different task panes. The commands include creating new presentations, opening existing ones, searching for documents, and using the Office clipboard. You can also perform basic formatting tasks from the task pane such as changing the slide layout, slide design, color scheme, or slide template of a presentation.

▶ The **Drawing toolbar**, located at the bottom of the PowerPoint window, contains buttons and menus that let you create lines, shapes, and special effects.

▶ The **view buttons**, at the bottom of the Outline tab and Slides tab area, allow you to quickly switch between PowerPoint views.

▶ The **status bar**, located at the bottom of the PowerPoint window, shows messages about what you are doing and seeing in PowerPoint, including which slide you are viewing.

FIGURE A-5: Presentation window in Normal view

Title bar
Menu bar
Outline tab
Slides tab
Slide pane
Notes pane
View buttons

Ask a Question box
Standard toolbar
Formatting toolbar
Task pane
Drawing toolbar
Status bar

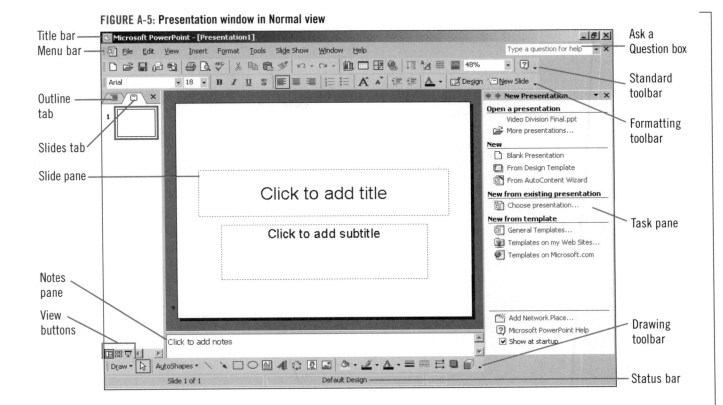

Toolbars in PowerPoint 2002

PowerPoint 2002 offers personalized toolbars and menus, which modify themselves to your working style. When you use personalized toolbars and menus, the Standard and Formatting toolbars appear on the same row and display only the most frequently used buttons. To use a button that is not visible on a toolbar, click the Toolbar Options button ⁘ at the end of the toolbar, and then click the button that you wish to appear on the Toolbar Options list. As you work, PowerPoint adds the buttons you use to the visible toolbars and drops the buttons you haven't used in a while to the Toolbar Options list. Similarly, PowerPoint menus adjust to your work habits, so that the commands you use most often appear on shortened menus. To view additional menu commands, click the double arrows at the bottom of a menu.

The lessons in this book assume you have turned off personalized menus and toolbars and are working with all menu commands and toolbar buttons displayed. To turn off personalized toolbars and menus so that you can easily find the commands that are referenced in this book, click Tools on the menu bar, click Customize, select the Show Standard and Formatting toolbars on two rows and Always show full menus checkboxes on the Options tab, and then click Close. The Standard and Formatting toolbars will then appear on separate rows and display all the buttons, and the menus will display the complete list of menu commands. (You can also quickly display the toolbars on two rows by clicking either Toolbar Options button and then clicking Show Buttons on Two Rows.)

Using the AutoContent Wizard

The quickest way to create a presentation is with the AutoContent Wizard. A **wizard** is a series of steps that guides you through a task (in this case, creating a presentation). Using the AutoContent Wizard, you choose a presentation type from the wizard's list of sample presentations. Then you indicate what type of output you want. Next, you type the information for the title slide and the footer. The AutoContent Wizard then creates a presentation with sample text you can use as a guide to help formulate the major points of your presentation. ✐ Maria decides to start her presentation by opening the AutoContent Wizard.

Steps 1234

1. In the New Presentation task pane, point to the **From AutoContent Wizard hyperlink** under New

The mouse pointer changes to 🖑. The pointer changes to this shape any time it is positioned over a hyperlink.

> **Trouble?**
>
> If the Office Assistant appears and asks if you would like help, click No.

2. Click the **From AutoContent Wizard hyperlink**

The AutoContent Wizard dialog box opens, as shown in Figure A-6. The left section of the dialog box outlines the contents of the AutoContent Wizard, and the text in the right section explains the current wizard screen.

3. Click **Next**

The Presentation type screen appears. This screen contains category buttons and types of presentations. Each presentation type contains suggested text for a particular use. By default, the presentation types in the General category are listed.

4. Click the category **Projects**, click **Reporting Progress or Status** in the list on the right, then click **Next**

The Presentation style screen appears, asking you to choose an output type.

5. If necessary, click the **On-screen presentation option button** to select it, then click **Next**

The Presentation options screen requests information that will appear on the title slide of the presentation and in the footer at the bottom of each slide.

6. Click in the **Presentation title text box**, then type **New Ad Campaign**

7. Press **[Tab]**, then type your name in the Footer text box

8. Make sure the **Date last updated** and **Slide number check boxes** are selected

9. Click **Next**, then click **Finish**

The AutoContent Wizard opens the presentation based on the Reporting Progress or Status presentation type you chose. Sample text for each slide is listed on the left in the Outline tab, and the title slide appears on the right side of the screen. A text box with information appears next to Slide 1. Notice that the task pane is no longer visible. The task pane can be easily opened the next time you need it. Compare your screen to Figure A-7.

FIGURE A-6: AutoContent Wizard opening screen

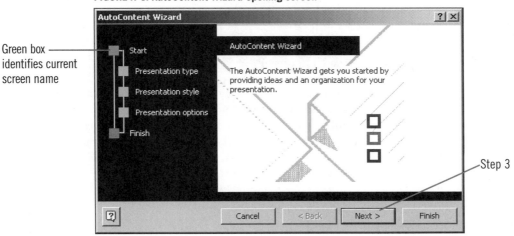

Green box identifies current screen name

Step 3

FIGURE A-7: Presentation created with AutoContent Wizard

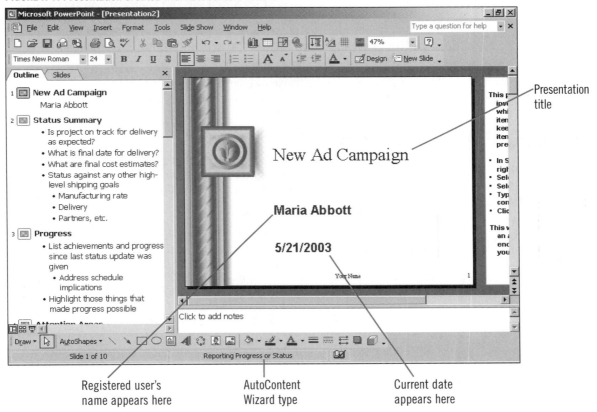

Presentation title

Registered user's name appears here

AutoContent Wizard type

Current date appears here

About Wizards and the PowerPoint installation

As you use PowerPoint, you may find that not all AutoContent Wizards are available to you. The wizards available depend on your PowerPoint installation. A typical installation gives you a minimal set of wizards, templates, and other features. Some may be installed so that the program requests the Office CD "on first use"; in other words, the first time you request that feature. If you find that a feature you want is not installed, insert the Office CD as directed. If you are working on a networked computer or in a lab, see your technical support person for assistance.

Viewing a Presentation

This lesson introduces you to the four PowerPoint views: Normal view, Slide Sorter view, Slide Show view, and Notes Page view. Each PowerPoint view shows your presentation in a different way and allows you to manipulate your presentation differently. To move easily among most of the PowerPoint views, use the view buttons located at the bottom of the pane containing the Outline and Slides tabs. Table A-3 provides a brief description of the PowerPoint views. ✐ Maria examines each PowerPoint view, starting with Normal view.

Steps 1234

1. **In the Outline tab, click the small slide icon 🔲 next to Slide 3**
   The text for Slide 3 is selected in the Outline tab and Slide 3 appears in the slide pane as shown in Figure A-8. Notice that the status bar also indicates the number of the slide you are viewing.

2. **Click the Previous Slide button ⏫ at the bottom of the vertical scroll bar twice so that Slide 1 (the title slide) appears**
   The scroll box in the vertical scroll bar moves back up the scroll bar. The gray slide icon on the Outline tab indicates which slide is displayed in the slide pane. As you scroll through the presentation, notice the sample text on each slide created by the AutoContent Wizard.

QuickTip

Click the right horizontal scroll arrow in the slide pane to view all of the text to the right of the slide.

3. **Click the Slides tab**
   Thumbnails of all the slides in your presentation appear on the Slide tab and the slide pane enlarges. A text box to the right of Slide 1 in the slide pane describes a tip for working with this presentation. Tips like this appear when you create some presentations using the AutoContent Wizard.

4. **Click the Slide Sorter View button 🔳**
   A thumbnail of each slide in the presentation appears as shown in Figure A-9. You can examine the flow of your slides and easily move them to change their order.

5. **Double-click the first slide in Slide Sorter view**
   The slide that you clicked appears in Normal view.

6. **Click the Slide Show (from current slide) button 🖵**
   The first slide fills the entire screen. In this view, you can practice running through your slides as they would appear in an electronic slide show.

7. **Click the left mouse button, press [Enter], or press [Spacebar] to advance through the slides one at a time until you see a black slide, then click once more to return to Normal view**
   After you view the last slide in Slide Show view, a black slide, indicating that the slide show is finished, appears. When you click the black slide (or press [Spacebar] or [Enter]), you automatically return to the view you were in before you ran the slide show, in this case, Normal view.

Trouble?

If you don't see a menu command, click the double arrow at the bottom of the menu.

8. **Click View on the menu bar, then click Notes Page**
   Notes Page view appears, showing a reduced image of the current slide above a large text box. You can enter text in this box and then print the notes page for your own use to help you remember important points about your presentation. To switch to Notes Page view, you must choose Notes Page from the View menu; there is no Notes Page View button.

FIGURE A-8: Normal view with the Outline tab displayed

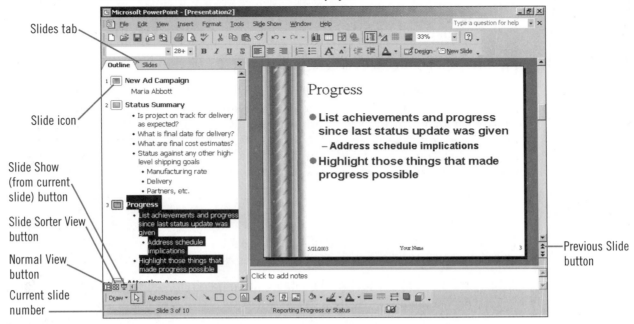

Slides tab

Slide icon

Slide Show (from current slide) button

Slide Sorter View button

Normal View button

Current slide number

Previous Slide button

FIGURE A-9: Slide Sorter view

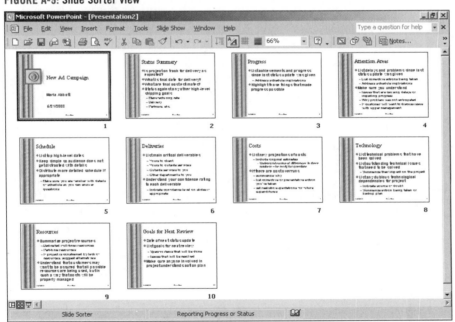

TABLE A-3: PowerPoint views

view name	button	button name	description
Normal	⊞	Normal View	Displays the pane that contains the Outline tab and Slide tab, slide pane, and notes panes at the same time; use this view to work on your presentation's content, layout, and notes concurrently
Slide Sorter	🔲	Slide Sorter View	Displays a thumbnail of all slides in the order in which they appear in your presentation; use this view to rearrange and add special effects to your slides
Slide Show	🖵	Slide Show (from current slide)	Displays your presentation as an electronic slide show
Notes Page			Displays a reduced image of the current slide above a large text box where you can enter notes

PowerPoint 2002

Saving a Presentation

To store your presentation permanently, you must save it as a file on a disk. As a general rule, you should save your work about every 10 or 15 minutes and before printing. You use either the Save command or the Save As command on the File menu to save your presentation for the first time. When you want to make a copy of an existing presentation under a different name, use the Save As command; otherwise, use the Save command to save your changes to a presentation file. ◢◢◣ Maria saves her presentation as New Ad Campaign.

Steps 1 2 3 4

1. Click **File** on the menu bar, then click **Save As**
The Save As dialog box opens, similar to Figure A-10.

2. Click the **Save in list arrow**, then navigate to the drive and folder where your Project Files are located
A default filename, which PowerPoint takes from the presentation title you entered, appears in the File name text box. If your drive or folder contains any PowerPoint files, their file-names appear in the white area in the center of the dialog box.

Trouble?

Don't worry if you see the extension .ppt after the filename in the list of filenames, even though you didn't type it. Windows can be set up to show or hide the file extensions.

3. If necessary, drag to select the default presentation name in the File name text box, type **New Ad Campaign**, then click **Save**
Filenames can be up to 255 characters long; you may use lower- or uppercase letters, symbols, numbers, and spaces. The Save As dialog box closes, and the new filename appears in the title bar at the top of the Presentation window. You decide you want to save the presentation in Normal view instead of in Notes Page view.

4. Click the **Normal View button** ▣
The presentation view changes from Notes Page view to Normal view.

QuickTip

To save a file quickly, you can press the shortcut key combination [Ctrl][S].

5. Click the **Save button** 🖫 on the Standard toolbar
The Save command saves any changes you made to the file to the same location you specified when you used the Save As command. Save your file frequently while working with it to protect the presentation.

FIGURE A-10: Save As dialog box

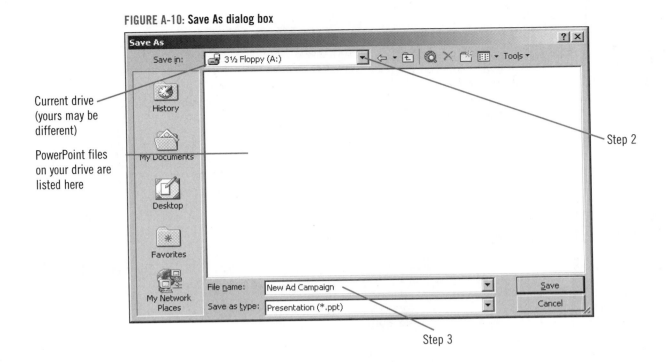

Current drive
(yours may be
different)

PowerPoint files
on your drive are
listed here

Step 2

Step 3

Saving fonts with your presentation

When you create a presentation, it uses the fonts that are installed on your computer. If you need to open the presentation on another computer, the fonts might look different if that computer has a different set of fonts. To preserve the look of your presentation on any computer, you can save, or embed, the fonts in your presentation. Click File on the menu bar, then click Save As. The Save As dialog box opens. Click Tools, click Save Options, then click the Embed TrueType fonts check box in the Save Options dialog box. Click OK to close the Save Options dialog box, then click Save. Now the presentation will look the same on any computer that opens it. Using this option, however, significantly increases the size of your presentation on disk, so only use it when necessary. You can freely embed any TrueType font that comes with Windows. You can embed other TrueType fonts only if they have no license restrictions.

PowerPoint 2002

Getting Help

PowerPoint has an extensive Help system that gives you immediate access to definitions, reference information, and feature explanations. Help information appears in a separate window that you can move and resize. ✎ Maria is finished working with her presentation for now, so she decides to learn about PowerPoint's printing capabilities.

QuickTip
Clicking the Ask a Question box list arrow displays a list of recently searched for Help topics.

1. **Click in the Ask a Question box** on the menu bar, type **printing**, then press **[Enter]**
   A list appears below the Ask a Question box displaying hyperlinks to Help topics related to printing. See Figure A-11.

2. Click the **About printing hyperlink**
   The Microsoft PowerPoint Help window opens and displays information in the right pane about printing in PowerPoint. See Figure A-12. The Help window on your screen might be a different size than the one shown in the figure. Three hyperlinks to subtopics, identified by small blue arrows, are listed below the Help information in the right pane. To see any of these topics, simply click the topic. The left pane of the Help window shows three tabs that you can use to continue searching for other Help topics. The Contents tab contains Help topics organized in outline form. To open a Help window about a topic, double-click it. On the Answer Wizard tab, you search for a key word in all the Help topics, similar to the Ask a Question box. The Index tab contains an alphabetical list of Help topics. Type the word you want help on in text box 1, and the list in box 2 scrolls to that word. Click Search to view related topics in text box 3, then click the topic you want to read about.

QuickTip
If the Office Assistant is visible, you can click it to open the dialog balloon and search PowerPoint Help to display the same topics as shown in Figure A-11. To quickly open the Office Assistant dialog balloon, click the animated character, click the Microsoft PowerPoint Help button 🔃 on the Standard toolbar, or press [F1].

3. Click each of the sub topics in the right pane, then read the information in the window
   You will need to scroll down to read all the information. After reading a particular Help topic, you can search for another topic using one of the tabs on the Help window.

4. Click the **Answer Wizard tab**, if necessary, select all of the text in the What would you like to do text box, if necessary, type **print slides**, then click **Search**
   Topics related to printing slides in PowerPoint appear in the Select topic to display list box.

5. Click the **Print slides topic**
   Read the information in the right pane on how to print slides.

6. Click the **Close button** 🗙 in the Microsoft PowerPoint Help window title bar
   The Help window closes, and you return to your presentation. The rest of the figures in this text do not show the Office Assistant.

QuickTip
To turn off the Office Assistant completely, right-click the Assistant, click Options, deselect the Use the Office Assistant check box, then click OK.

7. If the Office Assistant is visible, click **Help** on the menu bar, then click **Hide the Office Assistant**
   If you have hidden the Office Assistant several times, a dialog balloon may open asking if you want to turn it off permanently.

8. If a dialog balloon opens asking if you want to turn off the Office Assistant permanently, click the option you prefer in the Office Assistant dialog balloon, then click **OK**
   Selecting Hide the Office Assistant only hides it temporarily; it will reappear later to give you tips.

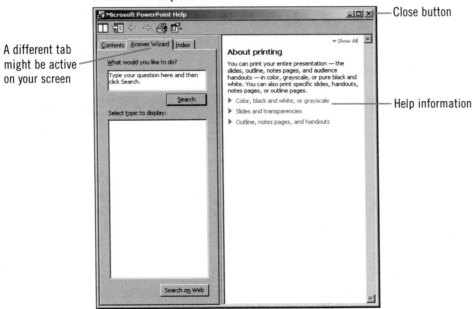

Type term to search for here

Topics related to search term

FIGURE A-12: **Help window**

Close button

A different tab might be active on your screen

Help information

Recovering lost presentation files

Sometimes while you are working on a presentation, PowerPoint may freeze, making it impossible to continue working on your presentation, or you may experience a power failure that causes your computer to shut down. If this type of interruption occurs, PowerPoint has a built-in recovery feature that allows you to open and save files that were open during the interruption. When you start PowerPoint again after an interruption, the Document Recovery task pane opens on the left side of your screen, displaying both original and recovered versions of the PowerPoint files that were open. If you're not sure which file to open (original or recovered), it's usually better to open the recovered file because it will have retained the latest information. You can, however, open and review all the versions of the file that was recovered and select the best one to save. Each file listed in the Document Recovery task pane has a list arrow with options that allow you to open the file, save the file, delete the file, or show repairs made to the file.

PowerPoint 2002

Printing and Closing the File, and Exiting PowerPoint

You print your presentation when you have completed it or when you want to review your work. Reviewing hard copies of your presentation at different stages of production gives you an overall perspective of its content and look. When you are finished working on your presentation, close the file containing your presentation and exit PowerPoint. Maria is done working on her presentation for now, so after saving her presentation, she prints the slides and notes pages of the presentation so she can review them later; then she closes the file and exits PowerPoint.

Steps

1. **Click File on the menu bar, then click Print**
   The Print dialog box opens, similar to Figure A-13. In this dialog box, you can specify which slide format you want to print (slides, handouts, notes pages, etc.) as well as the number of pages to print and other print options. The default options, Slides and Grayscale, are already selected in the Print what area at the bottom of the dialog box.

2. **In the Print range section in the middle of the dialog box, click the Slides option button to select it, type 3 to print only the third slide, then click OK**
   The third slide prints. If you have a black-and-white printer, the slide prints in shades of gray. To save paper, it's often a good idea to print in handout format, which lets you print up to nine slides per page.

3. **Click File on the menu bar, then click Print**
   The Print dialog box opens again. The options you choose in the Print dialog box remain there until you close the presentation.

4. **Click the All option button in the Print range section, click the Print what list arrow, click Handouts, click the Slides per page list arrow in the Handouts section, then click 6, if necessary**

5. **Click the Color/grayscale list arrow, click Pure Black and White, then click OK**
   The presentation prints as audience handouts on two pages. The presentation prints without any gray tones.

6. **Click File on the menu bar, then click Print**
   The Print dialog box opens again.

7. **Click the Print what list arrow, click Outline View, then click OK**
   The presentation outline prints.

8. **Click File on the menu bar, then click Close**
   If you have made changes to your presentation, a Microsoft PowerPoint alert box opens asking you if you want to save changes you have made to the New Ad Campaign file, as shown in Figure A-14.

9. **If necessary, click Yes to close the alert box**

10. **Click File on the menu bar, then click Exit**
    The presentation and the PowerPoint program close, and you return to the Windows desktop.

FIGURE A-13: Print dialog box

Your printer name may be different

Step 2

Click to select item to print

Step 5

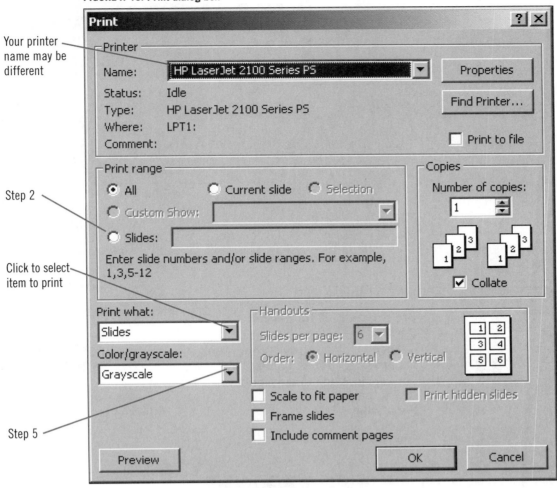

FIGURE A-14: Save changes message box

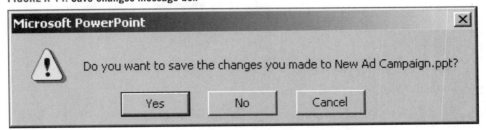

CLUES TO USE

Viewing your presentation in grayscale or black and white

Viewing your presentation in pure black and white or in grayscale (using shades of gray) is very useful when you will be printing a presentation on a black-and-white printer and you want to make sure your text is readable. To see how your color presentation looks in grayscale or black and white, click the Color/Grayscale button ▨ on the Standard toolbar, then select either the Grayscale command or the Pure Black and White command. The Grayscale View toolbar appears. You can use the Grayscale View toolbar to select different settings to view your presentation. If you don't like the way an object looks in black and white or grayscale view, you can change its color. Right-click the object, point to Black and White Setting or Grayscale Setting (depending on which view you are in), and choose from the options on the submenu.

Practice

▶ Concepts Review

Label the elements of the PowerPoint window shown in Figure A-15.

FIGURE A-15

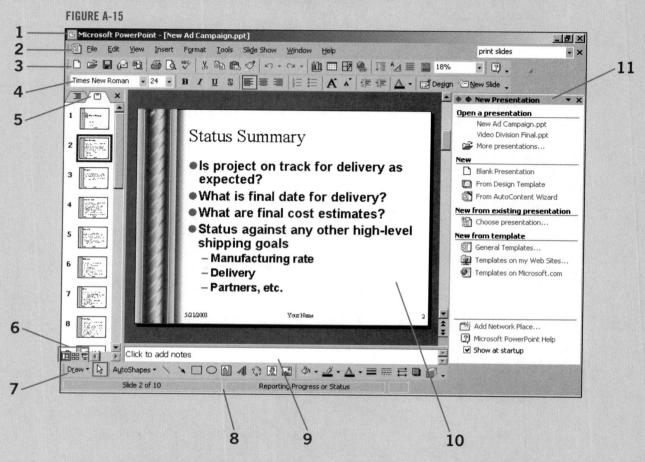

Match each term with the statement that describes it.

12. **AutoContent Wizard**
13. **Task pane**
14. **Slide Sorter view**
15. **Normal view**
16. **Outline tab**

a. Displays hyperlinks of common commands
b. Displays the text of your presentation in an outline form
c. Series of dialog boxes that guides you through creating a presentation and produces a presentation with suggestions for content
d. Displays the Outline and Slide tabs, as well as the slide and notes panes
e. Shows all your slides as thumbnails

Select the best answer from the list of choices.

17. PowerPoint can help you create all of the following, *except*:
- **a.** Notes pages.
- **b.** Outline pages.
- **c.** An on-screen presentation.
- **d.** A movie.

18. The buttons you use to switch between the PowerPoint views are called:
- **a.** Screen buttons.
- **b.** PowerPoint buttons.
- **c.** View buttons.
- **d.** Toolbar buttons.

19. All of the following are PowerPoint views, *except*:
- **a.** Slide Sorter view.
- **b.** Notes Page view.
- **c.** Current Page view.
- **d.** Normal view.

20. The view that allows you to view your electronic slide show with each slide filling the entire screen is called:
- **a.** Presentation view.
- **b.** Slide Sorter view.
- **c.** Slide Show view.
- **d.** Electronic view.

21. Which wizard helps you create and outline your presentation?
- **a.** Presentation Wizard
- **b.** OrgContent Wizard
- **c.** AutoContent Wizard
- **d.** Pick a Look Wizard

22. How do you switch to Notes Page view?
- **a.** Press [Shift] and click in the notes pane
- **b.** Click the Notes Page View button
- **c.** Click View on the menu bar, then click Notes Page
- **d.** All of the above

23. How do you save changes to your presentation after you have saved it for the first time?
- **a.** Click Save As on the File menu, select a filename from the list, then assign it a new name
- **b.** Click the Save button on the Standard toolbar
- **c.** Click Save As on the File menu, then click Save
- **d.** Click Save As on the File menu, specify a new location and filename, then click Save

PowerPoint 2002

▶ Skills Review

1. **Start PowerPoint and view the PowerPoint window.**
   a. Identify as many elements of the PowerPoint window as you can without referring to the unit material.
   b. For any elements you cannot identify, refer to the unit.

2. **Use the AutoContent Wizard.**
   a. Start the AutoContent Wizard, then select a presentation category and type. (*Hint*: If you see a message saying you need to install the feature, insert your Office CD in the appropriate drive and click OK. If you are working in a networked computer lab, see your technical support person for assistance. If you are unable to load additional templates, click No as many times as necessary, then select another presentation type.)
   b. Select the output options of your choice.
   c. Enter appropriate information for the opening slide, enter your name as the footer text, and complete the wizard to show the first slide of the presentation.

3. **View a presentation and run a slide show.**
   a. View each slide in the presentation to become familiar with its content.
   b. When you are finished, return to Slide 1.
   c. Click the Outline tab and review the presentation contents.
   d. Change to Notes Page view and see if the notes pages in the presentation contain text, then return to Normal view.
   e. Examine the presentation contents in Slide Sorter view.
   f. View all the slides of the presentation in Slide Show view, and end the slide show to return to Slide Sorter view.

4. **Save a presentation.**
   a. Change to Notes Page view.
   b. Open the Save As dialog box.
   c. Navigate to the drive and folder where your Project Files are located.
   d. Name your presentation **Practice**.
   e. Click Tools, then click Save Options.
   f. Choose the option to embed the fonts in your presentation, as shown in Figure A-16, then click OK.
   g. Save your file.
   h. Go to a different view than the one you saved your presentation in.
   i. Save the changed presentation.

FIGURE A-16

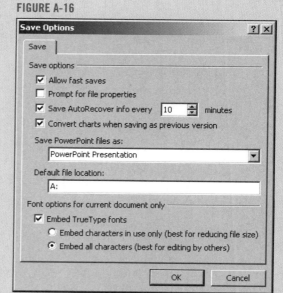

5. Get Help.

a. Type **creating presentations** in the Ask a Question box, then press [Enter].

b. Click the About creating presentations hyperlink.

c. Scroll down, and read the information.

d. Click the Index tab, then type a word you want help with in text box 1.

e. Click a word in the list in list box 2 if it did not jump to the correct word, then click Search.

f. Click a topic in the list in box 3 and read about it.

g. Explore a number of topics that interest you.

h. When you have finished exploring the Index tab, switch to the Contents tab.

i. On the Contents tab, double-click any book icon to view the Help subjects (identified by page icons), then click the page icons to review the Help information. Explore a number of topics that interest you.

j. When you have finished exploring the Contents tab, close the Help window and hide the Office Assistant, if necessary.

6. Print and close the file, and exit PowerPoint.

a. Print slides 2 and 3 as slides in grayscale. (*Hint*: In the Slides text box, type 2-3.)

b. Print all the slides as handouts, 9 slides per page, in pure black and white.

c. Print the presentation outline.

d. Close the file, saving your changes.

e. Exit PowerPoint.

▶ Independent Challenge 1

You have just gotten a job as a marketing assistant at Events, Inc, a catering firm specializing in clambakes and barbecues for large company events. John Hudspeth, the marketing manager, has some familiarity with PowerPoint. He has printed his presentation as grayscale, but he cannot see all of his text, and he wants to know how to solve this problem.

a. If PowerPoint is not already running, start it.

b. Use PowerPoint Help to find the answer to John's question.

c. Write down which Help feature you used (Ask a Question box, Index, etc.) and the steps you followed.

d. Print the Help window that shows the information you found. (*Hint*: Click the Print button at the top of the Help window.)

e. Exit PowerPoint.

PowerPoint 2002

► Independent Challenge 2

You are in charge of marketing for ArtWorks, Inc., a medium-size company that produces all types of art for corporations to enhance their work environment. The company has a regional sales area that includes areas throughout western Europe. The president of ArtWorks has asked you to plan and create the outline of the PowerPoint presentation he will use to convey his marketing plan to the sales department.

   a. If necessary, start PowerPoint.
   b. Start the AutoContent Wizard. (*Hint*: If the task pane is not visible, click View on the menu bar, then click Task Pane.)
   c. On the Presentation type screen, choose the Sales/Marketing category, then choose Marketing Plan from the list.
   d. Assign the presentation an appropriate title, and include your name as the footer text.
   e. Scroll through the outline that the AutoContent Wizard produces. Does it contain the type of information you thought it would?
   f. Plan and take notes on how you would change and add to the sample text created by the wizard. What information do you need to promote ArtWorks to companies?
   g. Switch views. Run through the slide show at least once.
   h. Save your presentation with the name **ArtWorks** to the drive and folder where your Project Files are located.
   i. Print your presentation as handouts (6 slides per page).
   j. Close the presentation and exit PowerPoint.

► Independent Challenge 3

You have recently been promoted to sales manager at Alison Industries. Part of your job is to train sales representatives to go to potential customers and give presentations describing your company's products. Your boss wants you to find an appropriate PowerPoint presentation template that you can use for your next training presentation to recommend strategies to the sales representatives for closing sales. She wants a printout so she can evaluate it.

   a. If necessary, start PowerPoint.
   b. Start the AutoContent Wizard. (*Hint*: If the task pane is not visible, click View on the menu bar, then click Task Pane.)
   c. Examine the available AutoContent Wizards and select one that you could adapt for your presentation. (*Hint*: If you see a message saying you need to install additional templates, insert your Office CD in the appropriate drive and click OK. If you are working in a networked computer lab, see your technical support person for assistance. If you are unable to load additional templates, click No as many times as necessary, then select another presentation type.)
   d. Enter an appropriate slide title and include your name as the footer text.
   e. Print the presentation as an outline, then print the first slide in pure black and white.
   f. Write a brief memo to your boss describing which wizard you think will be most helpful, referring to specific slides in the outline to support your recommendation.
   g. Save the presentation as **Sales Training** to the drive and folder where your project files are located.
   h. Close the presentation and exit PowerPoint.

Independent Challenge 4

In this unit, you've learned about PowerPoint basics such as how to start PowerPoint, view the PowerPoint window, use the AutoContent Wizard, and run a slide show. There are many Web sites that provide information about how to use PowerPoint more effectively.

Use the Web to access information about one of the following topics:

- Information on how to use PowerPoint effectively
- Tips on how to increase your productivity using PowerPoint

a. Connect to the Internet, then go to Microsoft's Web site at www.microsoft.com. Your screen should look similar to Figure A-17.

b. Click the Office hyperlink, then locate the Using Microsoft PowerPoint page.

c. Research and gather information on using PowerPoint.

d. Start a word processing program and create and save a new blank document as **PowerPoint Productivity Tips** to the drive and folder where your Project Files are located.

e. Type your name at the top of the document.

f. Write a brief summary report of the information you compile. Your report should include at least five tips or instructions on how to use PowerPoint more effectively or how to increase your productivity using PowerPoint. For each tip or instruction, include the exact URL where you found the tip. (*Hint*: Click in the Address or Location box in your browser window to select the current URL, click Edit on the menu bar, click Copy, then use the Paste command in the word processor to paste the exact URL in your document.)

g. Save your final document, print it, then close the document and exit the word processor.

FIGURE A-17

Click the Office link to locate information on PowerPoint

► Visual Workshop

Create the presentation shown in Figure A-18 using the Project Overview AutoContent Wizard in the Projects category. Make sure you include your name as the footer. Save the presentation as **Phase 3A** to the drive and folder where your Project Files are located. Print the slides as handouts, six slides per page, in pure black and white.

FIGURE A-18

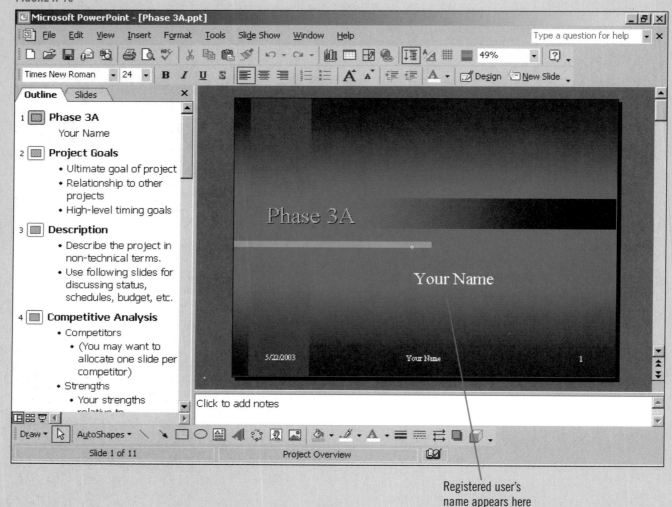

Registered user's name appears here

Unit B

Creating
a Presentation

Objectives

► **Plan an effective presentation**

MOUS ► **Enter slide text**

MOUS ► **Create a new slide**

MOUS ► **Enter text in the Outline tab**

MOUS ► **Add slide headers and footers**

MOUS ► **Choose a look for a presentation**

MOUS ► **Check spelling in a presentation**

MOUS ► **Evaluate a presentation**

Now that you are familiar with PowerPoint basics, you are ready to plan and create your own presentation. To do this, you first enter and edit the presentation text, and then you can focus on the design and look of your presentation. PowerPoint helps you accomplish these tasks with the AutoContent Wizard and with a collection of professionally prepared slide designs, called **design templates**, which can enhance the look of your presentation. In this unit, you create a presentation using a PowerPoint design template. Maria Abbott, general sales manager at MediaLoft, needs to prepare a marketing presentation on a new service that MediaLoft is planning to introduce later in the year. She begins by planning her presentation.

Planning an Effective Presentation

Before you create a presentation using PowerPoint, you need to plan and outline the message you want to communicate and consider how you want the presentation to look. When preparing the outline, you need to consider where you are giving the presentation and who your audience will be. It is also important to know what resources you might need, such as a computer or projection equipment. Using Figure B-1 and the planning guidelines below, follow Maria as she outlines the presentation message.

In planning a presentation, it is important to:

► **Determine the purpose of the presentation**
When you have a well-defined purpose, developing an outline for your presentation is much easier. Maria needs to present a marketing plan for a new Internet service that MediaLoft is planning to launch later in the year.

► **Determine the message you want to communicate, then give the presentation a meaningful title and outline your message**
If possible, take time to adequately develop an outline of your presentation content before creating the slides. Maria starts her presentation by defining the new service, describing the competition, and stating the product positioning. See Figure B-1.

► **Determine the audience and the delivery location**
The presentation audience and delivery location can greatly affect the type of presentation you create. For example, if you had to deliver a presentation to your staff in a small, dimly lit conference room, you may create a very simple presentation; however, if you had to deliver a sales presentation to a client in a formal conference room with many windows, you may need to create a very professional-looking presentation. Maria will deliver her presentation in a large conference room to MediaLoft's marketing management team.

► **Determine the type of output—black-and-white or color overhead transparencies, on-screen slide show, or an online broadcast—that best conveys your message, given time constraints and computer hardware availability**
Because Maria is speaking in a large conference room to a large group and has access to a computer and projection equipment, she decides that an on-screen slide show is the best output choice for her presentation.

► **Determine a look for your presentation which will help communicate your message**
You can choose one of the professionally designed templates that come with PowerPoint, modify one of these templates, or create one of your own. Maria wants a simple and artistic template to convey the marketing plan.

► **Determine what additional materials will be useful in the presentation**
You need to prepare not only the slides themselves but also supplementary materials, including speaker notes and handouts for the audience. Maria uses speaker notes to help remember a few key details, and she will pass out handouts for the audience to use as a reference.

FIGURE B-1: Outline of the presentation content

1. iMedia
   - Proposed Marketing Plan
   - Maria Abbott
   - May 26, 2003
   - General Sales Manager
2. Product Definition
   - Internet media service provider
     - Music and video
     - Articles and trade papers
     - Historical papers archive
   - Publishing service
     - Papers, articles, books, games, and more...
3. Competition
   - Bookstores
   - Internet stores
   - Media services
   - Ratings
4. Product Positioning
   - Only licensed media download service provider
   - Only interactive service provider
   - Only publishing service provider

CLUES TO USE

Using templates from the Web

When you create a presentation, you have the option of using one of the design templates supplied with PowerPoint, or you can use a template from another source, such as a Web server or Microsoft's Office Template Gallery Web site. To create a presentation using a template from a Web server, start PowerPoint, open the New Presentation task pane, then click the Templates on my Web Sites hyperlink. The New from Templates on my Web Sites dialog box opens. Locate and open the template you want to use, then save it with a new name. To use a template from Microsoft's Office Template Gallery, open the New Presentation task pane, then click the Templates on Microsoft.com hyperlink. Your Web browser opens to the Microsoft Office Template Gallery Web site. Locate the PowerPoint template you want to use, then click the Edit in Microsoft PowerPoint hyperlink to open and save the template in PowerPoint. The first time you use the Template Gallery, you must install Microsoft Office Template Gallery and accept the license agreement.

Entering Slide Text

Each time you start PowerPoint, a new presentation with a blank title slide appears in Normal view. The title slide has two **text placeholders** that are boxes with dashed-line borders where you enter text. The top text placeholder on the title slide is the **title placeholder**, labeled "Click to add title." The bottom text placeholder on the title slide is the **main text placeholder**, labeled "Click to add subtitle." To enter text in a placeholder, simply click the placeholder and then type your text. After you enter text in a placeholder, the placeholder becomes a text object. An **object** is any item on a slide that can be manipulated. Objects are the building blocks that make up a presentation slide. ✎ Maria begins working on her presentation by starting PowerPoint and entering text on the title slide.

Steps 1 2 3 4

1. **Start PowerPoint**

   A new presentation appears displaying a blank slide.

2. **Move the pointer over the title placeholder labeled "Click to add title" in the slide pane**

   The pointer changes to I when you move the pointer over the placeholder. In PowerPoint, the pointer often changes shape, depending on the task you are trying to accomplish.

3. **Click the title placeholder**

   The **insertion point**, a blinking vertical line, indicates where your text will appear in the title placeholder. A **selection box**, the slanted line border, appears around the title placeholder, indicating that it is selected and ready to accept text. See Figure B-2.

4. **Type iMedia**

   PowerPoint center-aligns the title text within the title placeholder, which is now a text object. Notice that text appears on the slide thumbnail on the Slides tab.

5. **Click the main text placeholder in the slide pane**

   A wavy, red line may appear under the word "iMedia" in the title object indicating that the automatic spellchecking feature in PowerPoint is active. Don't worry if it doesn't appear on your screen.

6. **Type Proposed Marketing Plan, then press [Enter]**

   The insertion point moves to the next line in the text placeholder.

7. **Type Maria Abbott, press [Enter], type May 26, 2003, press [Enter], then type General Sales Manager**

   Notice that the AutoFit Options button ⊞ appears near the text object. The AutoFit Options button on your screen tells you that PowerPoint has automatically decreased the size of all the text in the text object to fit in the text object.

8. **Click the Autofit Options button ⊞, then click Stop Fitting Text to This Placeholder on the shortcut menu**

   The text in the main text box changes back to its original size as shown in Figure B-3. The text object looks a little crowded.

9. **Position I to the right of 2003, drag to select the entire line of text, press [Backspace], then click outside the main text object in a blank area of the slide**

   The text and the line it occupied are deleted and the Autofit Options button closes. Clicking a blank area of the slide deselects all selected objects on the slide.

10. **Click the Save button ▣ on the Standard toolbar, then save your presentation as iMedia 1 to the drive and folder where your Project Files are stored**

Trouble?

If you press a wrong key, press [Backspace] to erase the character, then continue to type.

Trouble?

If the insertion point is blinking in a blank line after completing this step, press [Backspace] one more time.

FIGURE B-2: Slide with selected title placeholder

Selection box

Title placeholder

Insertion point

Main text placeholder

Mouse pointer

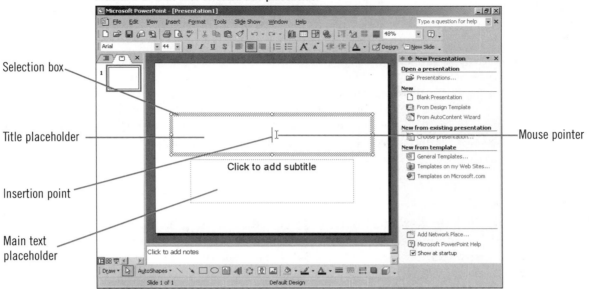

FIGURE B-3: Title slide with text

Red, wavy line indicates automatic spellchecking is on

iMedia

Proposed Marketing Plan
Maria Abbott
General Sales Manager

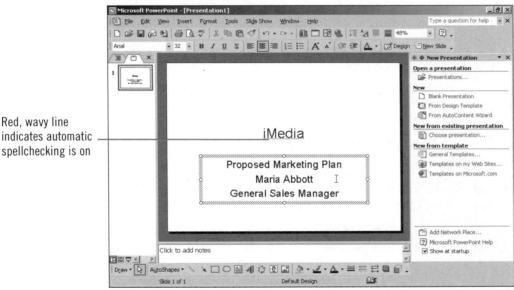

Using Speech Recognition

Speech recognition technology lets you enter text and issue commands by talking into a standard microphone connected to your computer. It is an Office-wide program that you must install and set up before you can use it. To start using Speech Recognition, start Word, click Tools on the menu bar, then click Speech. You might be prompted to install the Speech Recognition files using the Office CD. Once you have installed the Speech Recognition files, the Speech Recognition component will be available in all Office programs. The Training Wizard is a series of paragraphs that you read into your computer's microphone. These training sessions teach the Speech module to recognize your voice. They also teach you the speed and level of clarity with which you need to speak so that the program can understand you. Training sessions improve the performance of the Speech Recognition module. If you don't use the training sessions, the Speech Recognition module may be inaccurate.

Creating a New Slide

To help you create a new slide easily, PowerPoint offers 27 predesigned slide layouts. A **slide layout** determines how all of the elements on a slide are arranged. Slide layouts include a variety of place-holder arrangements for different objects, including titles, text, clip art, tables, charts, diagrams, and media clips, and are organized by layout type in the following categories: text layouts, content layouts, text and content layouts, and other layouts. You have already used the title slide layout in the previous lesson. Table B-1 describes some of the placeholders you'll find in the slide layouts. To continue developing the presentation, Maria needs to create a slide that defines the new service MediaLoft is developing.

You can also insert a new slide from the Slide Layout task pane: point to the slide layout you want, click the slide layout list arrow, then click Insert New Slide.

1. **Click the New Slide button on the Formatting toolbar**
   A new blank slide appears after the current slide in your presentation and the Slide Layout task pane opens, as shown in Figure B-4. The new slide in the slide pane contains a title placeholder and a **body text** placeholder for a bulleted list. Notice that the status bar indicates Slide 2 of 2 and that the Slides tab now contains two slide thumbnails. The Slide Layout task pane identifies the different PowerPoint slide layouts that you can use in your presentation. A selection box appears around the Title and Text slide layout identifying it as the currently applied layout for the slide. You can easily change the current slide's layout by clicking a slide layout icon in the Slide Layout task pane.

2. **Point to the Title and 2-Column Text layout (last layout in the Text Layouts section) in the Slide Layout task pane**
   When you place your pointer over a slide layout icon, a selection list arrow appears. You can click the list arrow to choose options for applying the layout. After a brief moment, a ScreenTip also appears that identifies the slide layout by name.

3. **Click the Title and 2-Column Text layout**
   A slide layout with two text placeholders replaces the Title and Text slide layout.

4. **Type Product Definition, then click the left body text placeholder in the slide pane**
   The text you type appears in the title placeholder, and the insertion point appears next to a bullet in the left body text placeholder.

5. **Type Internet media provider, then press [Enter]**
   A new first-level bullet automatically appears when you press [Enter].

6. **Press [Tab]**
   The new first-level bullet indents and becomes a second-level bullet.

If you mistype common words, PowerPoint automatically corrects them when you press [Spacebar] or [Enter]. You know PowerPoint has automatically corrected a word when you point to a word and a small rectangle appears under the word. To see a list of common typing errors that PowerPoint corrects automatically, click Tools on the menu bar, then click AutoCorrect Options.

7. **Type Music and video, press [Enter], type Articles and trade papers, press [Enter], then type Historical papers archive**
   The left text object has four bullet points.

8. **Press [Ctrl][Enter], then type Publishing service**
   Pressing [Ctrl][Enter] moves the insertion point to the next text placeholder. Because this is a two-column layout, the insertion point moves to the other body text placeholder on the slide.

9. **Press [Enter], press [Tab], type Papers, press [Enter], type Articles, press [Enter], type Books, press [Enter], type Games and more..., click in a blank area of the slide, then click the Save button on the Standard toolbar**
   Your changes to the file are saved. Compare your screen with Figure B-5.

FIGURE B-4: **New blank slide in Normal view**

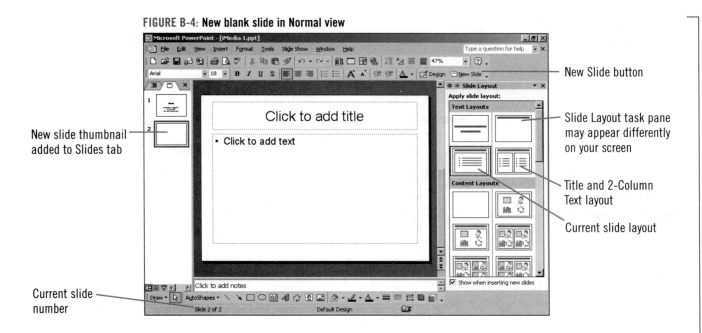

New slide thumbnail added to Slides tab

Current slide number

New Slide button

Slide Layout task pane may appear differently on your screen

Title and 2-Column Text layout

Current slide layout

FIGURE B-5: **New slide with Title and 2-Column Text slide layout**

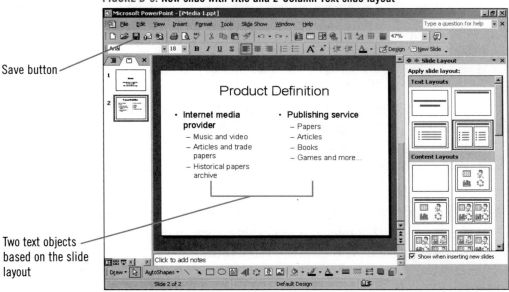

Save button

Two text objects based on the slide layout

TABLE B-1: **Slide Layout placeholders**

placeholder	symbol	description
Bulleted List		Inserts a short list of related points
Clip Art		Inserts a picture from the Clip Gallery
Chart		Inserts a chart created with Microsoft Graph
Diagram or Organization Chart		Inserts a diagram or organizational chart
Table		Inserts a table
Media Clip		Inserts a music, sound, or video clip
Content		Inserts objects such as a table, a chart, clip art, a picture, a diagram or organizational chart, or a media clip

Entering Text in the Outline Tab

You can enter presentation text on the slide, as you've learned already, or, if you'd rather focus on the presentation text without worrying about how it's arranged, you can enter it in the Outline tab. As in a regular outline, the headings, or titles, appear first; beneath the titles, the subpoints, or body text, appear. Body text appears as one or more lines of bulleted text indented under a title. ✐ Maria switches to the Outline tab to enter body text for two more slides.

Steps

QuickTip
The commands on the Outlining toolbar can be helpful when working in the Outline tab. To open the Outlining toolbar, click View on the menu bar, point to Toolbars, then click Outlining.

1. **Click the Outline tab to the left of the slide pane**
   The Outline tab enlarges to display the text of your slides. The slide icon for Slide 2 is highlighted, indicating that it's selected. Notice the numbers 1 and 2 that appear to the left of the first-level bullets for Slide 2, indicating that there are two body text objects on the slide.

2. **Point to the Title and Text layout (second row, first column) in the Slide Layout task pane, click the list arrow, then click Insert New Slide**
   A new slide, Slide 3, with the Title and Text layout appears as the current slide below Slide 2. A selected slide icon ▦ appears next to the slide number when you add a new slide to the outline. See Figure B-6. Text that you enter next to a slide icon becomes the title for that slide.

3. **Click next to the Slide 3 slide icon in the Outline tab, type Competition, press [Enter], then press [Tab]**
   A new slide was inserted when you pressed [Enter], but because you want to enter body text for the slide you just created, you indented this line to make it part of Slide 3.

4. **Type Bookstoes, press [Enter], type E-sites, press [Enter], type Media services, press [Enter], type Ratings, then press [Enter]**
   Make sure you typed "Bookstoes" without the "r" as shown.

5. **Press [Shift][Tab]**
   The bullet that was created when you pressed [Enter] changes to a new slide icon.

6. **Type Product Positioning, press [Ctrl][Enter], type Licensed media download provider, press [Enter], type Publishing service provider, press [Enter], type Interactive service provider, then press [Ctrl][Enter]**
   Pressing [Ctrl][Enter] while the cursor is in the body text object creates a new slide with the same layout as the previous slide. Two of the bulleted points you just typed for Slide 4 are out of order, and you don't need the new Slide 5 you just created.

QuickTip
If you click the Undo button list arrow, you can undo more actions.

7. **Click the Undo button 🔄 on the Standard toolbar**
   Clicking the Undo button undoes the previous action. Slide 5 is deleted and the insertion point moves back up to the last bullet in Slide 4.

8. **Position the pointer to the left of the last bullet in Slide 4 in the Outline tab**
   The pointer changes to ✛.

Trouble?
If your screen does not match Figure B-7, drag the text to the correct location.

9. **Drag the mouse pointer up until the pointer changes to ↕ and a vertical indicator line appears above the second bullet point in Slide 4, then release the mouse button**
   The third bullet point moves up one line in the outline and trades places with the second bullet point, as shown in Figure B-7.

10. **Click the Slides tab, click the Slide 2 icon in the Slides tab, then save your work**
    Slide 2 of 4 should appear in the status bar.

FIGURE B-6: Normal view with Outline tab open

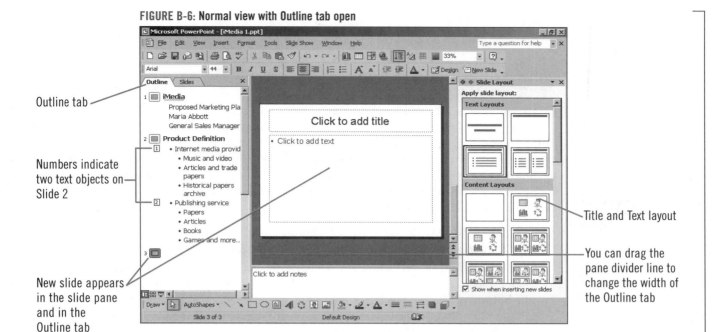

Outline tab

Numbers indicate two text objects on Slide 2

New slide appears in the slide pane and in the Outline tab

Title and Text layout

You can drag the pane divider line to change the width of the Outline tab

FIGURE B-7: Bulleted item moved up on the Outline tab

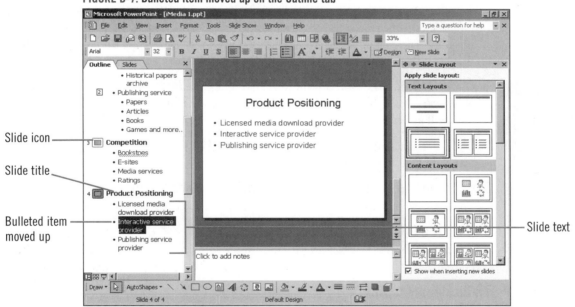

Slide icon

Slide title

Bulleted item moved up

Slide text

What do I do if I see a lightbulb on a slide?

If you have the Office Assistant showing, you may see a yellow lightbulb in your presentation window. The lightbulb is part of the PowerPoint Help system and it can mean several things. First, the Office Assistant might have a suggestion for an appropriate piece of clip art for that slide. Second, the Office Assistant might have a helpful tip based on the task you are performing. This is known as a context-sensitive tip.

Third, the Office Assistant might have detected a style, such as a word in the slide title that should be capitalized, which is inconsistent with preset style guidelines. When you see a lightbulb, you can click it, read the dialog balloon, and click the option you prefer, or you can ignore it. If the Office Assistant is hidden or turned off, the lightbulb will not appear.

Adding Slide Headers and Footers

Header and footer text, such as your company or product name, the slide number, and the date, can give your presentation a professional look and make it easier for your audience to follow. On slides, you can add text only to the footer; however, notes or handouts can include both header and footer text. Footer information that you apply to the slides of your presentation is visible in the PowerPoint views and when you print the slides. Notes and handouts header and footer text is visible when you print notes pages, handouts, and the outline. ✍ Maria wants to add footer text to the slides of her presentation.

Steps

1. **Click View on the menu bar, then click Header and Footer**

   The Header and Footer dialog box opens, as shown in Figure B-8. The Header and Footer dialog box has two tabs: one for slides and one for notes and handouts. The rectangles at the bottom of the Preview box identify the default position of the three types of footer text on the slides. Two of the Footer check boxes are selected by default, so two of the rectangles at the bottom of the Preview box are darkened.

2. **Click the Date and time check box to deselect it**

   The first dark rectangle at the bottom of the Preview box lightens. The middle dark rectangle identifies where the Footer text—the only check box still selected—will appear on the slide. The rectangle on the right, therefore, shows where the slide number will appear if that check box is selected.

QuickTip

If you want the original date that you opened or created the presentation to appear, select the Fixed date option and type the date in the Fixed text box.

3. **Click the Date and time check box, then click the Update automatically option button**

   Now every time you view the slide show or print the slides of the presentation, the current date will appear in the footer.

4. **Click the Update automatically list arrow, then click the fourth option in the list**

   The date format changes.

5. **Click the Slide number check box, click in the Footer text box, then type your name**

   The Preview box changes to show that all three footer placeholders are selected.

6. **Click the Don't show on title slide check box**

   Selecting this check box prevents the footer information you entered in the Header and Footer dialog box from appearing on the title slide. Compare your screen to Figure B-9.

7. **Click Apply to All**

   The dialog box closes and the footer information is applied to all of the slides in your presentation except the title slide. You can apply footer information to just one slide in the presentation if you want.

8. **Click the Slide 1 icon in the Slides tab, click View on the menu bar, then click Header and Footer**

   The Header and Footer dialog box opens displaying all of the options that you selected earlier in this lesson. You want to show your name in all the footer on the title slide.

Trouble?

If you click Apply to All in Step 10, click the Undo button on the Standard toolbar and repeat Steps 9 and 10.

9. **Click the Date and time check box, the Slide number check box, and the Don't show on title slide check box to deselect them**

   Only the text in the Footer text box will appear on the title slide.

10. **Click Apply, then save your work**

    Clicking Apply applies the footer information to just the current slide.

FIGURE B-8: Header and Footer dialog box

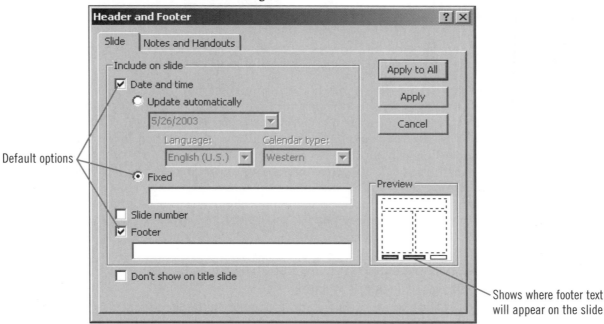

Default options

Shows where footer text will appear on the slide

FIGURE B-9: Completed Header and Footer dialog box

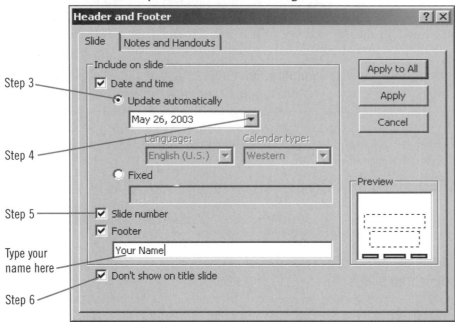

Step 3

Step 4

Step 5

Type your name here

Step 6

Entering and printing notes

You can add notes to your slides when there are certain facts you want to remember during a presentation or when there is information you want to hand out to your audience. Notes do not appear on the slides themselves when you run a slide show. Use the Notes pane in Normal view or Notes Page view to enter notes about your slides. To enter notes on a slide, click in the Notes pane, then type. If you want to insert graphics on the notes pages, you must use Notes Page view instead of the Notes pane. To open Notes Page view, click View on the menu, then click Notes Page. You can print your notes using the Notes Pages option in the Print dialog box. The notes page can also be a good handout to give your audience for their use. Don't enter any notes, and print the notes pages; the slides will print as thumbnails with space to the right for notes.

Choosing a Look for a Presentation

To help you design your presentation, PowerPoint provides a number of design templates so you don't have to spend time creating the right presentation look. A **design template** has borders, colors, text attributes, and other elements arranged in a specific format that you can apply to one or all the slides in your presentation. In most cases, you would apply one template to an entire presentation; you can, however, apply multiple templates to the same presentation. You can use a design template as is, or you can modify any element to suit your needs. Unless you know something about graphic design, it is often easier and faster to use or modify one of the templates supplied with PowerPoint. No matter how you create your presentation, you can save it as a template for future use. Maria decides to use an existing PowerPoint template.

Steps

1. **Click the Other Task Panes list arrow ▼ in the task pane title bar, then click Slide Design – Design Templates**

   The Slide Design task pane appears, similar to the one shown in Figure B-10. This task pane is split into sections: the three hyperlinks that open sub-task panes at the top of the pane; the Used in This Presentation section, which identifies the templates currently applied to the presentation (in this case, the Default Design template); the Recently Used section, which identifies up to five templates you have applied recently (this section will not appear on your screen if no one has used any other templates); and the Available For Use section, which lists all of the standard PowerPoint design templates that you can apply to a presentation.

2. **Scroll down to the Available For Use section of the Slide Design task pane, then place your pointer over the Balance template (first row, second column)**

   A selection list arrow appears next to the Balance template icon. The list arrow provides options for you to choose from when applying design templates. To really determine how a design template will look on your presentation, you need to apply it. You can apply as many templates as you want until you find one that you like.

3. **Click the Balance template list arrow, then click Apply to All Slides**

   The Balance template is applied to all the slides. Notice the new slide background color, the new graphic elements, and the new slide text color. The scales in the background of this template don't fit with the presentation content.

4. **Click the Fireworks template list arrow (sixth row, first column), then click Apply to Selected Slides**

   The Fireworks template is applied to the title slide of the presentation. This design template doesn't fit with the presentation content either.

5. **Click the Blends template list arrow (second row, first column), then click Apply to All Slides**

   This simple and colorful design template looks good with the presentation content and fits the MediaLoft company image.

6. **Click the Next Slide button ▼ three times**

   Preview all the slides in the presentation to see how they look.

7. **Click the Previous Slide button ▲ three times to return to Slide 1**

   Compare your screen to Figure B-11.

8. **Save your changes**

FIGURE B-10: Normal view with Slide Design task pane open

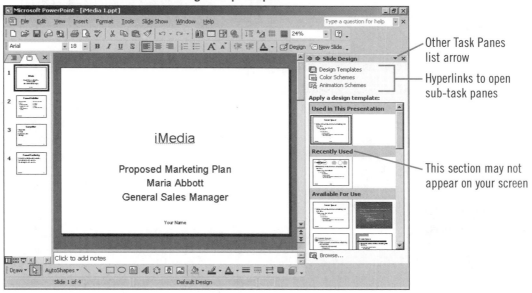

- Other Task Panes list arrow
- Hyperlinks to open sub-task panes
- This section may not appear on your screen

FIGURE B-11: Blends template design applied

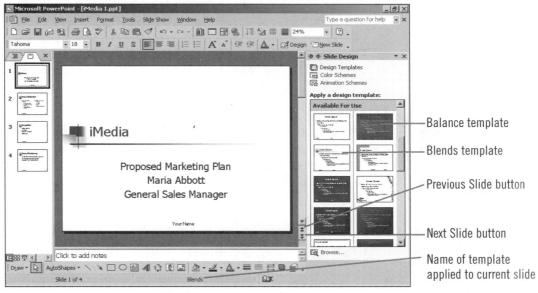

- Balance template
- Blends template
- Previous Slide button
- Next Slide button
- Name of template applied to current slide

Using design templates

You are not limited to using the templates PowerPoint provides; you can either modify a PowerPoint template or create your own. For example, you might want to use your company's color as a slide background or incorporate your company's logo on every slide. If you modify an existing template, you can keep, change, or delete any color, graphic, or font. To create a new template, click Blank Presentation on the New Presentation task pane. Add the design elements you want, then open the Save As dialog box. Click the Save as type list arrow, and choose Design Template, then name your template, and click Save. PowerPoint will automatically add the file extension .pot to the filename, save the template to the Office Templates folder, and add it to the Slide Design task pane. You can then use your customized template as a basis for future presentations. To apply a template that you created to an existing presentation, open the presentation, then choose the template in the Slide Design task pane. The design template will be applied to your current presentation.

Checking Spelling in the Presentation

As your work nears completion, you need to review and proofread your presentation thoroughly for errors. You can use the spellchecking feature in PowerPoint to check for and correct spelling errors. This feature compares the spelling of all the words in your presentation against the words contained in its electronic dictionary. You still must proofread your presentation for punctuation, grammar, and word-usage errors because the spellchecker recognizes only misspelled words, not misused words. For example, the spellchecker would not identify "The Test" as an error, even if you had intended to type "The Best." ⬥ Maria has finished adding and changing text in the presentation, so she checks her work.

Steps

1. Make sure that **Slide 1** is selected in the Slide tab, then click the **Spelling button** 🔲 on the Standard toolbar
   PowerPoint begins to check the spelling in your entire presentation. When PowerPoint finds a misspelled word or a word it doesn't recognize, the Spelling dialog box opens, as shown in Figure B-12. For an explanation of the commands available in the Spelling dialog box, see Table B-2. In this case, PowerPoint does not recognize "iMedia" on Slide 1. It suggests that you replace it with the word "Media." You want the word to remain as you typed it.

2. Click **Ignore All**
   Clicking Ignore All tells the spellchecker to ignore all instances of this word in this presentation. The next word the spellchecker identifies as an error is the word "Bookstoes" in the text body for Slide 3. In the Suggestions list box, the spellchecker suggests "Bookstores."

3. Click **Bookstores** in the Suggestions list box, then click **Change**
   If PowerPoint finds any other words it does not recognize, either change them or ignore them. When the spellchecker finishes checking your presentation, the Spelling dialog box closes, and a PowerPoint alert box opens with a message saying the spelling check is complete.

4. Click **OK**
   The alert box closes. Maria is satisfied with her presentation so far and decides to print it.

5. Click **File** on the menu bar, then click **Print**

6. Make sure **Slides** is selected in the Print what list box, click the **Color/grayscale list arrow**, then click **Pure Black and White**

7. Click the **Frame slides check box** to select it, as shown in Figure B-13
   The slides of your presentation print with a frame around each page.

8. Click **OK**, return to **Slide 1** in Normal view, then save your presentation

Checking spelling as you type

PowerPoint checks your spelling as you type. If you type a word that is not in the electronic dictionary, a wavy, red line appears under it. To correct the error, right-click the misspelled word. A pop-up menu appears with one or more suggestions. You can select a suggestion, add the word you typed to your custom dictionary, or ignore it. To turn off automatic spellchecking, click Tools on the menu bar, then click Options to open the Options dialog box. Click the Spelling and Style tab, and in the Spelling section, click the Check spelling as you type check box to deselect it. To temporarily hide the wavy, red lines, click the Hide all spelling errors check box to select it.

FIGURE B-12: Spelling dialog box

Unrecognized word

Selected word from Suggestions list

Alternate spellings

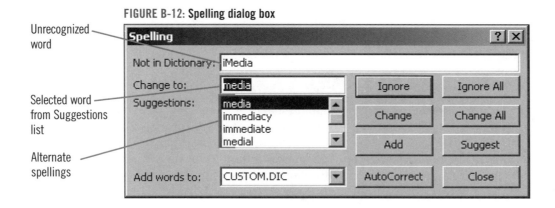

FIGURE B-13: Print dialog box

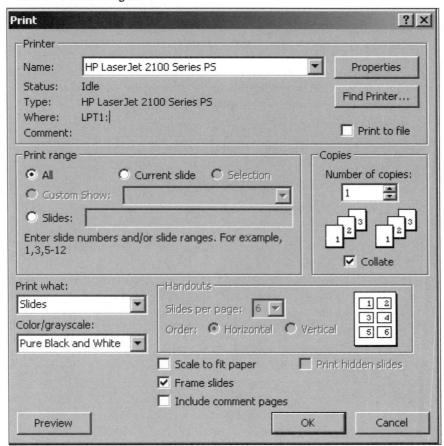

TABLE B-2: Spelling dialog box commands

command	description
Ignore/Ignore All	Continues spellchecking without making any changes to the identified word (or all occurrences of the identified word)
Change/Change All	Changes the identified word (or all occurrences) to the suggested word
Add	Adds the identified word to your custom dictionary; spellchecker will not flag it again
Suggest	Suggests an alternative spelling for the identified word
AutoCorrect	Adds the suggested word as an AutoCorrect entry for the highlighted word
Add words to	Lets you choose a custom dictionary where you store words you often use but that are not part of the PowerPoint dictionary

Evaluating a Presentation

As you create a presentation, keep in mind that good design involves preparation. An effective presentation is both focused and visually appealing—easy for the speaker to present and easy for the audience to understand. The visual elements (colors, graphics, and text) can strongly influence the audience's attention and interest and can determine the success of your presentation. See Table B-3 for general information on the impact a visual presentation has on an audience. ◢ Maria evaluates her presentation's effectiveness.

1. Click the **Slide Show button** 🖳, then press **[Enter]** to move through the slide show

2. When you are finished viewing the slide show, click the **Slide Sorter View button** 🖼
   Maria decides that Slide 4 should come before Slide 3.

3. Drag **Slide 4** between Slides 2 and 3, then release the mouse button
   The thin, black line that moved with the pointer indicates the slide's new position. The final presentation is shown in Slide Sorter view. Compare your screen to Figure B-14. For contrast, Figure B-15 shows a poorly designed slide.

4. When you are finished evaluating your presentation according to the following guidelines, save your changes, then close the presentation and exit PowerPoint

In evaluating a presentation, it is important to:

► **Keep your message focused**

Don't put everything you plan to say on your presentation slides. Keep the audience anticipating further explanations to the key points shown.

► **Keep your text concise**

Limit each slide to six words per line and six lines per slide. Use lists and symbols to help prioritize your points visually. Your presentation text provides only the highlights; use notes to give more detailed information. Maria's presentation focuses attention on the key issues. She will supplement the information with further explanation and details during her presentation.

► **Keep the design simple, easy to read, and appropriate for the content**

A design template makes the presentation consistent. If you design your own layout, keep it simple and use design elements sparingly. Use similar design elements consistently throughout the presentation; otherwise, your audience will get confused. Maria used a simple design template; the colored box cluster and horizontal line give the presentation an interesting, somewhat artistic, look, which is appropriate for a casual professional presentation.

► **Choose attractive colors that make the slide easy to read**

Use contrasting colors for slide background and text to make the text readable. If you are giving an on-screen presentation, you can use almost any combination of colors that look good together.

► **Choose fonts and styles that are easy to read and emphasize important text**

As a general rule, use no more than two fonts in a presentation and vary the font size, using nothing smaller than 24 points. Use bold and italic attributes selectively.

► **Use visuals to help communicate the message of your presentation**

Commonly used visuals include clip art, photographs, charts, worksheets, tables, and movies. Whenever possible, replace text with a visual, but be careful not to overcrowd your slides. White space on your slides is OK!

FIGURE B-14: The final presentation in Slide Sorter view

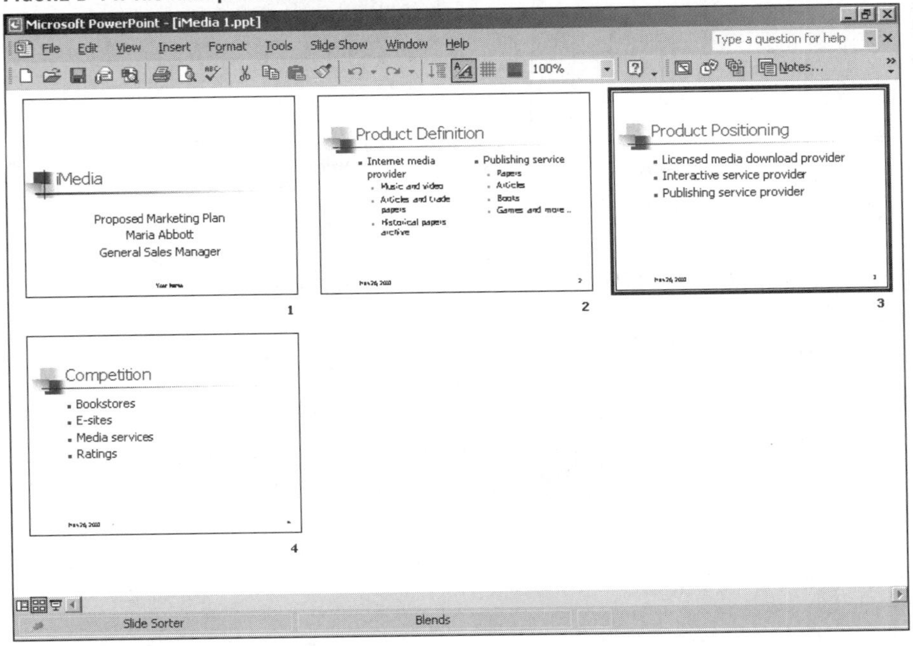

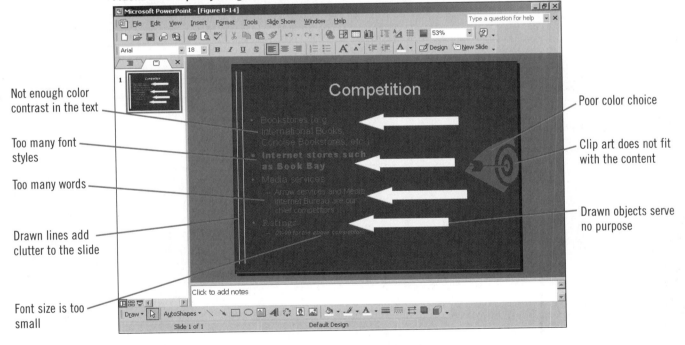

FIGURE B-15: A poorly designed slide in Normal view

Not enough color contrast in the text

Too many font styles

Too many words

Drawn lines add clutter to the slide

Font size is too small

Poor color choice

Clip art does not fit with the content

Drawn objects serve no purpose

TABLE B-3: Audience impact from a visual presentation

impact	description
Visual reception	Most people receive up to 75% of all environmental stimuli through the human sense of sight
Learning	Up to 90% of what an audience learns comes from visual and audio messages
Retention	Combining visual messages with verbal messages can increase memory retention by as much as 30%
Presentation goals	You are twice as likely to achieve your communication objectives using a visual presentation
Meeting length	You are likely to decrease the average meeting length by 25% when you use visual presentation

Source: Presenters Online, www.presentersonline.com

Practice

► Concepts Review

Label each element of the PowerPoint window shown in Figure B-16.

FIGURE B-16

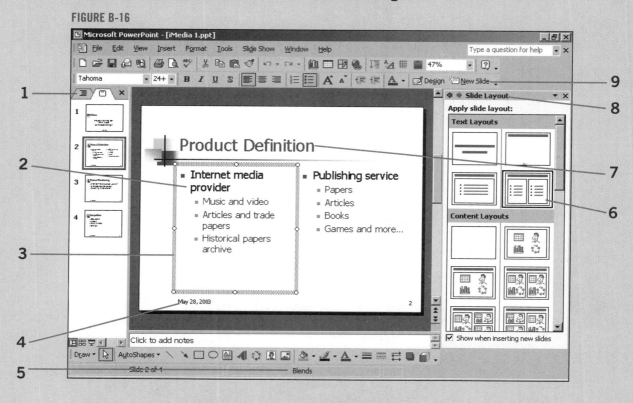

Match each term with the statement that describes it.

10. **Selection box**
11. **Insertion point**
12. **Slide icon**
13. **Design template**
14. **Text placeholder**
15. **Slide layout**

a. A specific design, format, and color scheme that is applied to all the slides in a presentation

b. A blinking vertical line that indicates where your text will appear in a text object

c. Determines how all of the elements on a slide are arranged

d. The slanted line border that appears around a text placeholder, indicating that it is ready to select text

e. A box with a dashed border in which you can enter text

f. In Outline view, the symbol that represents a slide

Select the best answer from the list of choices.

16. What is the definition of a slide layout?
   a. A slide layout automatically applies all the objects you can use on a slide.
   b. A slide layout determines how all the elements on a slide are arranged.
   c. A slide layout applies a different template to the presentation.
   d. A slide layout puts all your slides in order.

17. When you type text in a text placeholder, it becomes:
   a. A label.
   b. A text label.
   c. A selection box.
   d. A text object.

18. When the spellchecker identifies a word as misspelled, which of the following is not a choice?
   a. To ignore this occurrence of the error
   b. To change the misspelled word to the correct spelling
   c. To have the spellchecker automatically correct all the errors it finds
   d. To ignore all occurrences of the error in the presentation

19. When you evaluate your presentation, you should make sure it follows which of the following criteria?
   a. The slides should include every piece of information to be presented so the audience can read it.
   b. The slides should use as many colors as possible to hold the audience's attention.
   c. Many different typefaces will make the slides more interesting.
   d. The message should be clearly outlined without a lot of extra words.

20. According to the unit, which of the following is *not* a guideline for planning a presentation?
   a. Determine the purpose of the presentation
   b. Determine what you want to produce when the presentation is finished
   c. Determine which type of output you will need to best convey your message
   d. Determine who else can give the final presentation

21. Which of the following statements is *not* true?
   a. You can customize any PowerPoint template.
   b. The spellchecker will identify "there" as misspelled if the correct word for the context is "their."
   c. Speaker notes do not appear during the slide show.
   d. PowerPoint has many colorful templates from which to choose.

22. Where else can you enter slide text?
   a. Outline tab
   b. Outline view
   c. Notes Page view
   d. Slides tab

PowerPoint 2002

Skills Review

1. Enter slide text.
a. Start PowerPoint if necessary.
b. In the slide pane in Normal view, enter the text **Product Marketing** in the title placeholder.
c. In the main text placeholder, enter **Ian Kuvick**.
d. On the next line of the placeholder, enter **Manager**.
e. On the next line of the placeholder, enter **Oct. 11, 2003**.
f. Deselect the text object.
g. Save the presentation as **RouterJet Testing** to the drive and folder where your Project Files are located.

2. Create new slides.
a. Create a new slide.
b. Review the text in Table B-4, then select the appropriate slide layout.
c. Enter the text from Table B-4 into the new slide.
d. Create a new bulleted list slide using the Slide Layout task pane.
e. Enter the text from Table B-5 into the new slide.
f. Save your changes.

3. Enter text on the Outline tab.
a. Open the Outline tab.
b. Create a new bulleted list slide after the last one.
c. Enter the text from Table B-6 into the new slide.
d. Move the third bullet point in the text object to the second position.
e. Switch back to the Slides tab.
f. Save your changes.

4. Add slide headers and footers.
a. Open the Header and Footer dialog box.
b. Type today's date into the Fixed text box.
c. Add the slide number to the footer.
d. Type your name in the Footer text box.
e. Apply the footer to all of the slides.
f. Open the Header and Footer dialog box again, then click the Notes and Handouts tab.
g. Enter today's date in the Fixed text box.
h. Type the name of your class in the Header text box.
i. Type your name in the Footer text box.
j. Apply the header and footer information to all the notes and handouts.
k. Save your changes.

TABLE B-4

Text Object	Text to Insert
Slide title	RouterJet Project Tests - Ian
First indent level	Focus: Component System
Second indent level	User access components
	Security components
	Network components
	System components
First indent level	Data Files and Report
Second indent level	Compile component data files
	Define component interface parameters
	Write function data report

TABLE B-5

Text Object	Text to Insert
Slide title	RouterJet Project Tests - Elaine
First indent level	Focus: Network Integration
Second indent level	Server codes and routes
	File transfer
	Data conversion
	Platform functionality ratings

TABLE B-6

Text Object	Text to Insert
Slide title	RouterJet Project Tests - Rajesh
First indent level	Focus: Software QA
Second indent level	User access testing
	Software compatibility testing
	Platform testing

5. Choose a look for a presentation.
   a. Open the Slide Design task pane.
   b. Locate the Network template, then apply it to all the slides. (*Hint*: The template designs are sorted in alphabetical order.)
   c. Move to Slide 1.
   d. Locate the Crayons template, then apply it to Slide 1.
   e. Save your changes.

6. Check spelling in a presentation.
   a. Perform a spelling check on the document and change any misspelled words. Ignore any words that are correctly spelled but that the spellchecker doesn't recognize.
   b. Save your changes.

7. Evaluate a presentation.
   a. View Slide 1 in Slide Show view, then move through the slide show.
   b. Evaluate the presentation using the points described in the lesson as criteria.
   c. Preview your presentation.
   d. Print the outline of the presentation.
   e. Print the slides of your presentation in grayscale with a frame around each slide.
   f. Save your changes, close the presentation, and exit PowerPoint.

▶ Independent Challenge 1

You are an independent distributor of natural foods in Tucson, Arizona. Your business, Harvest Natural Foods, has grown progressively since its inception eight years ago, but sales and profits have leveled off over the last nine months. In an effort to stimulate growth, you decide to acquire two major natural food dealers, which would allow Harvest Natural Foods to expand its territory into surrounding states. Use PowerPoint to develop a presentation that you can use to gain a financial backer for the acquisition.

   a. Start PowerPoint. Choose the Maple design template. Enter **Growth Plan** as the main title on the title slide, and **Harvest Natural Foods** as the subtitle.
   b. Save the presentation as **Harvest Proposal** to the drive and folder where your Project Files are located.
   c. Add five more slides with the following titles: Slide 2—Background; Slide 3—Current Situation; Slide 4—Acquisition Goals; Slide 5—Our Management Team; Slide 6—Funding Required.
   d. Enter text into the text placeholders of the slides. Use both the slide pane and the Outline tab to enter text.
   e. Create a new slide at the end of the presentation. Enter concluding text on the slide, summarizing the main points of the presentation.
   f. Check the spelling in the presentation.
   g. View the presentation as a slide show, then view the slides in Slide Sorter view. Evaluate your presentation and make any changes you feel are necessary.
   h. Add your name as a footer on the notes and handouts, print handouts (6 slides per page), and then print the presentation outline.
   i. Save your changes, close your presentation, then exit PowerPoint.

PowerPoint 2002

▶ Independent Challenge 2

You have been asked to give a one-day course at a local adult education center. The course is called "Personal Computing for the Slightly Anxious Beginner" and is intended for adults who have never used a computer. One of your responsibilities is to create presentation slides that outline the course materials.

Plan and create presentation slides that outline the course material for the students. Create slides for the course introduction, course description, course text, grading policies, and a detailed syllabus. Create your own course material, but assume the following: the school has a computer lab with IBM-compatible computers and Microsoft Windows software; each student has a computer; the prospective students are intimidated by computers but want to learn; and the course is on a Saturday from 9 to 5, with a one-hour lunch break.

a. Think about the results you want to see, the information you need, and the type of message you want to communicate.

b. Write an outline of your presentation. What content should go on the slides? Remember that your audience has never used computers before and will need computer terms defined.

c. Start PowerPoint and create the presentation by entering the title slide text.

d. Create the required slides as well as an ending slide that summarizes your presentation.

e. Add a design template. Choose one that is appropriate to your presentation message and your intended audience.

f. Check the spelling in the presentation.

g. Save the presentation as **Class 1** to the drive and folder where your Project Files are located.

h. View the slide show.

i. View the slides in Slide Sorter view, and evaluate your presentation. Adjust it as necessary so that it is focused, clear, concise, and readable. Make sure none of the slides is too cluttered.

j. Add your name as a footer on the notes and handouts, print handouts (6 slides per page), and then print the presentation outline.

k. Save your changes, close your presentation, then exit PowerPoint.

▶ Independent Challenge 3

You are the training director for Events, Ltd, a German company in Berlin that coordinates special events, including corporate functions, weddings, and private parties. You regularly train groups of temporary employees that you can call on as coordinators, kitchen and wait staff, and coat checkers for specific events. The company trains 10 to 15 new workers each month for the peak season between May and September. One of your responsibilities is to orient new temporary employees at the next training session.

Plan and create presentation slides that outline your employee orientation. Create slides for the introduction, agenda, company history, dress requirements, principles for interacting successfully with guests, and safety requirements. Create your own presentation and company material, but assume the following: Events Ltd is owned by Jan Negd-Sorenson; the new employee training class lasts four hours, and your orientation lasts 15 minutes; the training director's presentation lasts 15 minutes; and the dress code requires uniforms, supplied by Events, Ltd (white for daytime events, black and white for evening events).

a. Think about the results you want to see, the information you need, and the message you want to communicate.

b. Write a presentation outline. What content should go on the slides?

c. Start PowerPoint and create the presentation by entering the slide text for all your slides.

d. Create a slide that summarizes your presentation.

e. Create an ending slide with the following information:
   Events, Ltd
   Gubener Strase 49, 10243 Berlin
   (Berlin-Friedrichshain)
   TEL.: 293755, FAX: 29375799
f. Check the spelling in the presentation.
g. Save the presentation as **Training Class** to the drive and folder where your Project Files are located.
h. View the slide show, then view the slides in Slide Sorter view. Evaluate your presentation, make any changes necessary so that the final version is focused, clear, concise, and readable.
i. Add your name as a footer on the notes and handouts, print the presentation as handouts (2 slides per page), then print the presentation outline.
j. Save your changes, close your presentation, then exit PowerPoint.

 # Independent Challenge 4

One of the best things about PowerPoint is the flexibility you have in creating your presentations, but that same flexibility can result in slides that may appear cluttered, unorganized, and hard to read. Unit B introduced you to some concepts that you can use to help create good presentations using PowerPoint. Use the Web to research more guidelines and tips on creating effective presentations.

Plan and create a presentation that explains these tips to an audience of beginning PowerPoint users. The information you find on the Web should include the following topics:

- Message organization
- Text arrangement and amount
- Slide layout and design
- Presentation development
- Room layout and delivery
- Equipment

a. Connect to the Internet, then use a search engine to locate Web sites that have information on presentations. Use the keywords **presentation tips** to conduct your search. If your search does not produce any results, you might try the following sites:
   www.presentersonline.com
   www.boxlight.com
   www.ljlseminars.com
b. Review at least two Web sites that contain information about presentation tips and guidelines.
c. Start PowerPoint. Title the presentation **Presentation Tips**.
d. Create a presentation with at least five slides. Each slide should contain one main tip with supporting information about that tip.
e. Add a final slide titled **Presentation Tip URLs**. List the URLs from which you obtained the information you used in your presentation.
f. Apply an appropriate design template.
g. Save the presentation as **Presentation Tips** to the drive and folder where your Project Files are located.
h. Add your name as a footer to the slides and notes and handouts, check the spelling in the presentation, then view the final presentation as a slide show.
i. View your presentation in Slide Sorter view and evaluate it. Make any changes necessary so that the final version is focused, clear, concise, and readable.
j. Save your final presentation, print the slides as handouts, 2 per page, then close the presentation and exit PowerPoint.

PowerPoint 2002

► Visual Workshop

Create the marketing presentation shown in Figures B-17 and B-18. Add today's date as the date on the title slide. Save the presentation as **Sales Project** to the drive and folder where your Project Files are located. Review your slides in Slide Show view, add your name as a footer to the slides and the notes and handouts. Print the first slide of your presentation as a slide, and print the outline. Save your changes, close the presentation, and exit PowerPoint.

FIGURE B-17

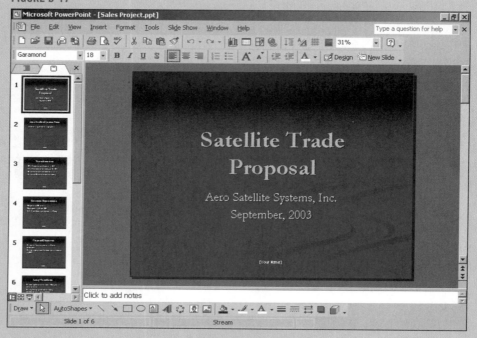

FIGURE B-18

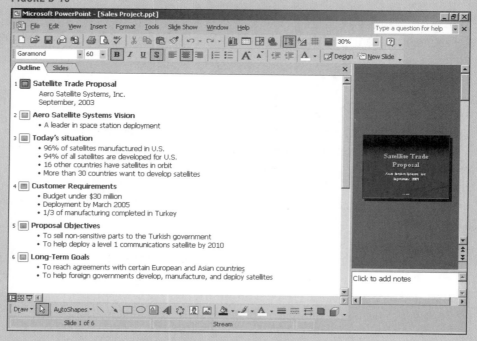

Modifying

a Presentation

Objectives

- ► **Open an existing presentation**
- [MOUS] ► **Draw and modify an object**
- [MOUS] ► **Edit drawing objects**
- ► **Align and group objects**
- [MOUS] ► **Add and arrange text**
- [MOUS] ► **Format text**
- [MOUS] ► **Import text from Microsoft Word**
- [MOUS] ► **Customize the color scheme and background**

After you create the basic outline of your presentation and enter text, you need to add visuals to your slides to communicate your message in the most effective way possible. In this unit, you open an existing presentation; draw and modify objects; add, arrange, and format text; change a presentation color scheme; and revise a presentation. Maria Abbott continues to work on the iMedia marketing presentation by drawing and modifying objects. Maria uses the PowerPoint drawing and text-editing features to bring the presentation closer to a finished look.

Opening an Existing Presentation

Sometimes the easiest way to create a new presentation is by changing an existing one. Revising a presentation saves you from typing duplicate information. You simply open the file you want to change, then use the Save As command to save a copy of the file with a new name. Whenever you open an existing presentation in this book, you will save a copy of it with a new name—this keeps the original file intact. Saving a copy does not affect the original file. Maria wants to add visuals to her presentation, so she opens the presentation she has been working on.

Steps

1. Start PowerPoint

2. Click the **Choose presentation hyperlink** in the New Presentation task pane under New from existing presentation
The New from Existing Presentation dialog box opens. See Figure C-1.

3. Click the **Look in list arrow**, then locate the drive and folder where your Project Files are stored
A list of your Project Files appears in the dialog box.

4. Click **PPT C-1**
The first slide of the selected presentation appears in the preview box on the right side of the dialog box.

5. Click **Create New**
A copy of the file named PPT C-1 opens in Normal view. The title bar displays the temporary filename "Presentation2."

6. Click **File** on the menu bar, then click **Save As**
The Save As dialog box opens. See Figure C-2.

7. Make sure the Save in list box shows the location of your Project Files and that the current filename in the File name text box is selected, then type **iMedia 2**
Compare your screen to the Save As dialog box in Figure C-2.

8. Click **Save** to close the Save As dialog box and save the file
The file is saved with the name iMedia 2.

9. Click the **Slide Design button** on the Formatting toolbar, click **Window** on the menu bar, then click **Arrange All**
You can work with the task pane opened or closed. Many of the figures in this book show only the window that contains the slide and notes panes and the Slide and Outline tabs.

FIGURE C-1: Open dialog box

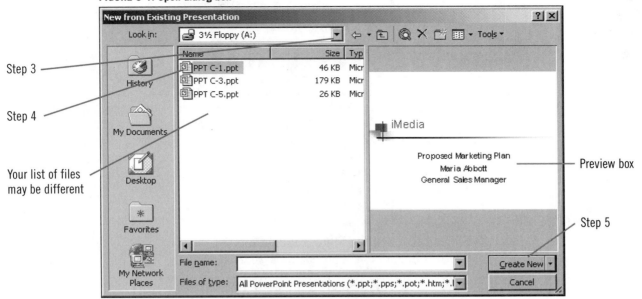

Step 3

Step 4

Your list of files may be different

Preview box

Step 5

FIGURE C-2: Save As dialog box

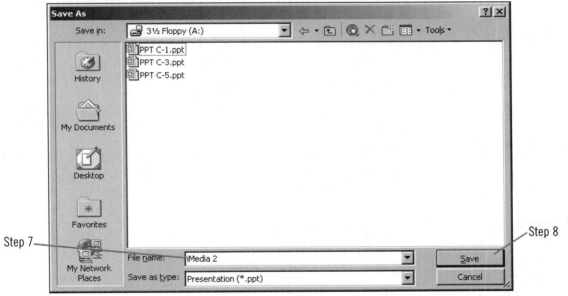

Step 7

Step 8

 CLUES TO USE

Searching for a Presentation

You click the Search button 🔍 on the Standard toolbar to open the Search task pane, where you can search for specific text in files located on your computer's hard drive, your local network, your Microsoft Outlook mailbox, and your network places. When you conduct a search from the Search task pane, all the files that contain the search text you specify are displayed. For example, a search for the text "book club" will yield a list of all the files in the locations you specified that contain the text "book club" in the filename, contents, or properties. Once you have found the file you want, you can open and edit the file in its application, create a new document based on the file, create a link from the file to the Office clipboard, or view the file's properties.

Drawing and Modifying an Object

Using the drawing commands in PowerPoint, you can draw and modify lines, shapes, and pictures to enhance your presentation. Lines and shapes that you create with the PowerPoint drawing tools are objects that you can modify and move at any time. These drawn objects have graphic attributes that you can change, such as fill color, line color, line style, shadow, and 3-D effects. To add drawing objects to your slides, use the buttons on the Drawing toolbar at the bottom of the screen above the status bar. ✏ Maria decides to draw an object on Slide 3 of her marketing presentation to add impact to her message.

Steps 1 2 3 4

1. In the Slides tab, click the **Slide 3 thumbnail**
   Slide 3, titled "Competition," appears in the slide pane.

2. Press and hold **[Shift]**, then click the **body text object**
   A dotted selection box with small circles called **sizing handles** appears around the text object. If you click a text object without pressing [Shift], a selection box composed of slanted lines appears, indicating that the object is active and ready to accept text, but it is not selected. When an object is selected, you can change its size, shape, or attributes by dragging one of the sizing handles.

Trouble?

If you are not satisfied with the size of the text object, resize it again.

3. Position the pointer over the right, middle sizing handle, then drag the sizing handle to the left until the text object is about half its original size as shown in Figure C-3
   When you position the pointer over a sizing handle, it changes to ↔. It points in different directions depending on which sizing handle it is positioned over. When you drag a sizing handle, the pointer changes to +, and a dotted outline representing the size of the text object appears.

QuickTip

Position the pointer on top of a button to see its name.

4. Click the **AutoShapes button** [AutoShapes ▾] on the Drawing toolbar, point to **Block Arrows**, then click the **Right Arrow button** ⇨ (first row, first item)
   After you select a shape from the AutoShapes menu and move the pointer over the slide, the pointer changes to +.

QuickTip

If your arrow object is not approximately the same size as the one shown in Figure C-4, press [Shift] and drag one of the corner sizing handles to resize the object.

5. Position + in the blank area of the slide to the right of the text object, press **[Shift]**, drag down and to the right to create an arrow object, as shown in Figure C-4, then release the mouse button and **[Shift]**
   When you release the mouse button, an arrow object appears on the slide, filled with the default color and outlined with the default line style, as shown in Figure C-4. Pressing [Shift] while you create the object maintains the object's proportions as you change its size.

6. Click the **Line Color list arrow** ✎▾ on the Drawing toolbar, then point to the **red square** (second square from the right)
   A ScreenTip appears identifying this color as the Follow Accent and Hyperlink Scheme Color.

7. Click the **red square**
   PowerPoint applies the red color to the selected object's outline.

8. Click the **Fill Color list arrow** ◻▾ on the Drawing toolbar, then click the **yellow square** (third square from the right, called Follow Accent Scheme Color)
   PowerPoint fills the selected object with yellow.

9. Click the **Save button** 🖫 on the Standard toolbar to save your changes

FIGURE C-3: Resizing a text object

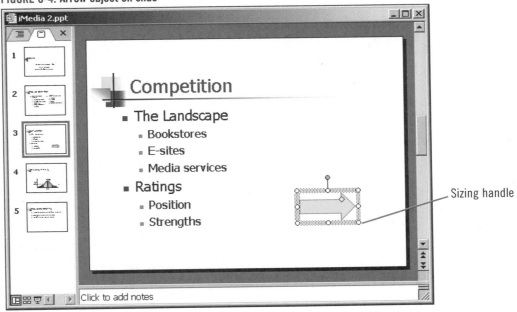

FIGURE C-4: Arrow object on slide

Understanding PowerPoint Objects

In PowerPoint, you often work with multiple objects on the same slide. These may be text objects or graphic objects, such as drawn objects, clip art, or charts. To help you organize objects on a slide, you can align, group, and stack the objects using the Align or Distribute, Group, and Order commands on the Draw menu on the Drawing toolbar. When you align objects, you place their edges (or their centers) on the same plane. For example, you might want to align two squares vertically (one above the other) so that their left edges are in a straight vertical line. When you group objects, you combine two or more objects into one object. It's often helpful to group objects into one when you have finished positioning them on the slide. When you stack objects, you determine their order, that is, which ones are in front and which are in back. You can use the stacking order of objects to overlap them to create different effects.

PowerPoint 2002

Editing Drawing Objects

PowerPoint allows you to manipulate the size and shape of objects on your slide. You can alter the appearance of any object by changing its shape or by adjusting its dimensions. You can add text to most PowerPoint objects. You also can move or copy objects. ✐ Maria wants three arrows on her slide, and she wants them all to be the same shape and size. She changes the shape of the arrow object, and then makes two copies of it. She then rotates one arrow to complete her graphic.

Steps 1 2 3 4

1. **Click the arrow object to select it, if necessary**
   In addition to sizing handles, two other handles appear on the selected object. You use the **adjustment handle**—a small yellow diamond—to change the appearance of an object, usually its most prominent feature, like the size of the head of an arrow. You use the **rotate handle**—a small green circle—to rotate the object.

2. **Press [Shift], then drag the right, middle sizing handle to the right approximately 1"**

3. **Position the pointer over the middle of the selected arrow object so that it changes to ⌖, then drag the arrow so that the bottom of the arrow aligns with the bottom of the word "Position" in the text box**
   A dotted outline appears as you move the arrow object to help you position it. Compare your screen to Figure C-5 and make any necessary adjustments.

4. **Position ⌖ over the arrow object, then press and hold [Ctrl]**
   The pointer changes to ⌖, indicating that PowerPoint will make a copy of the arrow object when you drag the mouse.

5. **While holding down [Ctrl], drag the arrow object up until the dotted lines indicate that the copy aligns with the bottom of the words "Media services" in the text box, then release the mouse button**
   A copy of the first arrow object appears.

6. **Position ⌖ over the second arrow object, press and hold [Ctrl], then drag a copy of the arrow object up the slide until it aligns with the bottom of the first bullet point in the text box**
   You now have three identical objects on your slide.

7. **Type Adopters**
   The text appears in the center of the active object, in this case, the top arrow. The text is now part of the object, so if you move or rotate the object, the text will move with it.

8. **Position the pointer over the rotate handle of the selected arrow object so that it changes to ↻, then drag the rotate handle to the left until the arrow head is pointing straight up**
   If you need to make any adjustments to the arrow object, drag the rotate handle again. Compare your screen with Figure C-6.

9. **Click the middle arrow object, type Price, click the bottom arrow object, type Performance, then click in a blank area of the slide**

10. **Click the Save button 🖫 on the Standard toolbar to save your changes**

Trouble?
PowerPoint uses a hidden grid to align objects; it forces objects to "snap" to the grid lines. If you have trouble aligning the object with the text, press and hold down [Alt] while dragging the object to turn off the grid.

QuickTip
You can use PowerPoint rulers to help you align objects. To display the rulers, position the pointer in a blank area of the slide, right-click, then click Ruler on the shortcut menu.

QuickTip
You can also use the Rotate or Flip commands on the Draw menu button on the Drawing toolbar to rotate or flip objects 90 or 180 degrees.

FIGURE C-5: Slide showing resized arrow object

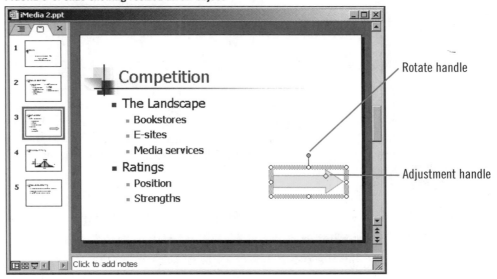

Rotate handle

Adjustment handle

FIGURE C-6: Slide showing duplicated arrow object

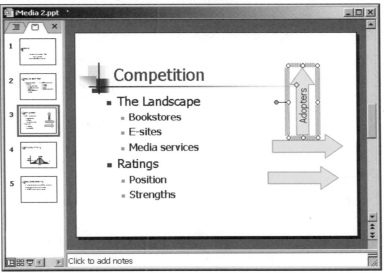

More Ways to Change Objects

You can layer objects over one another by changing their stacking order, or you can change the appearance of an object by making it three-dimensional or by applying a shadow effect. To change the stacking order of an object, select the object, click the Draw button on the Drawing toolbar, point to Order, then click one of the menu commands shown in Figure C-7. To make an object three-dimensional, select it, click the 3-D Style button 🔲 on the Drawing toolbar, then click one of the buttons on the pop-up menu shown in Figure C-8. To add a shadow to an object, select it, click the Shadow Style button 🔲 on the Drawing toolbar, then click one of the buttons on the pop-up menu shown in Figure C-9.

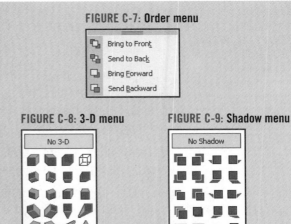

FIGURE C-7: Order menu

FIGURE C-8: 3-D menu

FIGURE C-9: Shadow menu

Aligning and Grouping Objects

After you create objects, modify their appearance, and edit their size and shape, you can position them on the slide, align them, and then group them. The Align command aligns objects relative to each other by snapping the selected objects to a grid of evenly spaced vertical and horizontal lines. The Group command groups objects into one object to make editing and moving them much easier. Maria positions, aligns, and groups the arrow objects on the slide.

Steps

1. Position 🖑 over the **Adopters arrow object**, then drag it down the slide until it is in the same position as in Figure C-10

2. Click the **Price arrow object**, press and hold **[Shift]**, then click the **Performance arrow object**
   The two objects are now selected.

3. Click the **Draw button** Draw ▾ on the Drawing toolbar, then point to **Align or Distribute**
   A menu of alignment and distribution options appears. The top three options align objects vertically; the next three options align objects horizontally.

4. Click **Align Center**
   The arrow objects align vertically on their centers.

5. Press and hold **[Shift]**, click the **Adopters arrow object**, click Draw ▾, then click **Group**
   The arrow objects group to form one object without losing their individual attributes. Notice the sizing handles now appear around the outer edge of the grouped object, not around each individual object.

6. Right-click a blank area of the slide, then click **Grid and Guides** on the shortcut menu
   The Grid and Guides dialog box opens.

7. Click the **Display drawing guides on screen check box**, then click **OK**
   The PowerPoint guides appear as dotted lines on the slide. (The dotted lines may be very faint on your screen.) The guides intersect at the center of the slide. They will help you position the arrow object.

8. Position 🖑 over the **horizontal guide** in a blank area of the slide, press and hold the mouse button until the pointer changes to a guide measurement, then drag the guide down until the guide measurement box reads approximately **0.50**

9. Press **[Shift]**, drag the **grouped arrow object** over the horizontal guide until the center sizing handles are approximately centered over the guide
   Pressing [Shift] while you drag an object constrains its movement to vertical or horizontal. Compare your screen with Figure C-11.

10. Right-click a blank area of the slide, click **Grid and Guides** on the shortcut menu, click the **Display drawing guides on screen check box**, click **OK**, then click the **Save button** 🖫 on the Standard toolbar to save your changes
    The guides are no longer displayed on the slide.

FIGURE C-10: Repositioned arrow object

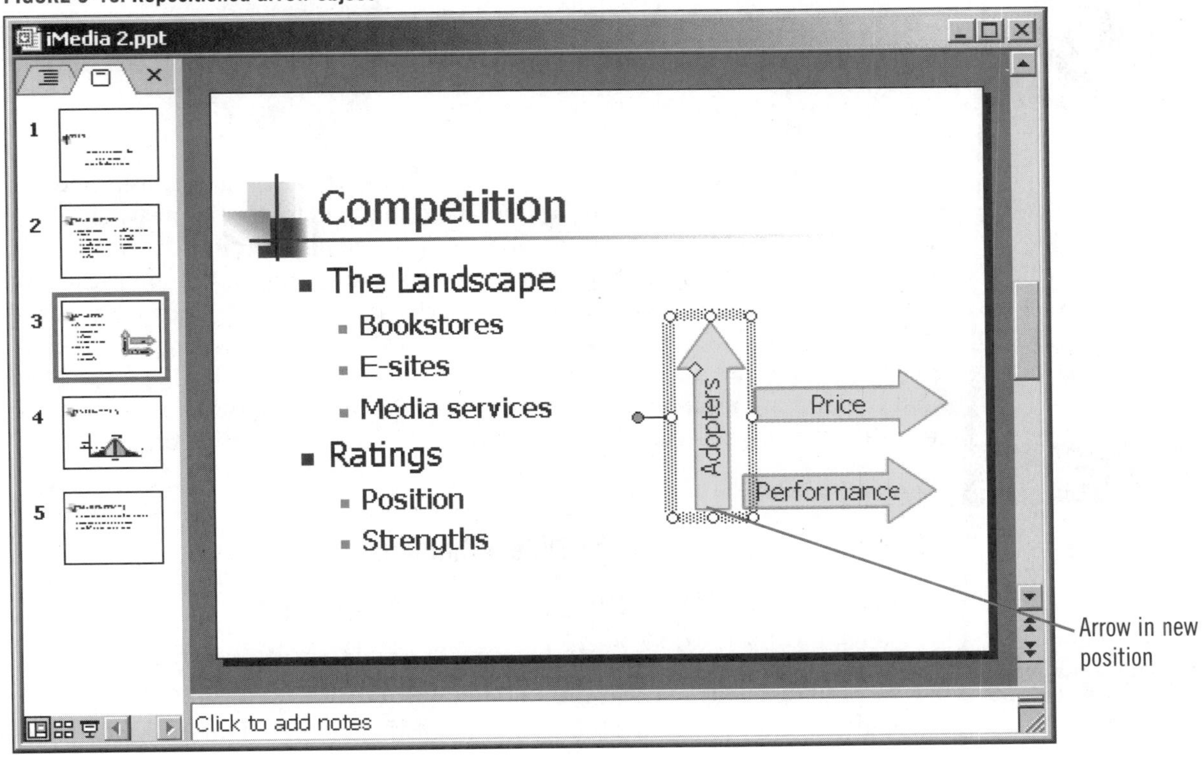

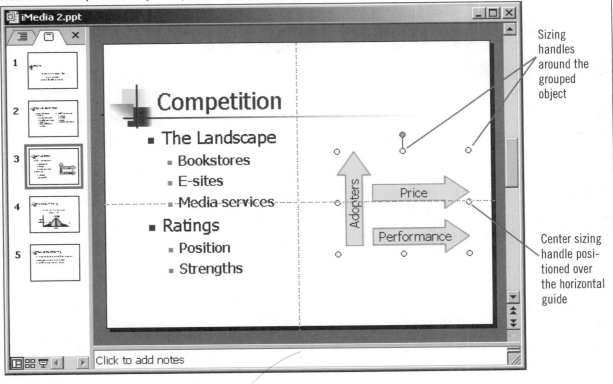

Arrow in new position

FIGURE C-11: Grouped arrow object re-positioned on the slide

Sizing handles around the grouped object

Center sizing handle positioned over the horizontal guide

Adding and Arranging Text

Using the advanced text-editing capabilities of PowerPoint, you can easily add, insert, or rearrange text. The PowerPoint slide layouts allow you to enter text in prearranged text placeholders. If these text placeholders don't provide the flexibility you need, you can use the Text Box button on the Drawing toolbar to create your own text objects. With the Text Box button, you can create two types of text objects: a text label, used for a small phrase where text doesn't automatically wrap to the next line inside the box; and a word-processing box, used for a sentence or paragraph where the text wraps inside the boundaries of the box. ✒ Maria has a slide that contains information on the typical cycle of a product. Now, she uses the Text Box button to create a word-processing box to enter a label for the information on the slide.

Steps 1 2 3 4

1. In the Slides tab, click the **Slide 4 thumbnail**

2. Click the **Text Box button** 🔳 on the Drawing toolbar
The pointer changes to ↓.

3. Position ↓ about 1" from the left side of the slide, above the top of the chart on the slide, then drag toward the right side of the slide to create a word-processing box
Your screen should look similar to Figure C-12. When you begin dragging, an outline of the box appears, indicating how wide a text object you are drawing. After you release the mouse button, an insertion point appears inside the text object, ready to accept text.

4. Type **Market, players, shifts and competition**
Notice that the word-processing box increases in size as your text wraps inside the object. There is a mistake in the text. It should read "Market shifts."

5. Double-click the word **shifts** to select it

6. Position the pointer on top of the selected word and press and hold the mouse button
The pointer changes to ⬚.

7. Drag the word **shifts** to the right of the word **Market** in the text box, then release the mouse button
A dotted insertion line appears as you drag, indicating where PowerPoint will place the word when you release the mouse button. The word "shifts" moves next to the word "Market."

8. Position ⬚ over the text box border, then drag it to the center of the slide
Your screen should look similar to Figure C-13.

9. Click a blank area of the slide outside the text object, then click the **Save button** 🔳 on the Standard toolbar to save your changes

FIGURE C-12: Word-processing box ready to accept text

Slanted lines indicate the word-processing box is ready to accept text

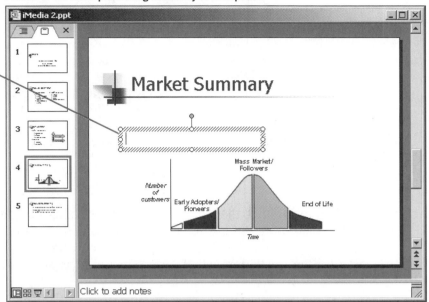

FIGURE C-13: Text added to the word-processing box

Your text might wrap differently depending on the size of your word-processing box

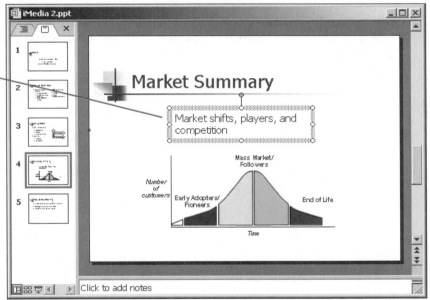

Revising a Presentation

You can send a copy of a presentation over the Internet to others for them to review, edit, and add comments. To send your presentation out for review, you can use Microsoft Outlook, which automatically tracks changes made by reviewers, or you can use any other compatible e-mail program. To send a presentation to reviewers using Outlook, click File on the menu bar, point to Send To, then click Mail Recipient (for Review). Outlook opens and a "Review Request" e-mail with the PowerPoint presentation attached to it is automatically created for you to send to reviewers. Reviewers can use any version of PowerPoint to review, edit, and comment on their copy of your presentation. Once a reviewer is finished with the presentation and sends it back to you, you can combine their changes and comments with your original presentation using PowerPoint's Compare and Merge Presentations feature. When you do this, the Revisions task pane opens with commands that allow you to accept or reject reviewers' changes.

Formatting Text

Once you have entered and arranged the text in your presentation, you can change and modify the way the text looks to emphasize your message. Important text needs to be highlighted in some way to distinguish it from other text or objects on the slide. Less important information needs to be de-emphasized. For example, if you have two text objects on the same slide, you could draw attention to one text object by changing its color or size. To change the way text looks, you need to select it, then choose a Formatting command. ◢ Maria uses some of the commands on the Formatting and Drawing toolbars to change the way the new text box looks on Slide 4.

Steps

1. **On Slide 4, press [Shift], then click the word-processing text box**
   If a text box is already active because you have been entering text in it, you can select the entire text box by clicking on its border with ↖. The entire text box is selected. Any changes you make will affect all the text in the selected text box. Changing the text's size and appearance will help emphasize it.

2. **Click the Increase Font Size button** Å **on the Formatting toolbar**
   The text increases in size to 28 points.

3. **Click the Italic button** *I* **on the Formatting toolbar**
   The text changes from normal to italic text. The Italic button, like the Bold button, is a toggle button, which you click to turn the attribute on or off.

4. **Click the Font Color list arrow** A̲ ▾ **on the Formatting toolbar**
   The Font Color menu appears, showing the eight colors used in the current presentation and the More Colors command, which lets you choose additional colors.

5. **Click More Colors, then click the green cell in the middle row of the color hexagon, second from the left, as shown in Figure C-14**
   The Current color and the New color appear in the box in the lower-right corner of the dialog box.

6. **Click OK**
   The text in the word-processing box changes to green, and the green is added as the ninth color in the set of colors used in the presentation.

7. **Click the Font list arrow on the Formatting toolbar**
   A list of available fonts opens with the font used in the text box selected in the list.

8. **Click the down scroll arrow, then click Times New Roman**
   The Times New Roman font replaces the original font in the text object.

9. **Click the Center button** ☰ **on the Formatting toolbar**
   All the text in the text box is aligned to the center of the text box.

10. **Drag the text box so it is centered over the chart, resize the text box so the text wraps as shown in Figure C-15, click a blank area of the slide outside the text object to deselect it, then click the Save button** 💾 **on the Standard toolbar**
    Compare your screen to Figure C-15.

FIGURE C-14: Colors dialog box

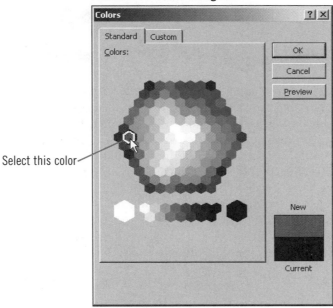

Select this color

FIGURE C-15: Slide showing formatted text box

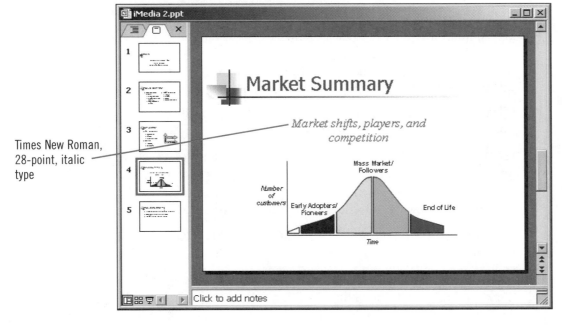

Times New Roman, 28-point, italic type

Market Summary

Market shifts, players, and competition

Click to add notes

Replacing Text and Attributes

As you review your presentation, you may decide to replace certain words throughout the entire presentation. You can automatically modify words, sentences, text case, and periods. To replace specific words or sentences, use the Replace command on the Edit menu. To automatically add or remove periods from title or body text and to automatically change the case of title or body text, click Options on the Tools menu, click the Spelling and Style tab, then click Style Options to open the Style Options dialog box. Click the Case and End Punctuation tab, if necessary. The options on the Visual Clarity tab in the Style Options dialog box control the legibility of bulleted text items on the slides.

Importing Text from Microsoft Word

PowerPoint makes it easy to insert information from other sources, such as Microsoft Word, into a presentation. If you have an existing Word document or outline, you can import it into PowerPoint to create a new presentation or additional slides in an existing presentation. Documents saved in Microsoft Word format (.doc), Rich Text Format (.rtf), plain text format (.txt), and HTML format (.htm) can be inserted into a presentation. When you import a Microsoft Word or a Rich Text Format document into a presentation, PowerPoint creates an outline structure based on the styles in the document. For example, a Heading 1 style in the Word document becomes a slide title in PowerPoint and a Heading 2 style becomes the first level of text in a bulleted list. If you insert a plain text format document into a presentation, PowerPoint creates an outline based on the tabs at the beginning of the document's paragraphs. Paragraphs with no tab become slide titles; paragraphs with one tab indent become first-level text in bulleted lists; paragraphs with two tabs become second-level text in bulleted lists; and so on. ✐ One of Maria's colleagues from the Product Fulfillment department sent her a Word document containing a description of the new product. Maria inserts this document into her presentation.

Steps

1. **Click the Outline tab, then click the Slide 5 icon** 🔲
   Slide 5 appears in the slide pane. Each time you click a slide icon in the Outline tab, the slide title and text are highlighted indicating the slide is selected. Before you insert information into a presentation, you must first designate where you want the information to be placed. The document will be inserted after the selected slide.

2. **Click Insert on the menu bar, then click Slides from Outline**
   The Insert Outline dialog box opens.

Trouble?

If a message dialog box opens telling you that you need to install a converter, click Yes, and insert the Office CD when prompted. Check with your instructor or technical support person if you have trouble.

3. **Locate the Word document PPT C-2 in the drive and folder where your Project Files are stored, then click Insert**
   Three new slides (6, 7, and 8) are added to the presentation as shown in Figure C-16. Slide 6 is highlighted showing you where the information from the Word document begins.

4. **Read the text for the new Slide 6 in the slide pane, click the Slide 7** 🔲 **icon in the Outline tab, then review the text on that slide**
   Slide 7 is selected.

5. **Click the Slides tab, then click the Slide 8 thumbnail**
   After reviewing the text on this slide, Maria realizes that someone else will cover this information in another presentation.

6. **Right-click the Slide 8 thumbnail, then click Delete Slide on the shortcut menu**
   Slide 8 is deleted from the presentation and Slide 7 appears in the slide pane again. Compare your screen to Figure C-17.

7. **Click the Save button** 🔲 **on the Standard toolbar to save your changes**

FIGURE C-16: Outline tab showing imported text

Imported text from Word

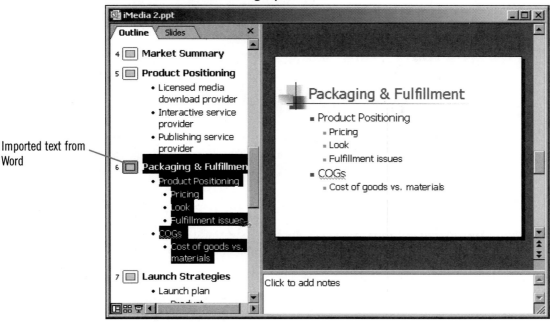

FIGURE C-17: Presentation after deleting slide

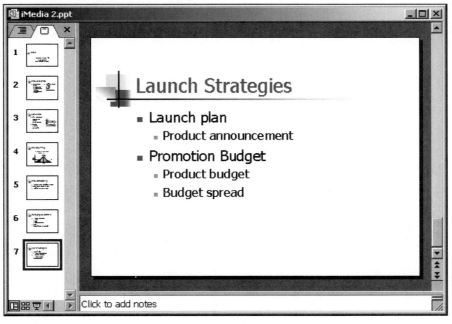

Inserting Slides from Other Presentations

To insert slides into the current presentation, click Insert on the menu bar, then click Slides from Files. Click Browse in the Slide Finder dialog box, then locate the presentation from which you want to copy slides. In the Select slides section, select the slide(s) you want to insert, click Insert, then click Close. The new slides automatically take on the design of the current presentation. If both presentations are open, you can copy the slides from one presentation to another. Change the view of each presentation to Slide Sorter view, select the desired slides, then copy and paste them (or use drag and drop) into the desired presentation. You can then rearrange the slides in Slide Sorter view if necessary.

Customizing the Color Scheme and Background

Every PowerPoint presentation has a **color scheme**, a set of eight coordinated colors, that determines the colors for the slide elements in your presentation: slide background, text and lines, shadows, title text, fills, accents, and hyperlinks. The design template that is applied to a presentation determines its color scheme. See Table C-1 for a description of the slide color scheme elements. The **background** is the area behind the text and graphics. Every design template in PowerPoint—even the blank presentation template—has a color scheme that you can use or modify. You can change the background color and appearance independent of changing the color scheme. 🖌 Maria changes the color scheme and modifies the background of the presentation.

Steps

1. Click the **Color Schemes hyperlink** in the Slide Design task pane
   The current, or default, color scheme is selected with a black border as shown in Figure C-18. Additional color schemes designed specifically for the applied design template (in this case, the Blends template) are also shown.

2. Click the **color scheme icon in the third row, first column** in the Slide Design task pane
   The new color scheme is applied to all the slides in the presentation. In this case, the new color scheme changes the color of the slide graphics and title text, but the bulleted text and background remain the same.

3. Click **Format** on the menu bar, then click **Background**
   The Background dialog box opens.

4. In the Background fill section, click the **list arrow** below the preview of the slide, click **Fill Effects**, then click the **Gradient tab**, if necessary

5. Click the **One color option button** in the Colors section, click the **Color 1 list arrow**, click the **purple square** (called Follow Accent and Hyperlink Scheme Color)
   The purple color fills the Color 1 list arrow and the four variant previews in the Variants section, showing that the background will be shaded with purple.

6. Drag the **Brightness scroll box** all the way to the right (towards Light) in the Colors section
   The four variant previews change color.

7. Click the **From corner option button** in the Shading Styles section, then click the **lower-right variant**
   Compare your screen to Figure C-19.

8. Click **OK**, then click **Apply to All**
   The slide background is now shaded from purple (lower-right) to white (upper-left).

9. Click the **Slide Sorter View button** 🔳, click the **Zoom list arrow** on the Standard toolbar, then click **50%**
   The final presentation appears in Slide Sorter view. Compare your screen to Figure C-20.

10. Add your name as a footer on the notes and handouts, print the slides as handouts (4 slides per page), click the **Save button** 🔲 on the Standard toolbar to save your changes, close the presentation, then exit PowerPoint

QuickTip
To apply a new color scheme to only selected slides, select the slides you want to change on the Slides tab or in Slide Sorter view, point to the color scheme in the Slide Design task pane, click the list arrow that appears, then click Apply to Selected Slides.

QuickTip
If you click the Preset option button, you can choose from a variety of predesigned backgrounds. You can also add other backgrounds by clicking one of the other tabs in the Fill Effects dialog box.

QuickTip
You can also apply a shaded background to an AutoShape by right-clicking the object, then clicking Format Autoshape in the shortcut menu.

FIGURE C-18: Slide Design task pane

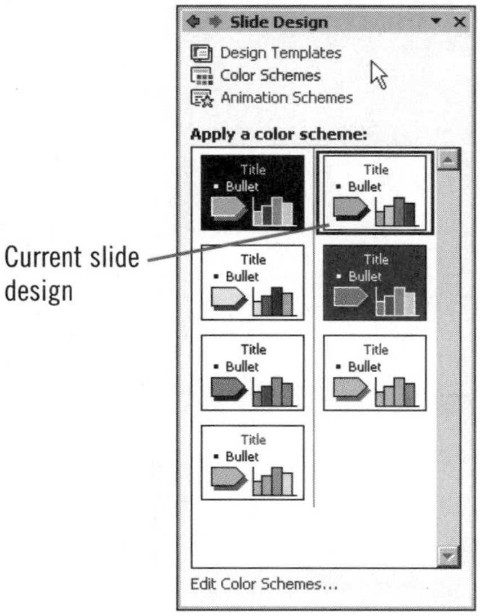

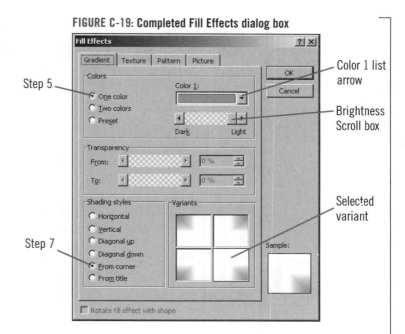

FIGURE C-19: Completed Fill Effects dialog box

Current slide design

Step 5 — Color 1 list arrow

Brightness Scroll box

Step 7

Selected variant

FIGURE C-20: Final presentation in Slide Sorter view

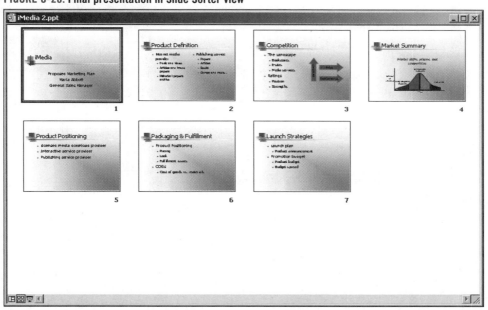

TABLE C-1: Color scheme elements

scheme element	description
Background color	Color of the slide's canvas, or background
Text and lines color	Used for text and drawn lines; contrasts with the background color
Shadows color	Color of the shadow of the text or other object; generally a darker shade of the background color
Title text color	Used for slide title; like the text and line colors, contrasts with the background color
Fills color	Contrasts with both the background and the text and line colors
Accent colors	Colors used for other objects on slides, such as bullets
Accent and hyperlink colors	Colors used for accent objects and for hyperlinks you insert
Accent and followed hyperlink color	Color used for accent objects and for hyperlinks after they have been clicked

PowerPoint 2002

Practice

► Concepts Review

Label the elements of the PowerPoint window shown in Figure C-21.

FIGURE C-21

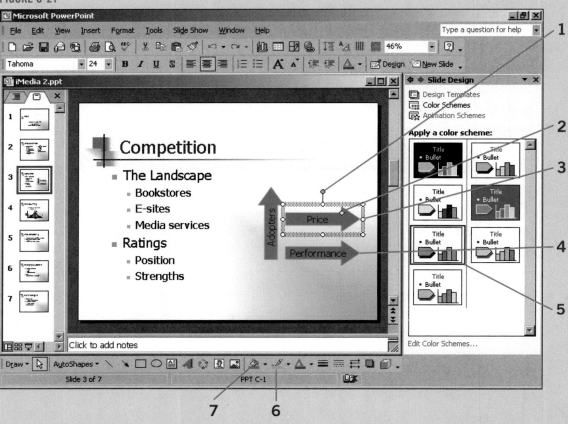

Match each term or button with the statement that describes it.

8. **Word-processing box**
9. **Text label**
10.
11. **Rotate handle**
12. **Adjustment handle**

a. Used to turn an object
b. Creates a text object on a slide
c. Used to change the shape of an object
d. A text object that does not word wrap
e. A text object made by dragging to create a box after clicking the Text Box button

Select the best answer from the list of choices.

13. How do you change the size of a PowerPoint object?
a. Drag a sizing handle
b. Click the Resize button
c. Drag the adjustment handle
d. You can't change the size of a PowerPoint object

14. What would you use to position objects at a specific place on a slide?
a. PowerPoint placeholders
b. PowerPoint guides and rulers
c. PowerPoint lines
d. PowerPoint anchor lines

15. PowerPoint objects can be:
a. Grouped and aligned.
b. Resized and modified.
c. Converted to pictures.
d. Both A and B.

16. What does the adjustment handle do?
a. Adjusts the size of an object
b. Adjusts the position of an object
c. Changes the appearance of an object
d. Changes the angle adjustment of an object

17. What is the easiest way to line objects along their centers on a slide?
a. Group the objects together
b. Use the Align Center command
c. Place the objects on the edge of the slide
d. Use PowerPoint anchor lines

18. What does *not* happen when you group objects?
a. Objects lose their individual characteristics.
b. Objects are grouped together as a single object.
c. Sizing handles appear around the grouped object.
d. The grouped objects have a rotate handle.

19. What is *not* true about guides?
a. Slides can have only one vertical and one horizontal guide.
b. You can press [Ctrl] and drag a guide to create a new one.
c. You can drag a guide off the slide to delete it.
d. A PowerPoint guide is a dotted line.

20. What is a slide background?
a. The pasteboard off the slide
b. A picture
c. The area behind text and graphics
d. The slide grid

21. What is *not* true about a presentation color scheme?
a. Every presentation has a color scheme.
b. The color scheme determines the colors of a slide.
c. You can't change the background color without changing the color scheme.
d. There are eight colors to every color scheme.

► Skills Review

1. Open an existing presentation.
a. Start PowerPoint.
b. Open the file PPT C-3 from the drive and folder where your Project Files are stored.
c. Save it as **Cafe Report** to the location where your Project Files are stored.

PowerPoint 2002

2. Draw and modify an object.

  a. On Slide 3, add the Lightning Bolt AutoShape from the Basic Shapes category on the AutoShapes menu. Make it as large as possible on the right side of the slide.

  b. On the Line Color menu, click No Line.

  c. Change the fill color to light green (named Follow Accent Scheme Color).

  d. Click the 3-D Style button on the Drawing toolbar, then click the 3-D Style 5 button.

  e. Rotate the bolt so it points from the upper-right to the lower-left.

  f. Move the object on the slide so it looks similar to Figure C-22.

  g. Deselect the object and save your changes.

3. Edit drawing objects.

FIGURE C-22

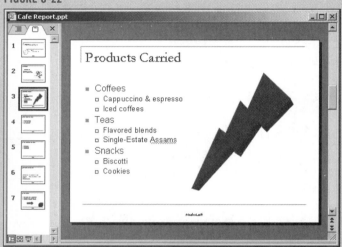

  a. On Slide 7, resize the arrow object so it is about ½" shorter. (*Hint*: You might want to resize the bulleted list text object so it does not interfere with your work.)

  b. Drag the arrow next to the left side of the box.

  c. Use the adjustment handle to lengthen the arrow's head about ¼", then insert the text **Satisfaction**. Enlarge the arrow object so that all the text fits inside it, if necessary.

  d. Make two copies of the arrow and arrange them to the left of the first one so that they are pointing in succession to the box.

  e. Replace the word **Satisfaction** on the middle arrow with the word **Growth**.

  f. Replace the word **Satisfaction** on the left arrow object with the word **Products**.

  g. Insert the word **Success** in the cube object.

  h. Change all the objects' text font to Arial italic. Enlarge the cube as necessary so the word **Success** fits in it.

  i. Save your changes.

4. Align and group objects.

FIGURE C-23

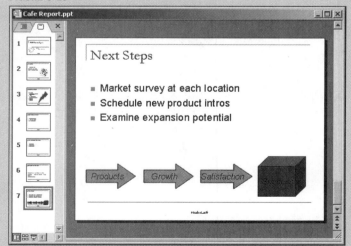

  a. Align the middles of the four objects.

  b. Group the arrow objects and the cube together.

  c. Display the guides, then move the vertical guide left to about 4.58 and the horizontal guide down to about 2.75.

  d. Align the grouped object so its bottom-left resize handle snaps to where the guides intersect. (*Hint*: If your object does not snap to the guides, open the Grid and Guides dialog box, and make sure the Snap objects to grid check box is checked.)

  e. Hide the guides, then save your changes. Compare your screen with Figure C-23.

5. Add and arrange text.

    a. Add a fourth item to the body text box on Slide 2 that reads **Next steps**.

    b. Near the bottom of the slide, below the graphic, create a word-processing box about 3" wide, and in it enter the text: **A relaxing café is a reading haven.** (If the AutoCorrect feature is active, the accent will be added to the *e* in *café* automatically when you press [Spacebar].)

    c. Drag the word **relaxing** in front of the word **reading**.

    d. Save your changes.

6. Format text.

    a. On Slide 2, select the word-processing text box that you added, so that formatting commands will apply to all the text in the box.

    b. Change the font color to the dark green color (named Follow Title Text Scheme Color), increase its font size to 28 points, then, if necessary, resize the word-processing box so the text fits on one line.

    c. Select the body text box to the left of the picture, then align the words to the center.

    d. Go to Slide 6, then align the words **Business Day, August 2003** to the right.

    e. Change the font color of the text box to the brown color (named Follow Accent and Hyperlink Scheme Color).

    f. Go to Slide 7, select the text in the cube, then change the font color to a light fluorescent green. (*Hint*: Use the Colors dialog box.)

    g. Go to Slide 1 and change the title text font to Arial Black, 48 points.

    h. Deselect the text object, then save your changes.

7. Import text from Microsoft Word.

    a. Click Slide 6 in the Slides tab.

    b. Import the Word file PPT C-4. Check the formatting of each new slide.

    c. In the Slides tab, drag Slide 9 below Slide 10.

    d. In the Slides tab, delete Slide 7, Market Surveys.

    e. Save your changes.

8. Customize the color scheme and background.

    a. Open the Slide Design task pane and click the Color Schemes hyperlink.

    b. Apply the bottom color scheme in the right column in the list to all the slides.

    c. Open the Background dialog box, then the Fill Effects dialog box.

    d. On the Gradient tab, select the Two colors option.

    e. Select the Diagonal up shading style and the upper-right variant.

    f. Apply this background to all slides.

    g. Add your name as a footer to the notes and handouts.

    h. Save your changes, then print the slides as handouts (4 slides per page). Your presentation in Slide Sorter view should look similar to Figure C-24.

    i. Close the file and exit PowerPoint.

FIGURE C-24

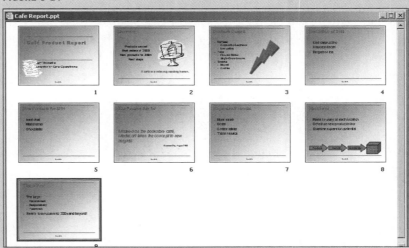

Independent Challenge 1

In this unit, you learned that when you work with multiple objects on a PowerPoint slide, there are ways to arrange them so your information appears neat and well-organized. Using a word-processing program, write a summary explaining how to perform each of these tasks in PowerPoint. Make sure you explain what happens to the objects when you perform these tasks. Also explain *why* you would perform these tasks.

a. Start the word processor, open a new document, then save the file as **Arranging Objects** to the drive and folder where your Project Files are stored.

b. Explain the six different ways to align objects.

c. Explain the concept of grouping objects.

d. Add your name as the first line in the document, save your changes, print the document, close the document, then exit the word processor.

 # Independent Challenge 2

You work for Chicago Language Systems, a major producer of language-teaching CD-ROMs with accompanying instructional books. Twice a year, the company holds title meetings to determine the new title list for the following production term and to decide which current CD titles need to be revised. As the director of acquisitions, you chair the September Title Meeting and present the basic material for discussion.

a. Start PowerPoint, open the file PPT C-5 from the drive and folder where your Project Files are stored, and save it as **Title Meeting 9-26-03**.

b. Add an appropriate design template to the presentation.

c. Insert the Word outline PPT C-6 after Slide 6.

d. Examine all of the slides in the presentation and apply italic formatting to all product and book titles.

e. Format the text so that the most important information is the most prominent.

f. Add appropriate shapes that emphasize the most important parts of the slide content. Format the objects using color and shading. Use the Align and Group commands to organize your shapes.

g. Evaluate the color scheme and the background colors. Delete any slides you feel are unnecessary, and make any changes you feel will enhance the presentation.

h. Spell check, view the final slide show, and evaluate your presentation. Make any necessary changes.

i. Add your name as footer text on the notes and handouts, save the presentation, print the slides as handouts, close the file, and exit PowerPoint.

 # Independent Challenge 3

The Software Learning Company is dedicated to the design and development of instructional software that helps college students learn software applications. You need to design five new logos for the company that incorporate the new company slogan: "Software is a snap!" The marketing group will decide which of the five designs looks best. Create your own presentation slides, but assume that the company colors are blue and green.

a. Sketch your logos and slogan designs on a piece of paper. What text and graphics do you need for the slides?

b. Start PowerPoint, create a new blank presentation, and save it as **Software Learning** to the drive and folder where your Project Files are stored.

c. Create five different company logos, each one on a separate slide. Use the shapes on the AutoShapes menu, and enter the company slogan using the Text tool. (*Hint*: Use the Title only layout.) The logo and the marketing slogan should match each other in tone, size, and color; and the logo objects should be grouped together to make it easier for other employees to copy and paste. Use shadings and shadows appropriately.

d. Add a background color if it is appropriate for your logo design.

e. Spell check, view the final slide show, and evaluate your presentation. Delete any slides you feel are unnecessary, and make any necessary changes.

f. Add your name as footer text, save the presentation, print the slides and notes pages (if any), close the file, and exit PowerPoint.

 # Independent Challenge 4

Your company is planning to offer 401(k) retirement plans to all its employees. The Human Resources Department has asked you to construct and deliver a brief presentation about 401(k) plans to the employees. To find the necessary information for the presentation, you decide to use the Web. The information you find on the Web should answer the following questions:

- What is a 401(k) plan?
- How does a 401(k) plan work?
- How much can I contribute to my 401(k) plan at work?
- When do I have to start taking money from my 401(k) account?
- Is there a penalty for early withdrawal?

a. Connect to the Internet, then use a search engine to locate Web sites that have information on 401(k) plans. If your search does not produce any results, you might try the following sites:
   www.401k.com
   www.quicken.com

b. Review at least two Web sites that contain information about 401(k) plans. Print the Home pages of the Web sites you use to gather data for your presentation.

c. Start PowerPoint. On the title slide, title the presentation **401(k) Plans: What Employees Need to Know**. The presentation should contain at least five slides, including the title slide. Refer to the bulleted list as you create your content.

d. Save the presentation as **401(k) Plans** to the drive and folder where your Project Files are stored.

e. Apply a template to the presentation, customize the slide background, create a new color scheme, and save the color scheme as a standard scheme.

f. Use text formatting as necessary to make text visible and help emphasize important points.

g. At least one slide should contain an object from the AutoShapes menu. Customize the object's size and color.

h. Add your name as a footer to the slides, spell check the presentation, and view the final presentation.

i. Save the final version of the presentation, print the slides, then close the file, and exit PowerPoint.

▶ Visual Workshop

Create a one-slide presentation that looks like the one shown in Figure C-24. Use a text box for each bullet. Group the objects in the bottom logo. (Hint: The top rectangle object uses the 3-D menu.) If you don't have the exact fonts, use something similar. Add your name as a footer on the slide, save the presentation as **SASLtd** to the drive and folder where your Project Files are stored, then print the slide.

FIGURE C-25

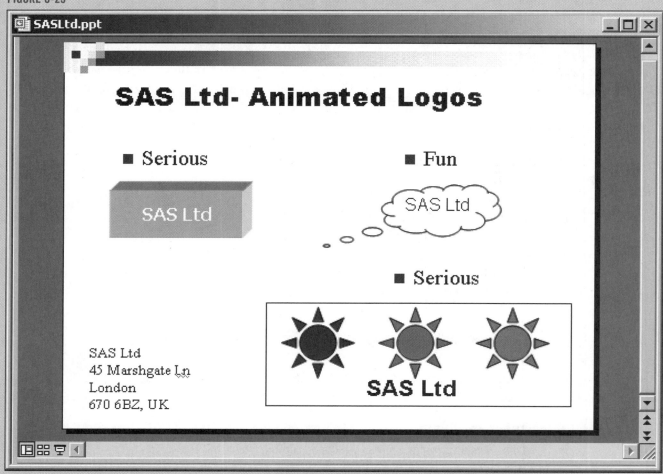

Enhancing
a Presentation

Objectives

- ► **Insert clip art**
- ► **Insert, crop, and scale a picture**
- ► **Embed a chart**
- ► **Enter and edit data in the datasheet**
- ► **Format a chart**
- ► **Create tables in PowerPoint**
- ► **Use slide show commands**
- ► **Set slide show timings and transitions**
- ► **Set slide animation effects**

After completing the content of your presentation, you can supplement your slide text with clip art or graphics, charts, and other visuals that help communicate your content and keep your slide show visually interesting. In this unit, you learn how to insert three of the most common visual enhancements: a clip art image, a picture, and a chart. These objects are created in other programs. After you add the visuals, you rehearse the slide show and add special effects. Maria Abbott has changed her presentation based on feedback from her colleagues. Now she wants to revise the marketing presentation to make it easier to understand and more interesting to watch.

PowerPoint 2002

Inserting Clip Art

PowerPoint includes many professionally designed images, called **clip art**, that you can place in your presentation. Using clip art is the easiest and fastest way to enhance your presentations. In Microsoft Office, clip art and other media files, including photographs, movies, and sounds, are stored in a file index system called the Microsoft Clip Organizer. The Clip Organizer sorts the clip art into groups, including My Collections, Office Collections, and Web Collections. The Office Collections group holds all the media files that come with Microsoft Office. You can customize the Clip Organizer by adding clips to a collection, moving clips from one collection to another, or creating a new collection. As with drawing objects, you can modify clip art images by changing their shape, size, fill, or shading. Clip art is available from many sources outside of the Clip Organizer, including Microsoft Design Gallery Live on Microsoft's Web site and collections on CD-ROMs. ✒ Maria wants to add a picture from the Media Gallery to one of the slides and then adjust its size and placement.

1. Start PowerPoint, open the presentation **PPT D-1** from the location where your Project Files are stored, save it as **iMedia 3**, click **View** on the menu bar, click **Task Pane**, click **Window** on the menu bar, then click **Arrange All**

Trouble?

If the Add Clips to Organizer dialog box opens asking if you want to catalog all media files, click Later.

2. Go to **Slide 7**, titled "Launch Strategies," then click the **Insert Clip Art button** 🖾 on the Drawing toolbar
   The Insert Clip Art task pane opens. Each piece of clip art in the Clip Organizer is identified by keywords that describe the clip art. At the top of the task pane in the Search For section, you can enter a keyword and search for specific types of clip art. If you want to search for specific clips, such as clip art, photographs, movies, or sounds, in certain collections, select options under Other Search Options in the task pane. At the bottom of the task pane, you can click one of the hyperlinks to locate other pieces of clip art or to read tips on how to find clip art.

3. Select any text in the **Search text box**, type **plans**, then click **Search**
   PowerPoint searches for clips identified by the keyword "plans."

QuickTip

You can change the slide layout prior to inserting a piece of clip art. Apply any of the "content" slide layouts except the Blank layout, then click the Insert Clip Art button in the Content placeholder to insert a piece of clip art.

4. Scroll down in the Insert Clip Art task pane, then click the **clip art thumbnail** shown in Figure D-1
   The clip art object appears on the slide and the Picture toolbar opens. PowerPoint automatically changes the slide layout to the Title, Text, and Content layout, which decreases the size of the body text box and positions the clip art object on the right side of the slide. The Automatic Layout Options button 📝 appears below the clip art, which tells you that the slide layout has been changed. You can click the Automatic Layout Options button to select commands that control the automatic changes to the slide layout. If you don't have the clip art picture shown in Figure D-1 in your Clip Organizer, select a similar picture.

5. Place the pointer over the **lower-left sizing handle** and drag the **handle** up to the right about ½"
   The clip art object proportionally decreases in size.

6. Place the pointer over the **Rotate handle** and drag the **handle** to the left so the clip art object is slightly tilted

QuickTip

You can also use the keyboard arrow keys or the Nudge command on the Draw menu button to reposition any selected object by small increments.

7. Drag the **clip art object** up to the right of the text object so it matches Fig D-2
   Compare your screen to Figure D-2 and make any necessary adjustments.

8. Click a blank area of the slide, then save your changes

FIGURE D-1: Screen showing Insert Clip Art task pane

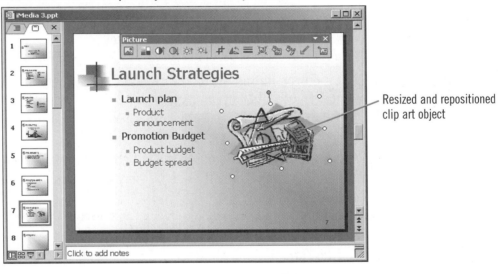

Select this clip

Scroll box about halfway down scroll bar

Indicates this image is from the Web collection of clip art

Click to locate clip art on the Microsoft Design Gallery Live Web site

FIGURE D-2: Slide with clip art object resized and repositioned

Resized and repositioned clip art object

Find more clips online

If you can't find the clips you need in the Clip Organizer, you can easily use clips from the Microsoft Design Gallery Live Web site. To get clips from the Design Gallery Live Web site, click the Clips Online hyperlink at the bottom of the Insert Clip Art task pane. This will launch your Web browser and automatically connect you to the site. Read the License Agreement carefully; it specifies how you are permitted to use clips from this site. Click Accept to agree to the terms of the License Agreement and continue using the site. The Design Gallery Live window opens. You can search the site by keyword or browse by category. Each clip you download is automatically inserted into the Clip Organizer Web Collections folder.

PowerPoint 2002

Inserting, Cropping, and Scaling a Picture

A picture in PowerPoint is a scanned photograph, a piece of line art, clip art, or other artwork that is created in another program and inserted into a PowerPoint presentation. You can insert 18 types of pictures. As with other PowerPoint objects, you can move or resize an inserted picture. You can also crop pictures. **Cropping** a picture means to hide a portion of the picture. Although you can easily change a picture's size by dragging a corner resize handle, you can also **scale** it to change its size by a specific percentage. ✐▬▬ Maria inserts a picture that has previously been saved to a file, crops and scales it, then adjusts its background.

Steps

QuickTip

You can also insert a picture by clicking the Insert Picture button on any of the Content layouts.

1. Go to **Slide 9**, titled "Distribution," then click the **Insert Picture button** 🖼 on the Drawing toolbar
   The Insert Picture dialog box opens.

2. Select the file **PPT D-2** from the location where your Project Files are stored, then click **Insert**
   The picture appears on the slide, and the Picture toolbar opens. The slide layout changes to the Title, Text, and Content layout. The slide might look better using the original slide layout.

3. Click the **Automatic Layout Options button** ⊞, then click **Undo Automatic Layout**
   The slide layout changes back to the original Title and Text layout and the picture moves to the center of the slide. The body text box is too large in this layout.

4. Click ⊞, then click **Redo Automatic Layout**
   The picture would fit better on the slide if it didn't show the boxes on the left side of the picture.

Trouble?

If the Picture toolbar is in the way, drag it by its title bar.

5. Click the **Crop button** ⊹ on the Picture toolbar, then place the pointer over the left, middle sizing handle of the picture
   When the Crop button is active, the sizing handles appear as straight black lines. The pointer changes to ⊣.

6. Press and hold **[Alt]**, then drag the left edge of the picture to the right until the dotted line indicating the left edge of the picture has cut out the boxes, as shown in Figure D-3, then click ⊹
   Pressing [Alt] while dragging or drawing an object in PowerPoint overrides the automatic snap-to-grid setting. Now the picture needs to be enlarged and positioned into place.

7. Click the **Format Picture button** 🖼 on the Picture toolbar, click the **Size tab**, make sure the **Lock aspect ratio check box** is selected, click and hold the **Height up arrow** until the Height and Width percentages reach **200%**, then click **OK**
   When you are scaling a picture and Lock aspect ratio is selected, the ratio of height to width remains the same. The white background is distracting.

QuickTip

You cannot change the colors in a bitmapped (.bmp) object in PowerPoint, but you can change the background colors of the object.

8. With the picture still selected, click the **Set Transparent Color button** ✐ on the Picture toolbar, then click the **white background** in the picture with the ✐ pointer
   The white background is no longer visible, and the picture contrasts well with the background.

9. Drag the **picture** to center it in the blank area on the right side of the slide, deselect it, then save your changes
   See Figure D-4.

FIGURE D-3: Using the cropping pointer to crop the picture

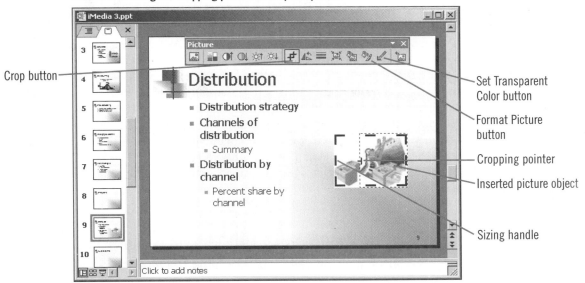

Crop button

Set Transparent Color button

Format Picture button

Cropping pointer

Inserted picture object

Sizing handle

FIGURE D-4: Completed slide with the cropped and resized graphic

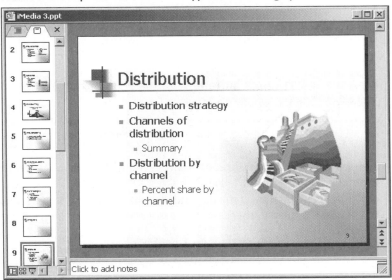

Ways to use graphics with PowerPoint

You can insert pictures with a variety of graphics file **formats**, or file types, in PowerPoint. Most of the clip art that comes with PowerPoint is in Windows metafile format and has the .wmf file extension. You can change the colors in a .wmf graphic object by selecting it, then clicking the Recolor Picture button on the Picture toolbar. You can then replace each color in the graphic with another color. A graphic in .wmf format can be ungrouped into its separate PowerPoint objects, then edited with any of the PowerPoint drawing tools. You cannot recolor or ungroup pictures (files with the .bmp or .tif

extension). The clip art you inserted in the last lesson is in .wmf format, and the picture you inserted in this lesson is in .tif format.

You can also save PowerPoint slides as graphics and later use them in other presentations, in graphics programs, and on Web pages. Display the slide you want to save, then click Save As from the File menu. In the Save As dialog box, click the Save as type list arrow, and scroll to the desired graphics format. Name the file, click OK, then click the desired option when the alert box appears asking if you want to save all the slides or only the current slide.

PowerPoint 2002

Embedding a Chart

Often, the best way to communicate information is with a visual aid such as a chart. PowerPoint comes with a program called **Microsoft Graph** that you can use to create charts for your slides. A **chart** is the graphical representation of numerical data. Every chart has a corresponding **datasheet** that contains the numerical data displayed by the chart. Table D-1 lists the chart types available in Microsoft Graph. When you insert a chart object into PowerPoint, you are actually embedding it. **Embedding** an object means that the object becomes part of the PowerPoint file, but you can double-click on the embedded object to display the tools of the program in which the object was created. If you modify the embedded object, the original object file does not change. Maria wants to embed a chart object into one of her slides.

Steps

1. Go to **Slide 10**, titled "Success Metrics," click the **Other Task Panes list arrow** ▼ on the task pane title bar, then click **Slide Layout**
   The Slide Layout task pane opens with the Title and Text layout selected.

2. Click the **Title and Content layout** in the Slide Layout task pane under Content Layouts
   Remember to use the ScreenTips to help locate the correct layout. A content placeholder appears on the slide displaying six buttons in the middle of the placeholder. Each of these buttons represents a different object, such as a table, picture, or chart, that you can apply to your slide.

3. Click the **Insert Chart button** 📊 in the content placeholder
   Microsoft Graph opens and embeds a default datasheet and chart into the slide, as shown in Figure D-5. The datasheet consists of rows and columns. The intersection of a row and a column is called a **cell**. Cells are referred to by their row and column location; for example, the cell at the intersection of column A and row 1 is called cell A1. Cells along the left column and top row of the datasheet typically contain **data labels** that identify the data in a column or row; for example, "East" and "1st Qtr" are data labels. Cells below and to the right of the data labels contain the data values that are represented in the chart. Each column and row of data in the datasheet is called a **data series**. Each data series has corresponding **data series markers** in the chart, which are graphical representations such as bars, columns, or pie wedges. The gray boxes along the left side of the datasheet are called **row headings** and the gray boxes along the top of the datasheet are called **column headings**. Notice that the PowerPoint Standard and Formatting toolbars have been replaced with the Microsoft Graph Standard and Formatting toolbars, and the menu bar has changed to include Microsoft Graph commands.

4. Move the pointer over the datasheet
   The pointer changes to ⊕. Cell A1 is the **active cell**, which means that it is selected. The active cell has a heavy black border around it.

5. Click cell **B3**, which contains the value 46.9
   Cell B3 is now the active cell.

6. Click a blank area of the slide to exit Graph then click again to deselect the chart object
   Graph closes and the PowerPoint menu bar and toolbars appear.

7. Save your changes

FIGURE D-5: Datasheet and chart in the PowerPoint window

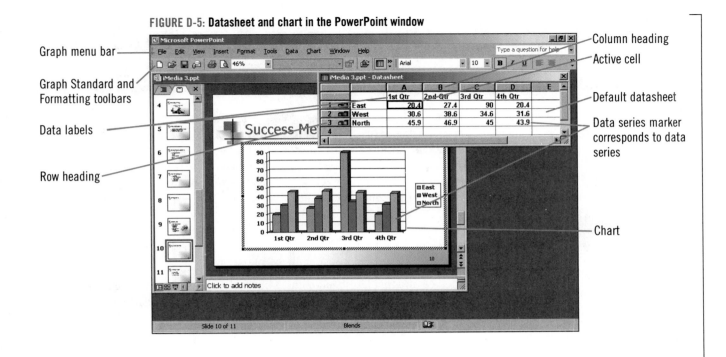

Graph menu bar

Graph Standard and Formatting toolbars

Data labels

Row heading

Column heading

Active cell

Default datasheet

Data series marker corresponds to data series

Chart

TABLE D-1: Microsoft Graph chart types

chart type	looks like	use to
Column		Track values over time or across categories
Bar		Compare values in categories or over time
Line		Track values over time
Pie		Compare individual values to the whole
XY (Scatter)		Compare pairs of values
Area		Show contribution of each data series to the total over time
Doughnut		Compare individual values to the whole with multiple series
Radar		Show changes in values in relation to a center point
Surface		Show value trends across two dimensions
Bubble		Indicate relative size of data points
Stock		Show stock market information or scientific data
Cylinder, cone, pyramid		Track values over time or across categories

Entering and Editing Data in the Datasheet

After you embed the default chart into your presentation, you need to replace the data labels and cell data in the sample datasheet with the correct information. If you have data in a spreadsheet or other source, you can import it into Microsoft Graph; otherwise you can type your own information into the datasheet. As you enter data or make changes to the datasheet, the chart automatically changes to reflect your alterations. ◢▬▬ Maria enters the projected revenue figures for the first year of iMedia operation.

Steps 1234

1. **Double-click the chart on Slide 10**
   The chart is selected and the datasheet opens. The labels representing the quarters across the top are correct, but the row labels need adjusting, and the data needs to be replaced with iMedia's projected quarterly sales figures for each product type.

QuickTip

Double-click the column divider lines between the column headings to automatically resize the column width to accommodate the widest entry.

2. **Click the East row label, type Media, then press [Enter]**
   After you press [Enter], the data label in row 2 becomes selected. Pressing [Enter] in the datasheet moves the active cell down one cell; pressing [Tab] in the datasheet moves the active cell to the right one cell.

3. **Type Publish, then press [Tab]**
   Cell A2 becomes active. Notice in the chart, below the datasheet, that the data labels you typed are now in the legend to the right of the chart. The information in row 3 of the datasheet is not needed.

4. **Click the row heading for row 3, then press [Delete]**
   Clicking the row heading for row 3 selects the entire row. The default information in row 3 of the datasheet is deleted and the columns in the chart adjust accordingly.

Trouble?

If you can't see a column or a row, resize the datasheet window or use the scroll bars to move another part of the datasheet into view.

5. **Click cell A1, type 36,000, press [Enter], type 47,000, press [Tab], then press [▲] to move to cell B1**
   Notice that the height of each column in the chart changes to reflect the numbers you typed.

6. **Enter the rest of the numbers shown in Figure D-6 to complete the datasheet**
   The chart currently shows the columns grouped by quarter, and the legend represents the rows in the datasheet. The icons in the row headings indicate that the row labels appear in the legend. It would be more effective if the columns were grouped by iMedia product with the legend representing the columns in the datasheet.

Trouble?

If you don't see the By Column button on the Standard toolbar, click a Toolbar Options button ▸▸ on a toolbar to locate buttons that are not visible on your toolbar.

7. **Click the By Column button ▦ on the Standard toolbar**
   The division labels are now on the horizontal axis of the chart, and the quarters are listed in the legend. The groups of data markers (the columns) now represent the projected revenue for each product by quarter. Notice that the small column chart graphics that used to be in the row headings in the datasheet have now moved to the column headings, indicating that the series are now in columns.

8. **Click the slide outside the chart area, compare your chart to Figure D-7, then save the presentation**
   The datasheet closes, allowing you to see your entire chart. This chart layout clearly shows iMedia's projected revenue for the first year it's in operation.

FIGURE D-6: Datasheet showing iMedia's projected revenue

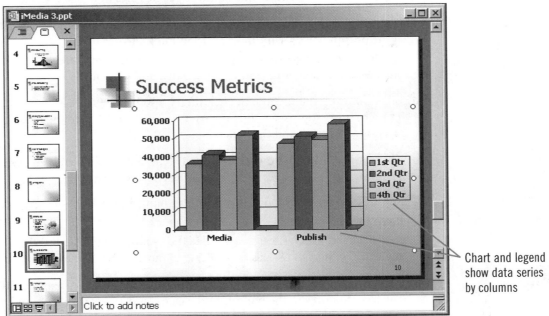

New values are automatically updated to match edited datasheet

Toolbar options button

Icons identify legend labels

Legend identifies the data series by rows

FIGURE D-7: Chart showing data grouped by division

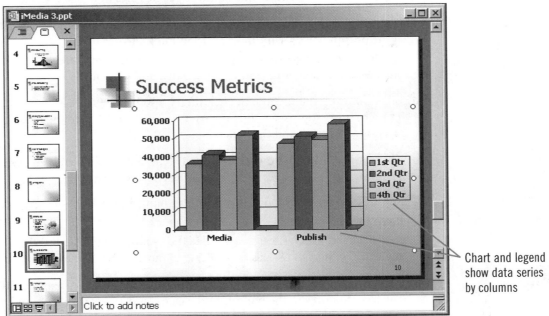

Chart and legend show data series by columns

Series in Rows vs. Series in Columns

If you have difficulty visualizing the difference between the Series in Rows and the Series in Columns commands on the Data menu, think about the legend. **Series in Rows** means that the information in the rows will become the legend in the chart, and the column labels will be on the horizontal axis.

Series in Columns means that the information in the columns will become the legend in the chart, and the row labels will be on the horizontal axis. Microsoft Graph places a small graphic representing the chart type on the axis items that are currently represented by the chart series items (bars, etc.).

Unit D

PowerPoint 2002

Formatting a Chart

Microsoft Graph lets you change the appearance of the chart to emphasize certain aspects of the information you are presenting. You can change the chart type (for example pie, column, bar, or line), create titles, format the chart labels, move the legend, add arrows, or format the data series markers. Like other objects in PowerPoint, you can change the fill color, pattern, line style and color, and style of most elements in a chart. ✐ Maria wants to improve the appearance of her chart by formatting the vertical and horizontal axes and by inserting a title.

Steps

1. **Double-click the chart** to reopen Microsoft Graph, then click the **Close button** ☒ in the Datasheet window to close the datasheet
   The Microsoft Graph menu and toolbar remain at the top of the window.

QuickTip

If you don't see the Currency Style button on the Formatting toolbar, click a Toolbar Options button ⯮ on a toolbar to locate buttons that are not visible on your toolbar.

2. **Click one of the revenue numbers** on the vertical axis to select the axis, then click the **Currency Style button** 🟤 on the Formatting toolbar
   Before you can format any object on the chart, you need to select it. The numbers on the vertical axis appear with dollar signs and two decimal places. You don't need to show the two decimal places, because all the values are whole numbers.

3. **Click the Decrease Decimal button** 🔢 on the Formatting toolbar twice
   The numbers on the vertical axis now have dollar signs and show only whole numbers. See Figure D-8. The division names on the horizontal axis would be easier to see if they were larger.

4. **Click one of the division names** on the horizontal axis, click the **Font Size list arrow** ▣ on the Formatting toolbar, then click **20**
   The font size changes from 18 points to 20 points for both labels on the horizontal axis. The chart would be easier to read if it had a title and axis labels.

5. **Click Chart** on the menu bar, click **Chart Options**, then click the **Titles tab**, if necessary
   The Chart Options dialog box opens. Here, you can change the chart title, axes, gridlines, legend, data labels, and the data table.

6. **Click in the Chart title text box**, then type **iMedia Projected Revenue**
   The preview box changes to show you the chart with the title.

7. **Press [Tab]** twice to move the insertion point to the Value (Z) axis text box, then type **Revenue**
   In a 3-D chart, the vertical axis is called the Z-axis, and the depth axis, which you don't usually work with, is the Y-axis. You decide to move the legend to the bottom of the chart.

8. **Click the Legend tab**, click the **Bottom option button**, then click **OK**
   The legend moves to the bottom of the chart, and a new chart title and axis title appear on the chart. The axis title would look better and take up less space if it were rotated 90 degrees.

9. **Right-click the "Revenue" label** on the vertical axis, click **Format Axis Title**, click the **Alignment tab**, drag the **red diamond** in the Orientation section up to a vertical position so the spin box reads 90 degrees, click **OK**, then click a blank area of the slide
   Graph closes and the PowerPoint toolbars and menu bar appear.

10. **Drag the chart** to the center of the slide, click a blank area of the slide, then save your changes
    Compare your screen to Figure D-9.

Currency style applied to chart numbers

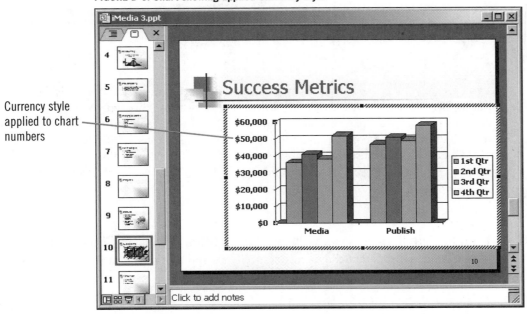

Chart title

Value (Z) axis title

Legend

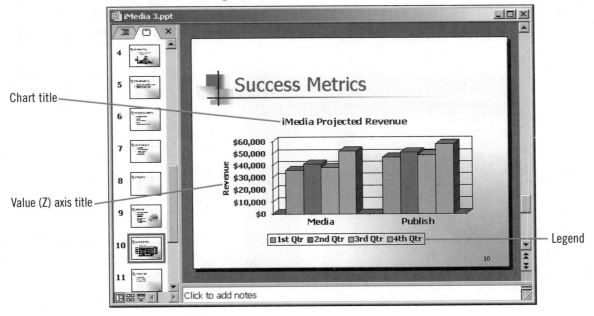

Customizing charts

You can easily customize the look of any chart in Microsoft Graph. Click the chart to select it, then double-click any data series element (a column, for example) to open the Format Data Series dialog box. Use the tabs to change the element's fill color, border, shape, or data label. You can even use the same fill effects you apply to a presentation background. In 3-D charts, you can change the chart depth as well as the distances between series.

Creating Tables in PowerPoint

As you create your PowerPoint presentation, you may need to insert information in a row and column format. A table you create in PowerPoint is ideal for this type of information layout. There are three ways to create a table in PowerPoint: the Insert Table button on the Standard toolbar, the Table command on the Insert menu and any of the content slide layouts. Once you have created a table, you can use the buttons on the Tables and Borders toolbar or on the Formatting toolbar to format it. ✐ Maria creates a table describing iMedia's different pricing plans.

Steps

1. Go to **Slide 8**, then click the **Insert Table button** ▦ on the Standard toolbar
   A cell grid appears that allows you to specify the number of columns and rows you want in your table.

2. Move your pointer over the grid to select a **3 × 3 cell area** ("3 × 3 Table" appears at the bottom of the cell grid), then click your mouse button
   A table with three columns and three rows appears on the slide, and the Tables and Borders toolbar opens. The first cell in the table is selected and ready to accept text.

Trouble?

If the Tables and Borders toolbar does not open, click View on the menu bar, point to Toolbars, then click Tables and Borders. If the toolbar obscures part of the table, drag it out of the way.

3. Type **Plan 1**, press **[Tab]**, type **Plan 2**, press **[Tab]**, type **Plan 3**, then press **[Tab]**
   Don't worry if the table borders seem to disappear. The text you typed appears in the top three cells of the table. Pressing [Enter] moves the insertion point to the next line in the cell.

4. Enter the rest of the table information shown in Figure D-10, pressing **[Tab]** after each entry except the last one
   The table would look better if it were formatted.

5. Drag to select the column headings in the top row of the table
   The text in the first row becomes highlighted.

QuickTip

You can change the height or width of any table cell by dragging its top or side borders.

6. Click the **Center Vertically button** ▤ on the Tables and Borders toolbar, then click the **Center button** ▤ on the Formatting toolbar
   The text is centered horizontally and vertically.

7. With the text in the first row still selected, click the **Fill Color list arrow** 🎨▾ on the Tables and Borders toolbar, click the **green color** in the second row, then click a blank area of the slide
   The top row is filled with the color green.

8. Select the text in the other two rows, vertically center the text, then fill these three rows with the **white color** in the first row of the Fill Color list
   The table would look better if the last two rows were a little farther away from the cell edges.

QuickTip

You can use the Format Table dialog box to apply a diagonal line through any table cell. Click the Borders tab, then click the diagonal line button.

9. With the bottom two rows still selected, click **Format** on the menu bar, click **Table**, click the **Text Box tab**, click the **Left up scroll arrow** until it reads **.25**, click **OK**, click a blank area of the slide, then save the presentation
   The Tables and Borders toolbar closes and the table is no longer selected. Compare your screen with Figure D-11.

FIGURE D-10: The new table before formatting

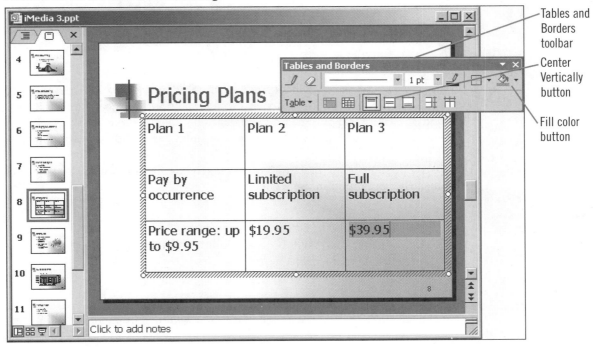

Tables and Borders toolbar

Center Vertically button

Fill color button

FIGURE D-11: Formatted table

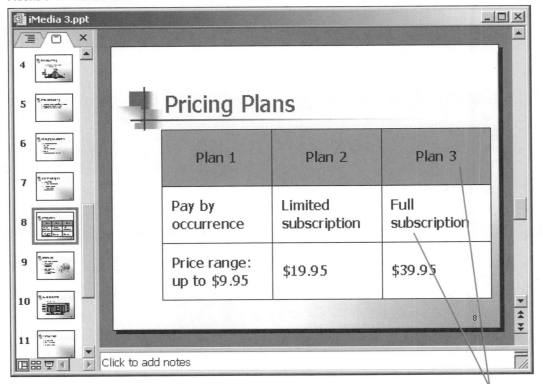

Text vertically centered in the cells

PowerPoint 2002

Using Slide Show Commands

With PowerPoint, you can show a presentation on any compatible computer using Slide Show view. As you've seen, Slide Show view fills your computer screen with the slides of your presentation, showing them one at a time, similar to how a slide projector shows slides. Once your presentation is in Slide Show view, you can use a number of slide show options to tailor the show. For example, you can draw on, or **annotate**, slides or jump to a specific slide. Maria runs a slide show of her presentation and practices using some of the custom slide show options to make her presentation more effective.

Steps 1234

1. Go to **Slide 1**, then click the **Slide Show button** 🖵

The first slide of the presentation fills the screen.

2. Press **[Spacebar]**

Slide 2 appears on the screen. Pressing [Spacebar] or clicking the left mouse button is the easiest way to move through a slide show. Another way is to use the keys listed in Table D-2. You can also use the Slide Show shortcut menu for on-screen navigation during a slide show.

3. Right-click anywhere on the screen, point to **Go** on the shortcut menu, then click **Slide Navigator**

The Slide Navigator dialog box opens and displays a list of the presentation slides.

> **QuickTip**
>
> You can also access the Slide Show shortcut menu by moving the mouse pointer, then clicking the Slide Show menu icon that appears in the lower-left corner of the screen.

4. Click **9. Distribution** in the Slide titles list box, then click **Go To**

The slide show jumps to Slide 9. You can emphasize major points in your presentation by annotating the slide during a slide show using the Pen tool.

5. Right-click the slide, point to **Pointer Options** on the shortcut menu, then click **Pen**

The pointer changes to ✎.

6. Press and hold **[Shift]** and drag ✎ to draw a line under each of the bulleted points on the slide

Holding down [Shift] constrains the Pen tool to straight horizontal or vertical lines. Compare your screen to Figure D-12. While the annotation pen is visible, mouse clicks do not advance the slide show; however, you can still move to the next slide by pressing [Spacebar] or [Enter].

7. Right-click the slide, point to **Screen** on the shortcut menu, click **Erase Pen**, then press **[Ctrl][A]**

The annotations on Slide 9 are erased and the pointer returns to ↖.

> **QuickTip**
>
> If you know the slide number of a slide you want to jump to during a slide show, type the number, then press [Enter].

8. Right-click the slide, point to **Go**, point to **By Title**, then click **3 Competition** on the shortcut menu

Slide 3 appears.

9. Press **[Home]**, then click the left mouse button, press **[Spacebar]**, or press **[Enter]** to advance through the slide show

After the black slide that indicates the end of the slide show appears, the next click ends the slide show and returns you to Normal view.

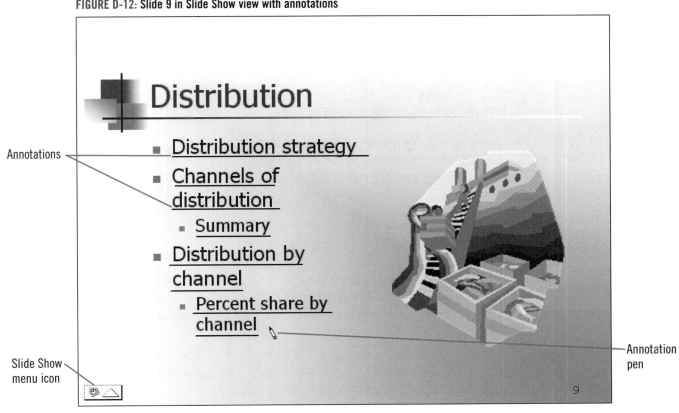

Annotations

Slide Show
menu icon

Annotation
pen

TABLE D-2: Slide Show keyboard controls

control	description
[Enter], [Spacebar], [PgDn], [N], [↓], or [→]	Advances to the next slide
[E]	Erases the annotation drawing
[Home], [End]	Moves to the first or last slide in the slide show
[H]	Displays a hidden slide
[↑] or [PgUp]	Returns to the previous slide
[W]	Changes the screen to white; press again to return
[S]	Pauses the slide show; press again to continue
[B]	Changes the screen to black; press again to return
[Ctrl][P]	Changes pointer to
[Ctrl][A]	Changes pointer to
[Esc]	Stops the slide show

PowerPoint 2002

Setting Slide Show Timings and Transitions

In a slide show, you can preset when and how each slide appears on the screen. You can set the **slide timing**, which is the amount of time a slide is visible on the screen. Each slide can have different timings. Setting the right slide timing is important because it determines how long you have to discuss the material on each slide. You can also set **slide transitions**, which are the special visual and audio effects you apply to a slide that determine how it moves in and out of view during the slide show. Maria decides to set her slide timings for 10 seconds per slide and to set transitions for all her slides.

Steps

1. Click the Slide Sorter View button 🔲

Slide Sorter view shows a thumbnail of the slides in your presentation. The number of slides you see on your screen depends on the current zoom setting in the Zoom box on the Standard toolbar. Notice that the Slide Sorter toolbar appears next to the Standard toolbar.

QuickTip

If you don't see the Slide Transition button on the Slide Sorter toolbar, click a Toolbar Options button 🔳 on a toolbar to locate buttons that are not visible on your toolbar.

2. Click the Slide Transition button 🔲 **on the Slide Sorter toolbar**

The Slide Transition task pane opens. The list box at the top of the task pane contains the slide transitions that you can apply to the slides of your presentation. You can change the speed of slide transitions or add a sound to a slide that plays during a slide show in the Modify transition section. Determine how slides progress during a slide show—either manually or with a slide timing—in the Advance slide section.

3. Make sure the On mouse click check box is selected in the Advance slide section, click the Automatically after check box to select it, select the number in the Automatically after text box, type 10, then click Apply to All Slides

The timing between slides is 10 seconds. The timing appears under each slide. When you run the slide show, each slide will remain on the screen for 10 seconds. You can override a slide's timing and speed up the slide show by pressing [Spacebar], [Enter], or clicking the left mouse button.

QuickTip

Click the transition icon under any slide to see its transition play.

4. Scroll down the list of transitions at the top of the task pane, click Wheel Clockwise, 4 Spokes, then click Apply to All Slides

You can apply a transition to one slide or to all of the slides in your presentation. The selected slide, Slide 1, displays the slide transition immediately after you apply the transition to all the slides. All of the slides now have the Wheel Clockwise transition applied to them as indicated by the transition icon under each slide. See Figure D-13. The slide transition would have more impact if it were slowed down.

5. Click the Speed list arrow under Modify Transition in the task pane, click Medium, then click Apply to All Slides

6. Scroll down the slide pane and click Slide 11, click the Sound list arrow under Modify transition in the task pane, scroll down the list, then click Chime

The sound plays when you apply the sound to the slide. The sound will now play when Slide 11 appears during the slide show.

QuickTip

To end a slide show, press [Esc] or click End Show in the Slide Show shortcut menu.

7. Press [Home], click Slide Show at the bottom of the task pane, and watch the slide show advance automatically

8. When you see the black slide at the end of the slide show, press [Spacebar]

The slide show ends and returns to Slide Sorter view with Slide 1 selected.

FIGURE D-13: Screen showing Slide Transition task pane

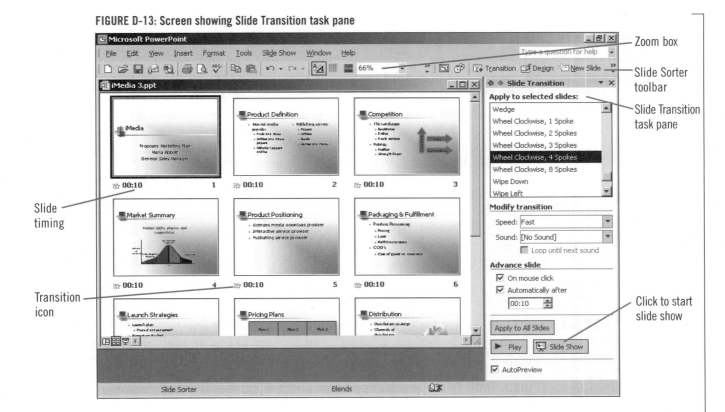

Zoom box

Slide Sorter toolbar

Slide Transition task pane

Click to start slide show

Slide timing

Transition icon

Rehearsing slide show timing

You can set different slide timings for each slide. For example, you can have the title slide appear for 20 seconds, the second slide for 3 minutes, and so on. You can set timings by clicking the Rehearse Timings button 🕑 on the Slide Sorter toolbar or by choosing the Rehearse Timings command on the Slide Show menu. The Rehearsal dialog box shown in Figure D-14 opens. It contains buttons to pause between slides and to advance to the next slide. After opening the Rehearsal dialog box, practice giving your presentation. PowerPoint keeps track of how long each slide appears and sets the timing accordingly. You can view your rehearsed timings in Slide Sorter view. The next time you run the slide show, you can use the timings you rehearsed.

FIGURE D-14: Rehearsal dialog box

Rehearsal 0:00:04 0:00:04

Click to pause

Time elapsed while viewing current slide

Click to reset the clock to zero for the current slide

Total elapsed time for all slides

PowerPoint 2002

Setting Slide Animation Effects

Animation effects let you control how the graphics and main points in your presentation appear on the screen during a slide show. You can animate text, images, or even individual chart elements, or you can add sound effects. You can set custom animation effects or use one of PowerPoint's animation schemes. An **animation scheme** is a set of predefined visual effects for the slide transition, title text, and bullet text of a slide. ✎ Maria wants to animate the text and graphics of several slides in her presentation using PowerPoint's animation schemes.

Steps 1 2 3 4

1. Click **Slide 2**, press and hold down **[Ctrl]**, then click **Slides 3**, **5**, **6**, **7**, and **9**
All of the selected slides have bulleted lists on them. The bullets can be animated to appear one at a time during a slide show.

> **QuickTip**
>
> Keep in mind that the animation effects you choose give a certain "flavor" to your presentation. They can be serious and businesslike or humorous. Choose appropriate effects for your presentation content and audience.

2. Click the **Other Task Panes list arrow** ▼, click **Slide Design – Animation Schemes**, scroll down the Apply to selected slides list to the **Exciting section**, then click **Neutron**
Each of the selected slides previews the Neutron animation scheme.

3. Click **Slide 1**, then click **Slide Show** at the bottom of the task pane
The Neutron animation scheme is displayed on the selected slides. You can also animate objects on a slide by setting custom animations. To set custom animation effects, the target slide must be in Slide view.

4. Double-click **Slide 3** in Slide Sorter view, click **Slide Show** on the menu bar, then click **Custom Animation**
The Custom Animation task pane opens, similar to Figure D-15. Objects that are already animated appear in the Custom Animation task pane list in the order in which they will be animated. **Animation tags** on the slide label the order in which elements are animated during a slide show.

> **QuickTip**
>
> If you want the parts of a grouped object to fly in individually, then you must ungroup them first.

5. Click the grouped **arrow object** to select it, then click **Add Effect** in the Custom Animation task pane
A menu of animation effects appears.

6. Point to **Entrance**, then click **More Effects**
The Add Entrance Effect dialog box opens. All of the effects in this dialog box allow an object to enter the slide using a special effect.

> **QuickTip**
>
> If you want to change the order in which objects are animated on the slide, select the object you want to change in the Custom Animation list in the task pane, then click the appropriate Re-Order arrow below the list.

7. Scroll down to the **Exciting section**, click **Pinwheel**, then click **OK**
The arrow object now has the pinwheel effect applied to it as shown in Figure D-15.

8. Run the Slide Show again from Slide 1
The special effects make the presentation more interesting to view.

9. Click the **Slide Sorter View button** ▦, click the **Zoom list arrow** on the Standard toolbar, then click **50**
Figure D-16 shows the completed presentation in Slide Sorter view at 50% zoom.

10. Add your name as a footer on the notes and handouts, save your presentation, print it as handouts, six slides per page, then close the presentation and exit PowerPoint

FIGURE D-15: Screen with Custom Animation task pane open

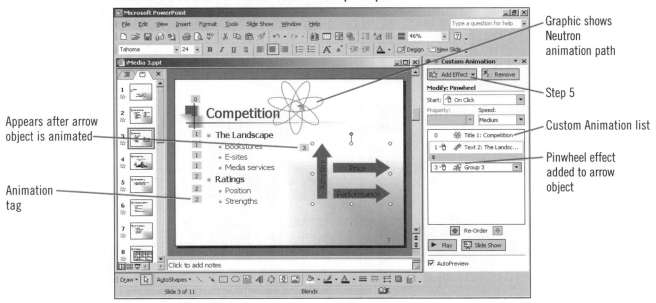

Appears after arrow object is animated

Animation tag

Graphic shows Neutron animation path

Step 5

Custom Animation list

Pinwheel effect added to arrow object

FIGURE D-16: Completed presentation in Slide Sorter view

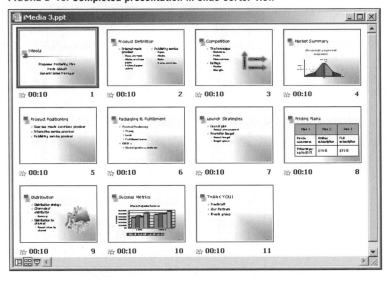

Presentation Checklist

You should always rehearse your slide show. If possible, rehearse your presentation in the room and with the computer that you will use. Use the following checklist to prepare for the slide show:

✓ Is PowerPoint or PowerPoint Viewer installed on the computer?

✓ Is your presentation file on the hard drive of the computer you will be using? Try putting a shortcut for the file on the desktop. Do you have a backup copy of your presentation file on a floppy disk?

✓ Is the projection device working correctly? Can the slides be seen from the back of the room?

✓ Do you know how to control room lighting so that the audience can see both your slides and their handouts and notes? You may want to designate someone to control the lights if the controls are not close to you.

✓ Will the computer be situated so you can advance and annotate the slides yourself? If not, designate someone to advance them for you.

✓ Do you have enough copies of your handouts? Bring extras. Decide when to hand them out, or whether you prefer to have them waiting at the audience members' places when they enter.

Practice

► Concepts Review

Label each element of the PowerPoint window shown in Figure D-17.

FIGURE D-17

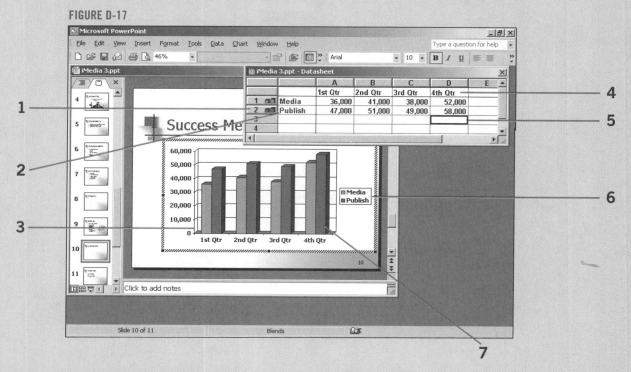

Match each term with the statement that describes it.

8. **Chart**
9. **Embedded object**
10. **Animation effect**
11. **Data series markers**
12. **Clip Organizer**
13. **Scaling**

a. Resizing an object by a specific percentage
b. A graphic representation of a datasheet
c. Graphic representations of data series
d. The special way text and objects appear on a slide
e. An object on a slide from which you can access another program's tools
f. A file index system that organizes images

Select the best answer from the list of choices.

14. **PowerPoint animation effects let you control:**
    a. The order in which text and objects are animated.
    b. The direction from which animated objects appear.
    c. Which text and images are animated.
    d. All of the above.

15. **Which of the following is *not* true of a Microsoft Graph chart?**
    a. A graph is made up of a datasheet and chart.
    b. You can double-click a chart to view its corresponding datasheet.
    c. An active cell has a black selection rectangle around it.
    d. You cannot import data from other programs into a datasheet.

► Skills Review

1. Insert clip art.
a. Open the presentation PPT D-3 from the drive and folder where your Project Files are stored, then save it as **CD Product Report**.
b. Go to Slide 2, search for CD clip art, then insert a piece of clip art.
c. On the Picture tab of the Format Picture dialog box, click the Color list arrow, then click Grayscale.
d. Drag the graphic so the top of the graphic aligns with the body text box and it is centered in the blank area on the right of the slide, then save your changes.

2. Insert, crop, and scale a picture.
a. Go to Slide 6 and insert the picture file PPT D-4.
b. Crop about ¾" off the left side of the picture.
c. Drag the graphic so its top is aligned with the top line of text.
d. Scale the graphic 25% larger than its original size.
e. Reposition the graphic, then make the white background transparent.
f. Save your changes.

3. Embed a chart.
a. Go to Slide 3, **2003 CD Sales by Quarter**, and apply the Title and Content layout.
b. Start Microsoft Graph.
c. Deselect the chart object and save your changes.

4. Enter and edit data in the datasheet.
a. Open Graph again.
b. Enter the information shown in Table D-4 into the datasheet.
c. Delete any unused rows of default data.
d. Place the data series in columns.
e. Save your changes.

TABLE D-4

	1st Qtr	2nd Qtr	3rd Qtr	4th Qtr
East Div.	12.5	10.6	11.9	15.2
West Div.	14.7	16.4	12.8	19.0

5. Format a chart.
a. Close the datasheet but leave Graph running.
b. Change the region names font on the X-axis to 20-point and regular font style (no bold).
c. Apply the Currency Style with no decimals to the values on the vertical axis.
d. Insert the chart title **Division Sales**.
e. Add the title **In Millions** to the Z-axis, then change the alignment of this label to vertical.
f. Change the legend text font to 16-point Arial font and regular font style (no bold).
g. Exit Graph and save your changes.

6. Create a table.
a. Insert a new slide after Slide 2 using the Title and Content slide layout.
b. Add the slide title **CD Sales by Type**.
c. Click the Insert Table button in the placeholder, then insert a table with two columns and five rows.
d. Enter **Type** in the first cell and **Sales** in the second cell in the first row.
e. In the left column, enter the following: **Rock, Pop, Classical**, and **Jazz/Blues**.
f. In the right column, add sales figures between 20,000 and 80,000 for each CD type.
g. Format the table using fills, horizontal and vertical alignment, and other features.
h. Save your changes.

7. Use slide show commands.

a. Begin the slide show at Slide 1, then proceed through the slide show to Slide 3.

b. On Slide 3, use the Pen to draw straight-line annotations under the labels on the horizontal axis.

c. Erase the pen annotations, then change the pointer back to an arrow.

d. Go to Slide 2 using the Go command on the Slide Show shortcut menu.

e. Press [End] to move to the last slide.

f. Return to Normal view.

8. Set slide show timings and transitions.

a. Switch to Slide Sorter view, then open the Slide Transition task pane.

b. Specify that all slides should advance after eight seconds.

c. Apply the Newsflash transition effect to all slides.

d. View the slide show to verify the transitions are correct, then save your changes.

9. Set slide animation effects.

a. Switch to Normal view, then open the Custom Animation task pane.

b. Switch to Slide 7, apply the (Entrance) Fly In animation effect to the Shuttle image, and the (Entrance) Ascend animation effect to the bulleted list. (*Hint*: Look in the Moderate section after clicking More effects.)

c. Go to Slide 2, apply the (Emphasis) Flicker animation effect to the text object. (*Hint*: Look in the Moderate section after clicking More effects.)

d. Apply the (Exit) Faded Zoom animation effect to the CD graphic. (*Hint*: Look in the Subtle section after clicking More effects.)

e. Run the slide show from the beginning to check the animation effects.

f. Add your name as a footer to the notes and handouts, then print the presentation as handouts (4 slides per page).

g. Save your changes, close the presentation, and exit PowerPoint.

► Independent Challenge 1

You are a financial management consultant for Pacific Coast Investments, located in San José, California. One of your primary responsibilities is to give financial seminars on different financial investments and how to determine which funds to invest in. In this challenge, you enhance the look of the slides by adding and formatting objects and adding animation effects and transitions.

a. Open the file PPT D-5 from the location where your Project Files are stored, and save it as **Fund Seminar**.

b. Add your name as the footer on all slides and handouts.

c. Apply the Title and Chart layout to Slide 6, and enter the data in Table D-5 into the datasheet.

d. Format the chart. Add titles as necessary.

e. Add an appropriate clip art item to Slide 2.

f. On Slide 4, use the Align and Group commands to organize the shapes.

g. Spell check the presentation, then save it.

TABLE D-5

	1 year	3 year	5 year	10 year
Bonds	4.2%	5.2%	7.9%	9.4%
Stocks	7.5%	8.3%	10.8%	12.6%
Mutual Funds	6.1%	6.3%	6.4%	6.1%

h. View the slide show, evaluate your presentation, and add a template of your choice. Make changes if necessary.

i. Set animation effects, slide transitions, and slide timings, keeping in mind that your audience includes potential investors who need the information you are presenting to make decisions about where to put their hard-earned money. View the slide show again.

j. Print the slides as handouts (6 slides per page), then close the presentation, and exit PowerPoint.

Independent Challenge 2

You are the manager of the Maryland University Student Employment Office. The office is staffed by work-study students; new students start every semester. Create a presentation that you can use to train them.

a. Plan and create the slide presentation. As you plan your outline, make sure you include slides that will help explain to the work-study staff the main features of the office, including its employment database, library of company directories, seminars on employment search strategies, interviewing techniques, and resume development, as well as its student consulting and resume bulk-mailing services. Add more slides with more content if you wish.

b. Use an appropriate design template.

c. Add clip art and photographs available in the Clip Organizer to help create visual interest.

d. Save the presentation as **Student Employment** to the location where your Project Files are stored. View the slide show and evaluate the contents of your presentation. Make any necessary adjustments.

e. Add transitions, special effects, and timings to the presentation. Remember that your audience is university students who need to assimilate a lot of information in order to perform well in their new jobs. View the slide show again to evaluate the effects you added.

f. Add your name as a footer to slides and handouts. Spell check, save, and print the presentation as handouts (4 slides per page), then close the presentation and exit PowerPoint.

Independent Challenge 3

You are the managing development engineer at JM Design, Inc, an international sports design company located in Ottawa, Ontario, Canada. JM Design designs and manufactures items such as bike helmets, bike racks, and kayak paddles, and markets these items primarily to countries in North America and Western Europe. You need to create a quarterly presentation that outlines the progress of the company's newest technologies, and present it.

a. Plan and create a slide show presentation that includes two new technologies.

b. Use an appropriate design template.

c. Add one chart and one table in the presentation that shows details (such as performance results, testing criteria, etc.) about the new technologies.

d. Include at least two slides that explain how the new technologies will appeal specifically to individual countries in the European and North American markets.

e. Use slide transitions, animation effects, and slide timings. View the slide show to evaluate the effects you added.

f. Add your name as a footer to the handouts. Save the presentation as **JM Design** to the location where your Project Files are stored. Print it as handouts (4 slides per page), then close the presentation and exit PowerPoint.

Independent Challenge 4

You work for Asset Advisors, a small investment firm. You have been asked to complete a basic investing presentation started by your boss. Most of the information has already been entered into the PowerPoint presentation; you just need to add a template and a table to complete the presentation. To find the data for the table, you need to use the Web to locate certain information.

You'll need to find the following information on the Web:
- Data for a table that compares the traditional IRA with the Roth IRA.
- Data for a table that compares at least two other retirement plans.

a. Open the file PPT D-6 from the location where your Project Files are stored, and save it as **Retirement Presentation**.

b. Connect to the Internet, then use a search engine to locate Web sites that have information on retirement plans. If your search does not produce any results, you might try the following sites:

www.vanguard.com
www.investorguide.com
www.quicken.com

c. Review at least two Web sites that contain information about retirement plans. Print the Home pages of the Web sites you use to gather data for your presentation.

d. Apply the Title and Table layout to Slide 7, then enter the data you found that compares the IRA retirement plans.

e. Apply the Title and Table layout to Slide 8, then enter the data you found that compares the other retirement plans.

f. Apply a template to the presentation, then customize the slide background and the color scheme.

g. Format the Autoshape objects on Slides 4 and 5.

h. Use text formatting to help emphasize important points, then add your name as a footer to the handouts.

i. Spell check the presentation, view the final presentation, save the final version, then print the handouts.

▶ Visual Workshop

Create a slide that looks like the example in Figure D-18. Add your name as a footer on the slide. Save the presentation as **Costs** to the location where your Project Files are stored.

FIGURE D-18

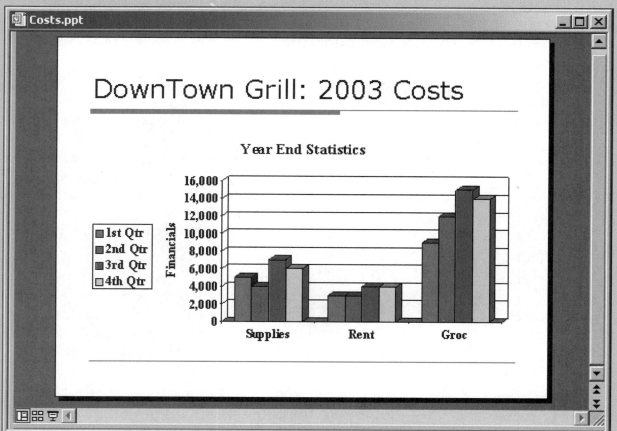

Unit
E

Customizing
Your Presentation

Objectives

MOUS ► **Understand PowerPoint masters**

MOUS ► **Format master text**

MOUS ► **Change master text indents**

MOUS ► **Adjust text objects**

MOUS ► **Use advanced drawing tools**

MOUS ► **Use advanced formatting tools**

► **Use the Style Checker**

MOUS ► **Create a template**

Design features such as text spacing and color are some of the most important qualities of a professional-looking presentation. It is important, however, to make design elements consistent throughout a presentation to hold the reader's attention and to avoid confusion. PowerPoint helps you achieve the look you want by providing ways to customize and enhance your slides, notes pages, and handouts. ◢━━ Maria Abbott, the general sales manager of MediaLoft, is working on a marketing presentation that she will give later this month. After receiving feedback from her coworkers, she revises her presentation by customizing the format of her slides and enhancing the graphics.

Understanding PowerPoint Masters

Each presentation in PowerPoint uses **Master views** to store information about the design template, including font styles, text placeholder position and size, and color scheme. Design elements that you place in the Slide Master view appear on every slide in the presentation. For example, you could insert a company logo in the upper-right corner of the Slide Master and that logo would then appear on every slide in your presentation. There are three Master views—Slide Master view, Handout Master view, and Notes Master view. Changes made to the slide master are reflected on all the slides, changes made to the notes master are reflected in the Notes Page view, and changes made to the handout master are reflected when you print your presentation using one of the Handout print options. Slide Master view actually has two master slides: one for the slide master and one for the title master. These two masters are called a **slide-title master pair**. ▰▰▰ Maria wants to make a few changes and add an optional design template to the presentation, so she opens her presentation and examines the Slide Master.

Steps 1 2 3 4

1. Start PowerPoint, open the presentation **PPT E-1** from the drive and folder where your Project Files are stored, then save it as **iMedia 5**

The title slide of the presentation appears.

QuickTip

You can also hold down [Shift] and click the Normal View button ▣ to display the slide master.

2. Click **View**, point to **Master**, then click **Slide Master**

The presentation's Slide Master view appears, showing the title master in the slide pane. The slide-title master pair appears as thumbnails to the left of the slide pane. The title master controls the title, subtitle, and footer placeholders for any slide in the presentation with the Title Slide layout. You can add more than one design template to the same presentation.

QuickTip

A slide master is preserved by default when you insert, paste, or drag a design template into Slide Master view or when you add a new design template in Slide Master view.

3. Click the **Slide Design button** ▣ on the Formatting toolbar, click the **Compass design template list arrow** in the Slide Design task pane under the Available For Use section, then click **Add Design**

There are now two slide-title master pairs to the left of the slide pane indicating that there are two design templates available in this presentation. You can apply a different template for different audiences or situations. You can also use multiple templates in one presentation at the same time.

4. Click the **top slide master thumbnail**

The slide master for the presentation appears. It contains a **Master title placeholder** and a **Master text placeholder**, as shown in Figure E-1. These placeholders control the format for each title text object and main text object for each slide in the presentation that doesn't have the Title layout. Figure E-2 shows Slide 6 of the presentation. Examine Figures E-1 and E-2 to better understand the relationship between the slide master and the slide.

- The Master title placeholder, labeled "Title Area for AutoLayouts," indicates the position of the title text object and its font size, style, and color. Compare this to the slide title shown in Figure E-2.
- The Master text placeholder, labeled "Object Area for AutoLayouts," determines the characteristics of the body text objects on all the slides in the presentation. Notice how the bullet levels in the body text object of Figure E-2 compare to the corresponding bullet levels of the Master text placeholder in Figure E-1.
- You can resize and move Master title and text placeholders as you would any placeholder in PowerPoint.
- The Slide Master can contain background objects, such as AutoShapes, clip art, or pictures, that will appear on every slide in the presentation behind the text and objects you place on the slides. In Maria's presentation, the iMedia logo appears on the slide master, so that it shows on every slide in the presentation, except the title slide.

FIGURE E-1: Slide Master

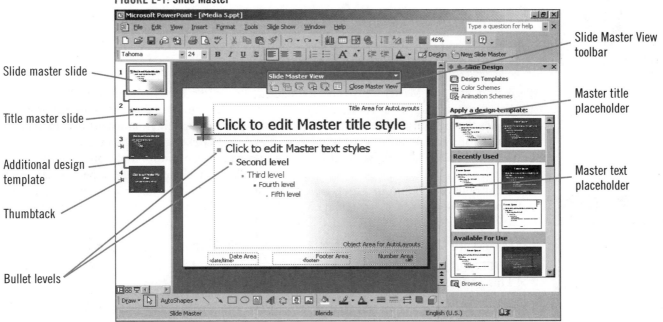

Slide master slide

Title master slide

Additional design template

Thumbtack

Bullet levels

Slide Master View toolbar

Master title placeholder

Master text placeholder

FIGURE E-2: Slide 2 in Normal view

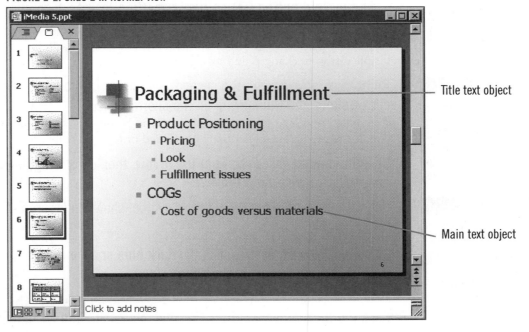

Title text object

Main text object

Restoring the master layout

If a master placeholder is missing or deleted from a master view, you can click the Master Layout button  on the master toolbar to reapply the placeholder. Clicking the Master Layout button opens the Master Layout dialog box, as shown in Figure E-3. Click the placeholder check box to reapply the placeholder. Each master view has its own Master Layout dialog box.

FIGURE E-3: Master Layout dialog box

PowerPoint 2002

Formatting Master Text

Formatting text in a Master view works the same as it does in other views, but PowerPoint applies the changes you make to the whole presentation. This ensures that you don't use a mixture of fonts and styles throughout the presentation. For example, if your presentation is part of a marketing campaign for a travel tour to the Middle East, you may decide to switch the title text font of the entire presentation from the standard Times New Roman font to a script font. You can change text color, style, size, and bullet type in the master view. When you change a bullet type, you can use a character bullet symbol from a font, a picture bullet from the Clip Gallery, or an image that you scan in. ✎   Maria decides to make a few formatting changes to the text of her slide master.

Steps

1. **Make sure the slide master is still visible, click Window on the menu bar, then click Arrange All**
   This ensures that your screen will match the figures in this book.

2. **Move I anywhere in the first line of text in the Master text placeholder, then click**
   Clicking I in a Master view selects the entire line of text. The first line of text could be more prominent.

3. **Click the Bold button B on the Formatting toolbar, then click the Shadow button S on the Formatting toolbar**
   The first line of text becomes bold with a shadow. The second-level bullet would be more visible if it were changed and formatted.

4. **Right-click anywhere in the second line of text in the Master text placeholder, then click Bullets and Numbering on the shortcut menu**
   The Bullets and Numbering dialog box opens. Notice that there is also a Numbered tab that you can use to create sequentially numbered or lettered bullets.

5. **Click Customize, click the Font list arrow, then click Wingdings 2**
   The available bullet choices change.

6. **Use the scroll arrows to locate the x symbol shown in Figure E-4, click the x symbol, then click OK**

7. **Click the Color list arrow, click the dark blue square (fourth from the left), click OK, then click a blank area of the slide**
   A dark blue arrow replaces the third-level bullet.

8. **Click the Normal View button ⊞, then click the Slide 2 thumbnail**
   Compare your screen to Figure E-5.

9. **Click the Save button 🖫 on the Standard toolbar to save your changes**

> **QuickTip**
>
> To insert a picture bullet, click Picture in the Bullets and Numbering dialog box, then click the desired bullet. You may need access to the Office CD to use picture bullets.

> **QuickTip**
>
> A bullet looks best if it is smaller than the text it identifies. Use the Size spin arrows to specify the percentage of the text size you want the bullet to be.

FIGURE E-4: Symbol dialog box

Choose this bullet style

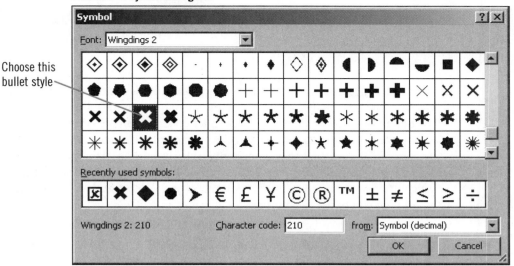

FIGURE E-5: Slide 2 with modified text and bullet styles

First-level text is bold and shadowed

New bullet

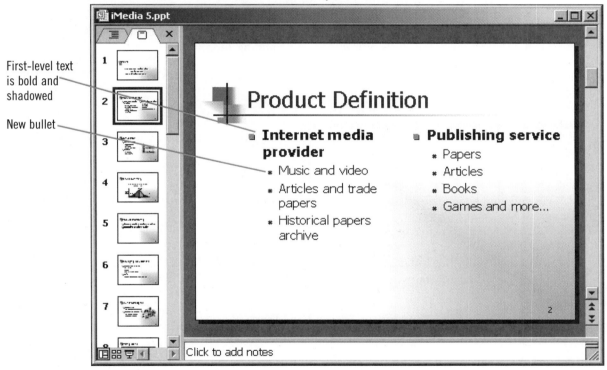

PowerPoint 2002

Applying a template from another presentation

When you apply a design template from another presentation, you automatically apply the master layouts, fonts, and colors over the existing presentation's design template. To apply a template from another presentation, open the Slide Design – Design Templates task pane, then click the Browse hyperlink at the bottom of the pane. In the Apply Design Template dialog box, click All PowerPoint Files in the Files of type list box, then use the Look in list arrow to navigate to the presentation whose design you want to apply. (It does not have to be a template.) Click the presentation or template name, then click Apply.

Changing Master Text Indents

The Master text placeholder in every presentation has five levels of text, called **indent levels**. You can use the horizontal slide ruler to control the space between the bullets and the text or to change the position of the whole indent level. Each indent level is represented by two small triangles called **indent markers** on the ruler that identify the position of each indent level in the Master text placeholder. You can also set tabs on the horizontal ruler by clicking the tab indicator to the left of the horizontal ruler. Table E-1 describes the indent and tab markers on the ruler. Maria decides to change the distance between the bullet symbols and the text in the first two indent levels of her presentation to emphasize the bullets.

Steps

1. Press **[Shift]**, then click the **Normal View button**
   Slide Master view appears.

Trouble?
If your rulers are already visible, skip Step 2.

2. Click anywhere in the Master text placeholder to place the insertion point, click **View** on the menu bar, then click **Ruler**
   The rulers and indent markers for the Master text placeholder appear. The indent markers are set so that the first line of text in each level—in this case, the bullet—begins to the left of subsequent lines of text. This is a **hanging indent**.

Trouble?
If you accidentally drag an indent marker into another marker, click the Undo button to restore the indent levels to their original position.

3. Position the pointer over the left indent marker of the first indent level, then drag to the right to the ½" mark
   Compare your screen to Figure E-6.

4. Position the pointer over the left indent marker of the second indent level, then drag to the right to the 1⅛" mark
   See Figure E-7. The rulers take up valuable screen area.

Trouble?
You can add tabs to any level text by clicking on the ruler where you want the tab. Click the tab indicator to the left of the ruler to cycle through the different tab alignment options.

5. Click the right mouse button in a blank area of the slide, then click **Ruler** on the shortcut menu
   The rulers are no longer visible.

6. Click the **Close Master View button** on the Master toolbar
   Slide Master view closes and Slide 2 appears, showing the increased indents in the main text object.

7. Click the **Save button** on the Standard toolbar

Exceptions to the slide master

If you change the format of text on a slide and then apply a different template to the presentation, the slide that you formatted retains the text formatting changes you made. These format changes that differ from the slide master are known as exceptions. Exceptions can only be changed on the individual slides where they occur. For example, you might change the font and size of a particular piece of text on a slide to make it stand out and then decide later to add a different template to your presentation. The text you formatted before you applied the template is an exception, and it is unaffected by the new template. Another way to override the slide master is to remove the master graphics on one or more slides. You might want to do this to get a clearer view of your slide text. Click Format on the menu bar, click Background, then click the Omit background graphics from master check box to select it.

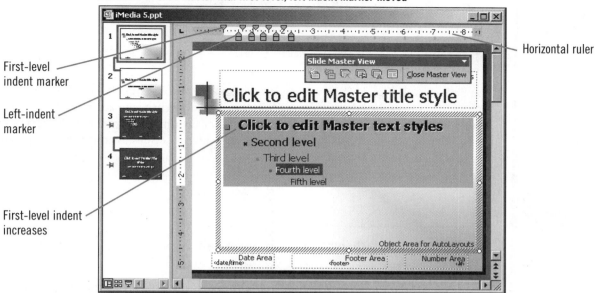

FIGURE E-6: Slide Master with first-level, left indent marker moved

First-level indent marker

Left-indent marker

First-level indent increases

Horizontal ruler

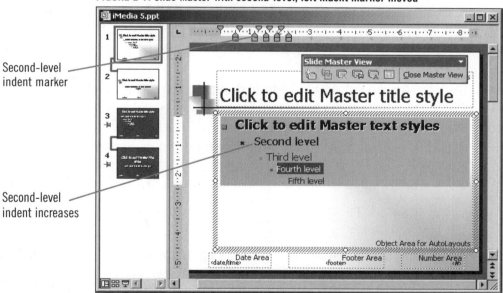

FIGURE E-7: Slide Master with second-level, left indent marker moved

Second-level indent marker

Second-level indent increases

TABLE E-1: Indent and Tab Markers

symbol	name	function
▽	First line indent marker	Controls the position of the first line of text in an indent level
△	Left indent marker	Controls the position of subsequent lines of text in an indent level
▢	Margin marker	Moves both indent markers of an indent level at the same time
⌐	Left-aligned tab	Aligns tab text on the left
⌐	Right-aligned tab	Aligns tab text on the right
⊥	Center-aligned tab	Aligns tab text in the center
⊥	Decimal-aligned tab	Aligns tab text on a decimal point

Adjusting Text Objects

You have complete control over the placement of your text in PowerPoint. With the **text anchor** feature, you can adjust text position within text objects or shapes to achieve the best look. If you want your text to fill more or less of the slide, you can adjust the spacing between lines of text, called **leading** (rhymes with "wedding"). Maria decides to adjust the text position and line spacing of the text object on Slide 5.

Steps 1 2 3 4

1. Click the **Slide 5 thumbnail** in the Slides tab
   Slide 5 appears.

2. Press **[Shift]**, right-click the **main text object**, then click **Format Placeholder** on the shortcut menu
   The Format AutoShape dialog box opens. The text would look better centered in the text box.

Trouble?

If the Format AutoShape dialog box prevents you from seeing the slide, drag it out of the way.

3. Click the **Text Box tab**, click the **Text anchor point list arrow**, click **Middle Centered**, then click **Preview**
   Compare your Format AutoShape dialog box to Figure E-8. The text moves to the middle center of the text object. To make it easier to select, resize the text object.

4. Click the **Resize AutoShape to fit text check box**, then click **Preview**
   The text object shrinks to fit the text. The text object would look better placed more in the center of the slide.

5. Click the **Position tab**, click the **Horizontal down arrow** until **0.79** appears, then click **OK**
   The text object moves to the center of the slide. The bullets are a little too close together.

6. Click **Format** on the menu bar, then click **Line Spacing**
   The Line Spacing dialog box opens.

7. In the After paragraph section, click the **up arrow** four times so that **0.2** appears, click **Preview**, then drag the dialog box out of the way
   The space, or leading, after each paragraph increases. The text is easier to read.

8. In the Line spacing section, click the **up arrow** until **2** appears, then click **Preview**
   Compare your Line Spacing dialog box to Figure E-9. The line spacing between the text lines increases.

9. Click **OK**, then click in a blank area of the slide to deselect the main text object, then save your changes
   Compare your screen to Figure E-10.

Changing margins around text in shapes

You can also use the Text Anchor Point command to change the margins around a text object to form a shape that suits the text better. Right-click the shape, click Format Placeholder, click the Text Box tab, then adjust the Internal margin settings. Click Preview to see your changes before you apply them to the shape.

FIGURE E-8: Format AutoShape dialog box

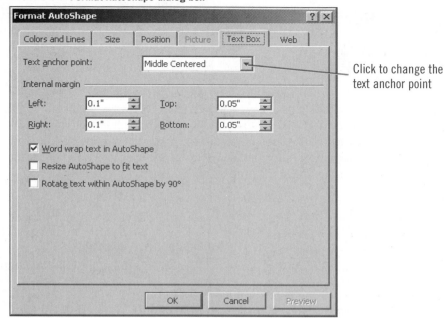

Click to change the text anchor point

FIGURE E-9: Line Spacing dialog box

Step 8

Step 7

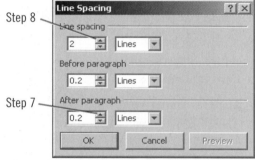

FIGURE E-10: Slide showing formatted body text object

Formatted text object

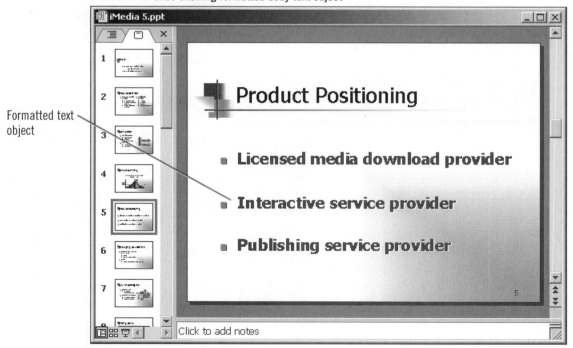

Using Advanced Drawing Tools

PowerPoint has a number of powerful drawing tools on the AutoShapes menu to help you draw all types of shapes. For example, the Curve drawing tool allows you to create a freeform curved line, the Arc tool helps you draw smooth, curved lines and pie-shaped wedges, and the Connector line tool allows you to connect AutoShape objects with a line. Once you have drawn a shape, you can format and rearrange it to create the effect you want. Maria uses the Connector line tool to complete the diagram on Slide 11.

Steps

1. Click the **Slide 11 thumbnail**, click the **AutoShapes button** on the Drawing toolbar, point to **Connectors**, then click the **Straight Arrow Connector button**
   The pointer changes to +.

2. Move + to the right side of the **Phase 2 object** until it changes to ⬦ and blue dots appear around the object, then click the **blue dot** on the right side of the Phase 2 object
   See Figure E-11. The blue dots are anchor points for the connector arrow.

Trouble?

If a green box appears at either end of the line, drag the green square until the blue connection point on the object appears.

3. Move the pointer to the left side of the **diamond object**, then, when you see the blue dot inside the pointer, click again to place the right side of the connector arrow
   A red circle appears at either end of the connector arrow, indicating that the arrow connects the two objects.

4. Click the **Line Style button** on the Drawing toolbar, then click the **2¼ pt line style**
   The line style of the arrow connector changes to a thicker weight.

5. Click the **Arrow Style button** on the Drawing toolbar, click **More Arrows**, then click the **Colors and Lines tab**
   The Format AutoShape dialog box opens. The arrow would look better with a more distinct shape.

QuickTip

To change the default attributes of a particular AutoShape, format the AutoShape, select it, click Draw on the Drawing toolbar, then click Set AutoShape Defaults.

6. Under the Arrows section, click the **End size list arrow**, click the **Arrow R Size 8 button** (second button, last row), then click **OK**
   The style of the arrow connector line changes to a more distinct style.

7. Place + over the head of the arrow, drag the connector arrow to the left side of the **Phase 3 object**, then release the mouse button when you see the blue dot on the left side of the Phase 3 object inside the pointer
   The arrow connector now connects the Phase 2 and Phase 3 objects.

8. Click the **Draw button** on the Drawing toolbar, point to **Order**, then click **Send to Back**
   The arrow connector line moves behind the diamond shape.

9. Click in a blank area of the slide, then save the presentation
   Compare your screen to Figure E-12.

FIGURE E-11: Slide showing Connector anchor points

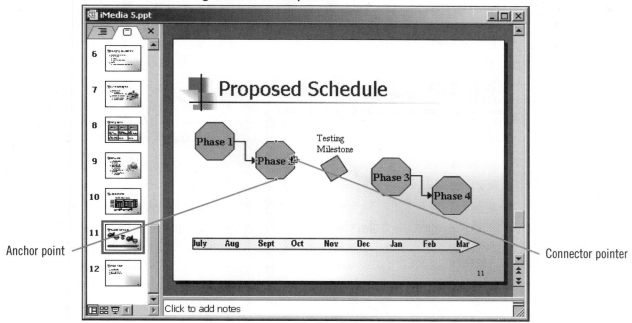

Anchor point

Connector pointer

FIGURE E-12: Slide showing formatted connector arrow

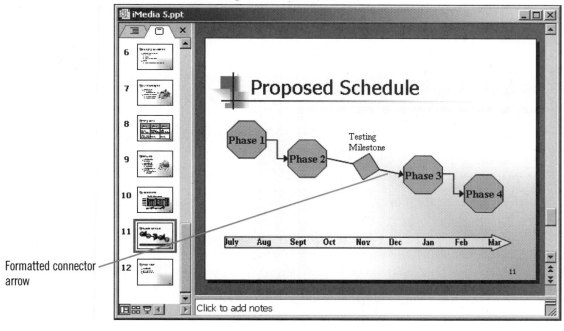

Formatted connector arrow

CLUES TO USE

Drawing a freeform shape

A freeform shape can consist of straight lines, freehand (or curved) lines, or a combination of the two. To draw a freeform shape, click the AutoShapes menu button, point to Lines, then click the Freeform button ⬚. Drag the mouse to draw the desired shape (the cursor changes to a pencil as you draw), then double-click when you are done. To draw a straight line with the Freeform tool, click where you want to begin the line, move the mouse, then double-click to deactivate the Freeform tool. To edit a freeform object, right-click the object, then click Edit Points on the shortcut menu.

Using Advanced Formatting Tools

With PowerPoint's advanced formatting tools, you can change formatting attributes such as fill texture, 3-D effects, and shadow for text and shapes. If you like the attributes of an object, you can use the Format Painter button to pick up the attributes and apply them to another object. ✐ Maria wants to use the advanced formatting tools to enhance the diagram on the slide.

Steps 1 2 3 4

1. Press **[Shift]**, right-click the **Phase 1 object**, click **Format AutoShape** on the shortcut menu, click the **Colors and Lines tab**, click the **Color list arrow** in the Fill section, then click **Fill Effects**
   The Fill Effects dialog box opens.

2. Click the **Texture tab**, click the **Newsprint square** (first square in the top row), click **OK**, then click **OK** again
   The newsprint texture fills the shape.

QuickTip

When you click the 3-D Style button on the Drawing toolbar, you can click one of the 3-D styles on the pop-up menu. The default 3-D style is Style 1, the first style in the first row.

3. Click the **3-D Style button** on the Drawing toolbar, then click **3-D Settings**
   The 3-D Settings toolbar appears.

4. Click the **Depth button** on the 3-D Settings toolbar, then click **36 pt.**
   A 3-D effect is applied and the depth of the 3-D effect lengthens from the default of 36 points.

5. Click the **Direction button** on the 3-D Settings toolbar, click the right effect in the middle row, as shown in Figure E-13, then click the **Close button** on the 3-D Settings toolbar
   The 3-D effect changes to the left side of the object.

6. With the Phase 1 object still selected, click the **Font Color list arrow** on the Drawing toolbar, then click the **dark blue square** (labeled Follow Title Text Scheme Color)
   The other four objects would look better if they matched the one you just formatted.

7. Double-click the **Format Painter button** on the Standard toolbar, click each of the other four objects, then click again to turn off the Format Painter
   Now all the objects on the slide have the same fill effect. When you use the Format Painter tool, it "picks up" the attributes of the object that is selected and copies them to the next object that you click. If you click the Format Painter button only once, it pastes the attributes of the selected object to the next object you select, then turns off automatically. The Phase 3 object is now on top of the arrowhead.

8. Click the **Phase 3 object**, click the **Draw button** on the Drawing toolbar, point to **Order**, click **Send to Back**, click in a blank area of the slide, then save your changes
   Compare your screen to Figure E-14.

9. Press **[Home]** to move to Slide 1, click the **Slide Show button**, then press **[Spacebar]** or click the left mouse button to run through the presentation

FIGURE E-13: Slide showing formatted 3-D object

Formatted object

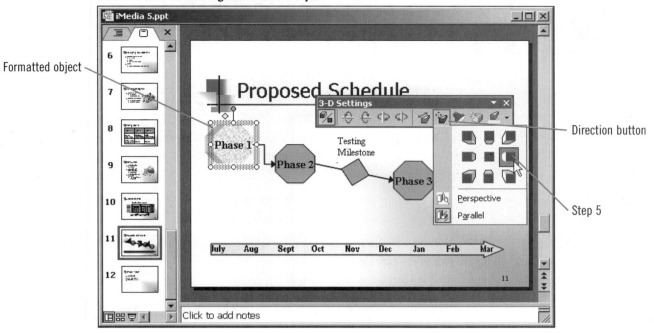

Direction button

Step 5

FIGURE E-14: Slide with formatted objects

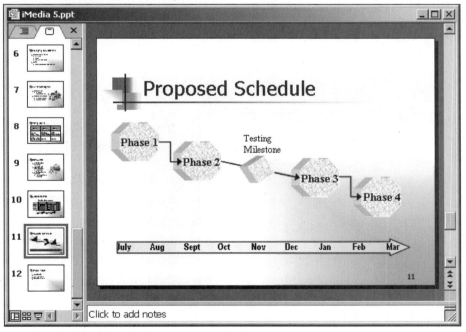

Applying a color scheme to another presentation

If you develop a custom color scheme that you like, you can use the Format Painter tool to apply it to another presentation. To apply a color scheme from one presentation to another, open each presentation in Slide Sorter view, then use the Arrange All command on the Windows menu to arrange the Presentation windows side by side. Select a slide in the presentation with the color scheme you want to copy, double-click the Format Painter button on the Standard toolbar, then click each slide that you want to change in the other presentation.

Using the Style Checker

To help you correct common design mistakes, the Style Checker feature in PowerPoint reviews your presentation for typical errors such as incorrect font sizes, use of too many fonts, extra words, errors in punctuation, and other readability problems. When you activate the Style Checker, PowerPoint checks your presentation for style inconsistencies and flags potential problem areas with a lightbulb. If you see the lightbulb, click it to see a list of suggested options for handling the problem or improving the presentation. ✒ Maria knows it's easy to overlook mistakes while preparing a presentation, so she reviews the Style Checker settings, then looks for errors she may have missed.

Steps

Trouble?

If a dialog box opens asking if you want to enable the Office Assistant, click Enable Assistant.

1. Click **Tools** on the menu bar, click **Options**, click the **Spelling and Style tab**, then click the **Check style check box**
   Now the Style Checker is activated.

2. Click **Style Options**, click check boxes as necessary so that your screen matches the dialog box shown in Figure E-15

3. Click the **Visual Clarity tab**, click **Defaults**, then review the options
   The Style Checker Options dialog box indicates the current option settings for visual clarity.

4. Click **OK**, then click **OK** again

5. Click the **Slide 12 thumbnail**, click the slide anywhere, then click the **lightbulb** on Slide 12
   The Office Assistant tells you that the text in the title text placeholder should use title case capitalization, in other words, that only the first letter in each word should be uppercase. See Figure E-16. You know this is not a problem.

Trouble?

Read the Style Checker suggestions carefully. Be sure that the Style Checker doesn't make changes that you don't expect. For example, the "Change the text to sentence case" option changes all uppercase letters in bulleted lists to lowercase.

6. Click **OK** in the Office Assistant dialog balloon, go to **Slide 6**, click the slide anywhere, click the **lightbulb** on the slide, then click the **Change the text to sentence case option** in the Help dialog balloon
   The word "positioning" correctly changes so the first letter is lowercase, but the letters in the acronym in the second bullet also change.

7. Change the second bullet to **COGs**, click the lightbulb, then click **OK** in the dialog balloon

8. Click **Tools** on the menu bar, click **Options**, click the **Check style check box**, then click **OK**
   The Style Checker is no longer active.

9. Hide the Office Assistant, if necessary, click the **Slide Sorter View button** 🔳, then add your name in the notes and handouts footer
   Figure E-17 shows the final presentation.

10. Click the **Normal View button** 🔲, save your changes, then print the presentation as handouts (4 per page)

FIGURE E-15: Style Options dialog box

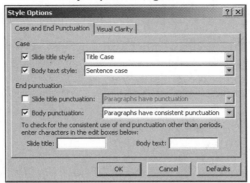

FIGURE E-16: Capitalization tip displayed by the Office Assistant

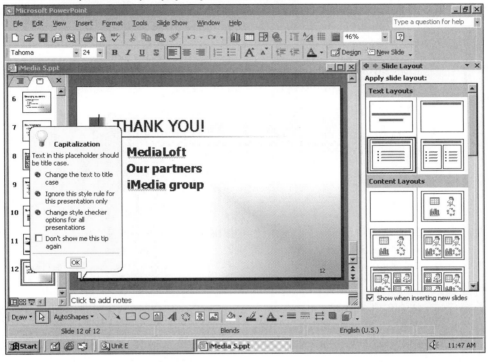

FIGURE E-17: Final presentation in Slide Sorter view

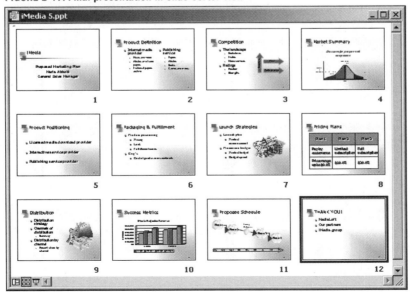

Creating a Template

You are not limited to using the standard templates PowerPoint provides or the ones you find on the Internet. You can create your own template from scratch using a blank presentation, or you can modify any existing PowerPoint template or presentation that you have access to. For example, you might want to use your company's color as a slide background or incorporate your company's logo on the slides of a presentation. If you modify an existing template, you can keep, change, or delete any color, graphic, or font as necessary. When you are finished with your template, you can save it as a special template file in PowerPoint, which adds the .pot extension to the file. You can then use your customized template as a basis for future presentations. ✐ Maria is finished customizing her presentation. Now she wants to insert the new iMedia logo into the presentation and save it as a template for future use.

Steps

1. Click **View**, point to **Master**, then click **Slide Master**
   Slide Master view appears.

2. Click **Insert** on the menu bar, point to **Picture**, click **From File**, locate the logo file **PPT E-2** where your Project Files are stored, then click **Insert**
   The iMedia logo appears on the slide. The logo needs to be enlarged and positioned on the slide.

3. Click the **bottom-right sizing handle** and drag it down ½", then drag the logo to the upper-right corner of the slide
   Compare your screen with Figure E-18. Adjust the logo as necessary to make it look similar to Figure E-18. You are now ready to save this presentation as a PowerPoint template.

4. Click **File**, click **Save As**, click the **Save as type list arrow**, click the **down scroll arrow**, then click **Design Template**
   The Save As dialog box opens. Because this is a template, PowerPoint automatically opens the Templates folder on your hard drive as shown in Figure E-19. Templates saved in this folder appear in the Slide Design task pane in PowerPoint.

5. Navigate to the location where your Project Files are stored, change the filename to **iMedia Template**, then click **Save**
   The presentation is saved as a PowerPoint template to the drive and folder where your Project Files are stored, and it appears in the PowerPoint window. Notice the .pot extension on the filename in the title bar, which identifies this presentation as a template. Because this presentation will be used as a template for other presentations, the slide content is no longer needed.

6. Click the **Slide Sorter View button** ⊞, click **Slide 3**, press **[Shift]**, click **Slide 12**, then press **[Delete]**
   Slides 3 through 12 are deleted.

7. Double-click **Slide 2**, press **[Shift]**, click **each text box**, then press **[Delete]**
   The content on Slide 2 is deleted.

8. Go to **Slide 1**, delete the text in the text boxes, type **iMedia Template** in the title text placeholder, then save your changes

9. Click ⊞, click the **Zoom button list arrow** [100% ▾] on the standard toolbar, then click **100%**
   Figure E-20 shows the final template presentation in Slide Sorter view.

10. Print the template presentation as handouts (2 per page), close the presentation, and exit PowerPoint

FIGURE E-18: Slide showing new iMedia logo

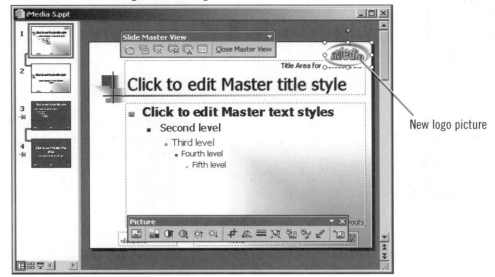

New logo picture

FIGURE E-19: Save As dialog box showing Templates folder

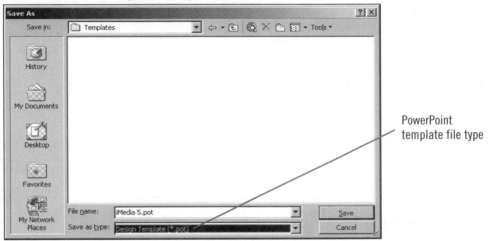

PowerPoint
template file type

FIGURE E-20: Completed template presentation in Slide Sorter view

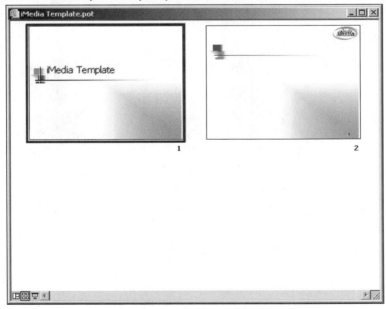

Practice

► Concepts Review

Label each of the elements of the PowerPoint window shown in Figure E-21.

FIGURE E-21

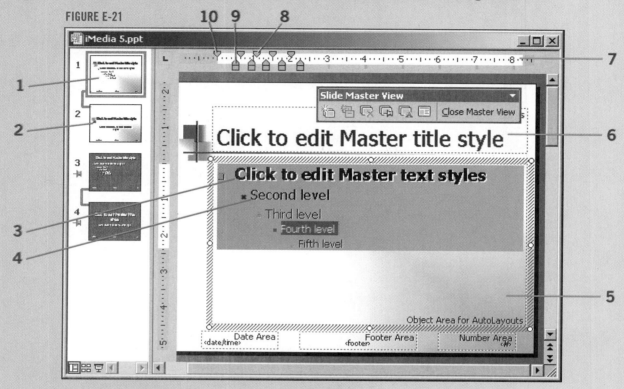

Match each of the terms with the statement that describes its function.

11. Line spacing
12. Indent levels
13. Text anchor
14. Margin marker
15. Master
16. Bottom indent marker

a. The five levels of text in a master text placeholder
b. Moves the whole indent level
c. Controls subsequent lines of text in an indent level
d. A template for all the slides in a presentation
e. Adjusts the distance between text lines
f. Adjusts the position of text in a text object

Select the best answer from the list of choices.

17. **A hanging indent is an indent in which the:**
    a. First line of text begins to the right of subsequent lines of text.
    b. First line of text begins to the left of subsequent lines of text.
    c. The bullet symbol is to the left of the first line of text.
    d. The bullet symbol is to the right of the first line of text.

18. **A background item on the title master:**
    a. Changes all views of your presentation.
    b. Is visible on slides with Title Slide layouts.
    c. Is a simple way to place an object on every slide of your presentation.
    d. Does not affect the slides of your presentation.

19. **The Style Checker checks for all of the following except:**
    a. Case and punctuation.
    b. The number of fonts in a presentation.
    c. The number of bullets in a presentation.
    d. Incorrect color scheme colors.

20. **What is leading?**
    a. Vertical space between lines of text
    b. Horizontal space between letters
    c. Diagonal space between letters
    d. Space between graphics on the slide master

21. **In PowerPoint, tabs:**
    a. Can be aligned on the left, right, or center of a character or on a decimal.
    b. Determine the location of margins.
    c. Have symbols for top and bottom tabs.
    d. Can be only left- or center-aligned.

22. **The Format Painter button:**
    a. Is the feature you use to paint objects in PowerPoint.
    b. Allows you to change the type of AutoShape.
    c. Picks up and applies formatting attributes from one object or slide to another.
    d. Changes the order of AutoShapes on a slide.

▶ Skills Review

1. **Format Master text.**
   a. Start PowerPoint and open the presentation PPT E-3, then save it as **Book Presentation**.
   b. Go to Slide 2, switch to Slide Master view, then make the first-level bulleted item in the Master text placeholder bold.
   c. Change the bullet symbol of the first-level bullet to a character bullet in Wingdings, the third bullet from the right in the last row.
   d. Click the Size up arrow in the Bullets and Numbering dialog box once to 75%.
   e. Change the bullet color to the green color (far right color).
   f. Take the shadow attribute off the second-level bulleted item and change its font to Arial.
   g. Save the presentation.

2. Change Master text indents.

   a. Display the rulers.

   b. Move the left indent marker of the first-level bullet to ½" and the second-level bullet to 1⅛" as shown in Figure E-22.

   c. Hide the rulers, switch to Normal view, then save the presentation.

3. Adjust text objects.

   a. Right-click anywhere in the main text object on Slide 2, then click Format Placeholder on the shortcut menu.

   b. Click the Text Box tab.

   c. Set the text anchor point to Top Centered.

   d. Adjust the internal margin on the left and right sides to 0.5 and preview your change.

   e. Select the Resize AutoShape to fit text check box, preview it, and click OK.

   f. Select the entire text object. (*Hint:* Press [Shift] while clicking the object.)

   g. Change the line spacing to 0.75, preview it, then click OK.

   h. Move the text object up and to left about ½".

   i. Save your changes.

4. Use advanced drawing tools.

   a. Go to Slide 4.

   b. Use the Elbow Connector to connect the left corner of the Warehouse diamond to the top corner of the MediaLoft Regional Warehouse diamond.

   c. Use the Straight Connector to connect the right side of the MediaLoft Regional Warehouse diamond to the left side of the Individual Stores diamond.

   d. Use the Elbow Connector to connect the top corner of the Individual Stores diamond to the right corner of the Warehouse diamond.

   e. Select all three of the connector lines, make them 3 points wide, then deselect them.

   f. Change the arrow style of the connector line connecting the MediaLoft Regional Warehouse diamond to the Individual Stores diamond to the Square Dot, dashed line style. (*Hint*: Click More Arrows from the Arrow Styles button, then click the Dashed list arrow.)

   g. Deselect all objects, then save your changes.

5. Use advanced formatting tools.

   a. Go to Slide 1.

   b. Select the entire text object in the lower-right corner of the slide.

   c. Use the Texture tab in the Fill Effects dialog box to apply the Green Marble texture to the object. (*Hint:* Read the description of the selected texture in the box under the textures.)

   d. Change the font to 20 pt. Arial.

   e. Double-click the Format Painter to pick up the format of the selected text box on the title slide and apply it to each of the diamond objects on Slide 4, then deselect the Format Painter and all objects.

   f. Use the 3-D Style button to apply 3-D Style 7 to the objects on Slide 4.

   g. Click the 3-D Color list arrow on the 3-D Settings toolbar, then click the dark green color (Follow Background Scheme Color).

   h. Deselect all objects, close the 3-D Settings toolbar, then save your changes.

FIGURE E-22

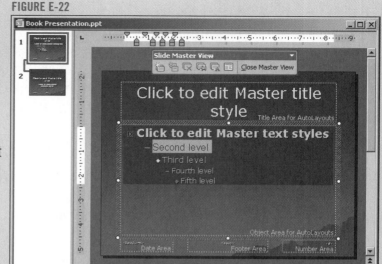

6. Use the Style Checker.

    a. Activate the Style Checker, open the Style Options dialog box, and on the Visual Clarity tab, make sure there is a check mark next to Title text size should be at least, select 48 from the list, then click OK twice.

    b. Go to Slide 1, then click the lightbulb on the title slide. Notice that the title text font is too small based on your adjustment to the style options.

    c. In the Office Assistant dialog balloon, click Change text to be at least 48 point.

    d. Scroll through the presentation clicking the lightbulbs that appear on the screen. Decide whether to accept the Office Assistant's suggestions or to ignore them.

    e. Turn the Style Checker off, then hide the Office Assistant, if necessary.

    f. Add your name to the footer in the slides and notes and handouts, save the presentation, then print the presentation as handouts, 3 slides per page.

7. Create a template.

    a. Open the Save As dialog box, then save the presentation as **MediaLoft Template** where your Project Files are stored.

    b. Delete Slides 3, 4, and 5, delete all the text in the text objects on Slide 2, then delete the clip art on Slide 2.

    c. Type **MediaLoft Template** in the title text object on Slide 1 in place of the current text.

    d. Save the presentation template, then print the presentation as handouts, 2 slides per page.

    e. Close the presentation and exit PowerPoint.

▶ Independent Challenge 1

You are the owner of Premier Catering in Brisbane, Queensland, Australia. You have built your business on private parties, wedding receptions, and special events over the last five years. To expand, you decide to cater to the business community by offering executive meals and business luncheons. Use PowerPoint to develop a presentation that you can use to gain corporate catering accounts.

In this independent challenge, you will create an outline and modify the look of a presentation. You will create your own material to complete the slides of the presentation. Assume the following about Premier Catering:

- Premier Catering has 10 full-time employees and 15 on-call staff.
- Premier Catering handles catering jobs up to 500 people.
- Premier Catering is a full-service catering business providing cost estimates, setup, complete preparation, service personnel, and cleanup.

a. Open the file PPT E-4, then save it as **Premier**. Add your name to the notes and handout footer.

b. Switch to the Outline tab and create a presentation outline. Add your name to the notes and handout folder.

c. Customize your presentation by formatting the Slide Master.

d. Search PowerPoint clip art and add a koala bear to both the slide master and the title master. Format the clip art as necessary.

e. Use PowerPoint's advanced drawing and formatting tools to give your presentation a unique look.

f. Add clip art and format the presentation using PowerPoint's formatting tools.

g. Switch to the last slide and change the text anchor and line spacing to create the best look.

h. Review the Style Checker options, then check the style of the presentation.

i. Create a template from this presentation. Delete all the slides except the first slide and the last slide.

j. Add two additional title-master pairs to the template.

k. Name the template **Catering 1** and save it to the location where your Project Files are stored.

l. Print the slides of your final template.

m. Close the presentation template and exit PowerPoint.

Independent Challenge 2

You are the finance director at Splat Records in Los Angeles, California. Splat Records specializes in alternative music. As an emerging record company, your business is looking for investment capital to expand its talent base and increase sales. It is your responsibility to develop the outline and basic look for a standard presentation that the president can present to various investors.

In this independent challenge, you will complete an outline and choose a custom background for the presentation. You'll need to create a presentation consisting of at least six slides. Assume the following about Splat Records:

- Splat Records has been in business for eight years.
- Splat Records currently has 22 recording contracts. Splat wants to double that during the next year and a half.
- Splat Records has six superstar recording groups including the groups: RIM and InHand.

a. Open the file PPT E-5, then save it as **Splat**.
b. Enter text into the title and main text placeholders of the slides.
c. Format the Master text placeholder by changing master text indents and bullet styles.
d. Add clip art and format the presentation using PowerPoint's formatting tools.
e. Use advanced drawing and formatting tools to create a unique look.
f. Check the style of the presentation.
g. Add your name to the notes and handouts footer, save the presentation, then print the slides of your final presentation as handouts in pure black and white.
h. Close the presentation and exit PowerPoint.

Independent Challenge 3

You are a computer game designer for GameNet, an interactive game developer. One of your jobs is to develop new interactive game concepts and present the information at a company meeting. Develop a 10- to 15-slide presentation that promotes two of the new interactive games concepts you've developed. Use PowerPoint clip art and shapes to enhance your slides. Use one of PowerPoint's templates, design one of your own, or copy one from another presentation. You can use one of the following, or you can develop your own.

- **Showdown** is an interactive game that puts you in one of six different historical situations, where you are either a US Marshal or a gunman.
- **Spy for US** is an adventure game in which you are a spy for the Axis Powers or the Allies during World War II; assume there are four different situations to choose from for each political side.

Create your own information, but assume the following:

- The product is designed for adults and children ages 13 and up.
- The cost of product development is estimated to be $250,000.
- Development time is four months.

a. Open a new presentation and save it as **Games** to the location where your Project Files are stored.
b. Plan the story line of how the software was developed using five or more slides. Plan the beginning and ending slides. What do you want your audience to know about the product idea?
c. Use clip art and shapes to enhance the presentation. Change the bullet and text formatting in the Master text and title placeholders to fit the subject matter.
d. Use advanced drawing and formatting tools to create a unique look.
e. Add your name to the notes and handouts footer, save the presentation, then print the final slide presentation as handouts in pure black and white.
f. Close the presentation and exit PowerPoint.

Independent Challenge 4

You are the Travel Coordinator for Bandwidth Inc., a large graphic multimedia development company in Seattle, Washington. One of the benefits Bandwidth offers its employees is the option to vacation at a destination planned by the company. Your job is to find a reasonable vacation spot and then negotiate with travel companies for reduced group rates that are charged to Bandwidth employees if they choose to utilize the benefit. Once you negotiate a contract with a travel organization, you create a brief presentation that outlines the vacation benefit packages for the employees.

Plan and create an 8- to 10-slide presentation that details the vacation package for the current year. Develop your own content, but assume the following:
- The vacation package is a 7-day Alaskan cruise or a 7-day Mexican cruise.
- Air travel originates from the Seattle/Tacoma Airport (SeaTac).
- Cruises can be booked on one of two different cruise lines.
- The price is 30% off the listed price based on double occupancy.
- Bandwidth employees can book a cruise anytime during the current year.

You'll need to find the following information on the Web:
- Price and schedule information. (*Hint:* Remember the price you list in the presentation is 30% lower than the listed price you find on the Internet.)
- A list of ships with a brief description of at least one ship from each cruise line.
- Ports of call for one Mexican cruise and one Alaskan cruise.

a. Open a new presentation, and save it as **Bandwidth** to the location where your Project Files are stored.
b. Add your name as the footer on all slides and handouts.
c. Connect to the Internet, then use a search engine to locate Web sites that have information on Mexican and Alaskan cruises. If your search does not produce any results, you might try the following sites:
    www.carnival.com
    www.hollandamerica.com
    www.ncl.com
    www.royalcaribbean.com
    www.celebrity-cruises.com
d. Review at least two Web sites that contain information about Mexican cruises and Alaskan cruises. Print the Home pages of the Web sites you use to gather data for your presentation.
e. Decide on two cruise lines to use in your presentation, then create slides that present the information.
f. Use clip art and shapes to enhance the presentation. Change the bullet and text formatting in the Master text and title placeholders to fit the subject matter.
g. Apply a template to the presentation and customize the slide background appropriately.
h. Use advanced drawing and formatting tools to create a unique look.
i. Use text formatting as necessary to make text visible and help emphasize important points.
j. Spell check the presentation, view the final presentation, save the final version, then print the slides and handouts.
k. Close the presentation and exit PowerPoint.

► Visual Workshop

Create two slides that look like the examples in Figures E-23 and E-24. Be sure to use connector lines. Add your name to the handout footer, then save the presentation as **New Products**. Print the Slide view of the presentation. Submit the final presentation output.

FIGURE E-23

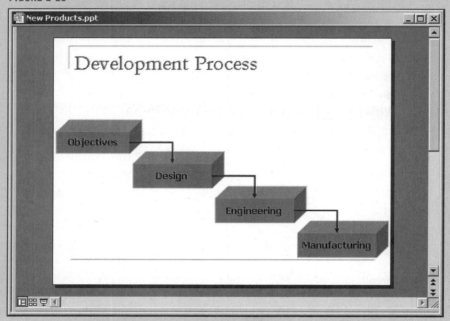

FIGURE E-24

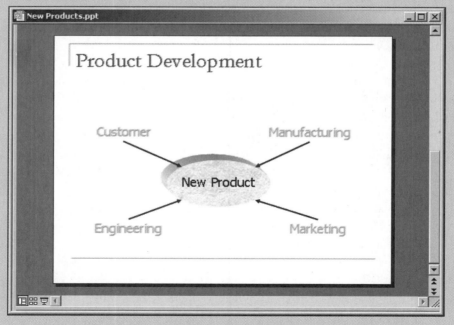

Enhancing

Charts

Objectives

- ► **Insert data from a file into a datasheet**
- ► **Format a datasheet**
- ► **Change a chart's type**
- ► **Change a chart display**
- [MOUS] ► **Work with chart elements**
- [MOUS] ► **Animate charts and sounds**
- [MOUS] ► **Embed an organizational chart**
- [MOUS] ► **Modify an organizational chart**

A PowerPoint presentation is a visual communication tool. A slide that delivers information with a relevant graphic object has a more lasting impact than a slide with plain text. Graphs and charts often communicate information more effectively than words. Microsoft Graph and Microsoft Organization Chart are built-in PowerPoint programs that allow you to easily create and embed charts in your presentation. ✧ In this unit, Maria Abbott updates the data and enhances the appearance of a Microsoft Graph chart and then creates and formats an organizational chart showing the management structure of the iMedia group.

Inserting Data from a File into a Datasheet

With Microsoft Graph, you can enter your own data into a datasheet using the keyboard, or you can import existing data from a spreadsheet program like Microsoft Excel. ✐ The accounting department gave Maria updated sales projection information in an Excel file. Maria wants to insert this data into the chart on Slide 11. To do this, she will open Graph and import the data from Excel.

Steps

1. Start PowerPoint, open the presentation **PPT F-1** from the location where your Project Files are stored, then save it as **iMedia 6**

2. Click **View** on the menu bar, click **Task Pane**, click **Window** on the menu bar, then click **Arrange All**

3. Click the **Slide 11 thumbnail**, then double-click the **chart object**
   The data in the datasheet needs to be replaced with the updated data in the Excel worksheet.

4. Click the **first cell** in the datasheet (labeled Dept.)
   This indicates where the imported data will appear in the datasheet.

QuickTip

If you don't see the Import File button on the Standard toolbar, click a Toolbar Options button 》, on a toolbar to locate buttons that are not visible on your toolbar.

5. Click the **Import File button** 📇 on the Graph Standard toolbar
   The Import File dialog box opens.

6. Click the Excel file **PPT F-2** from the location where your Project Files are stored, then click **Open**
   The Import Data Options dialog box opens. Because you want to import the entire sheet and overwrite the existing cells, all the options are correctly marked.

7. Click **OK**
   The chart changes to reflect the new data you inserted into the datasheet. Compare your screen to Figure F-1. Notice the **column headings**, the gray boxes along the edges of the datasheet. The data in column D does not need to be included in the chart.

Trouble?

To include data that you've previously excluded, double-click the control box again.

8. Double-click the **column D column heading**
   The data in column D is grayed out, indicating that it is excluded from the datasheet and will not appear in the chart. See Figure F-2.

9. Click the **Save button** 💾 on the Graph Standard toolbar

FIGURE F-1: Datasheet showing imported data

Step 5

Column heading

Row heading

New data

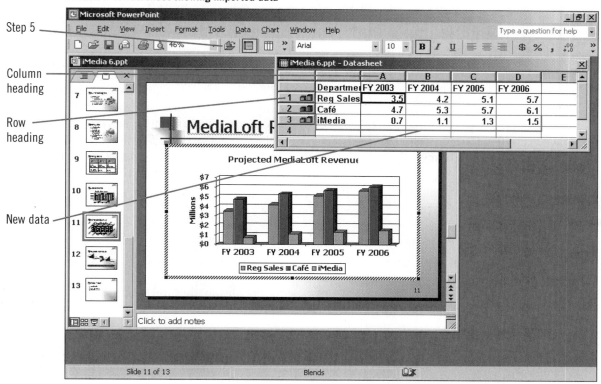

FIGURE F-2: Datasheet showing excluded column

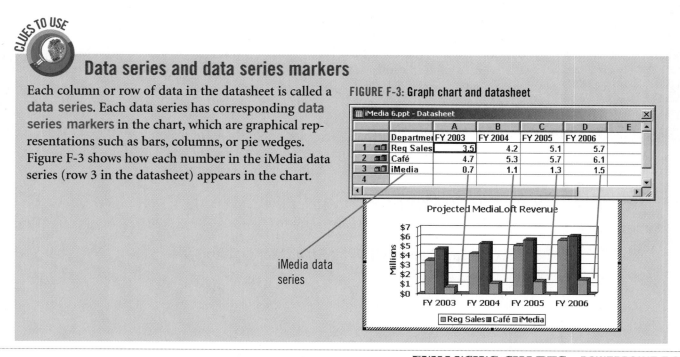

Excluded column

CLUES TO USE

Data series and data series markers

Each column or row of data in the datasheet is called a **data series**. Each data series has corresponding **data series markers** in the chart, which are graphical representations such as bars, columns, or pie wedges. Figure F-3 shows how each number in the iMedia data series (row 3 in the datasheet) appears in the chart.

FIGURE F-3: Graph chart and datasheet

iMedia data series

PowerPoint 2002

Formatting a Datasheet

Once you've imported the data from another file, it can be helpful to modify and format the datasheet to make your data easier to view and use. With Graph, you can make simple formatting changes to the font, number format, and column size in your datasheet. To format the data in the datasheet, you must first select the data. ⬦⬤⬤⬤ Maria changes the number format to show the sales numbers correctly, then she changes the chart to show the sales by department rather than by year.

Steps 1 2 3 4

1. Click cell **A1** in the datasheet, then drag to cell **D3**
All the data in this group of continuous cells, or **range**, is selected.

2. Right-click the selection, then click **Number** on the shortcut menu
The Format Number dialog box opens. The Category list on the left side of the dialog box indicates the format categories.

3. Click **Currency** in the Category list
The Sample box at the top of the dialog box shows you how your data will appear in the selected format. See Figure F-4.

4. Click **OK**
The data in the datasheet and in the chart change to the currency format. The numbers indicate millions of dollars, so the number of digits after the decimal place needs to be adjusted.

QuickTip

To quickly change the number format to Currency, click the Currency Style button 💲 on the Graph Formatting toolbar.

5. Click **Format** on the menu bar, click **Number**, click the **Decimal places down arrow** once to display **1**, click **OK**, then click anywhere in the datasheet
The datasheet would look better if the columns containing the numbers were not so wide and if the first column were wide enough to accommodate the column head.

QuickTip

To quickly adjust the column width to fit the widest cell of data in a column, double-click the border to the right of the column control box.

6. Drag to select the first cell in each column, click **Format** on the menu bar, click **Column Width**, then click **Best Fit**
The selected column widths automatically resize to fit the widest label in each column. The chart would be more helpful if it showed the sales figures along the vertical axis, in a series by column.

Trouble?

If you don't see the By Column button on the Standard toolbar, click a Toolbar Options button 》 on a toolbar to locate buttons that are not visible on your toolbar.

7. Click the **By Column button** 🔲 on the Graph Standard toolbar
The icons now appear in the column headings in the datasheet to indicate that the fiscal year in the columns is now the legend. Compare your datasheet to Figure F-5.

8. Click the **Close button** ✕ in the datasheet
The datasheet closes, but Graph is still open.

9. Click the **Save button** 💾 on the Graph Standard toolbar

FIGURE F-4: Format Number dialog box

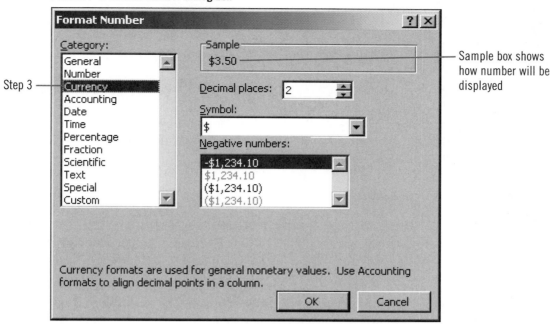

Step 3 →

Sample box shows
how number will be
displayed

FIGURE F-5: Datasheet showing formatted data

Icon indicates
that data is
displayed in a
series by
column

Formatting datasheets and charts

You can format data in both datasheets and in charts created by Graph. Sometimes it's easier to view the numbers in the datasheet after they have been formatted; other times, you may want to manipulate the numbers after they have been placed into a chart to get a better picture. After you've formatted the data in the datasheet, the formatting changes will be reflected in the chart; however, formatting changes made to the data in the chart will not be reflected in the datasheet.

Changing a Chart's Type

The type of chart you choose depends on the amount of information you have and how it's best depicted. For example, a chart with more than six or seven data series does not fit well in a pie chart. You can change a chart type quickly and easily by using the Chart Type command on the Chart menu. ◢◣◢◣ Maria decides that a bar chart on Slide 11 would communicate the information more clearly than a column chart.

1. With Graph still open, click **Chart** on the menu bar, then click **Chart Type**

   The Chart Type dialog box opens, as shown in Figure F-6. The current chart type is a clustered column chart with a 3-D effect.

QuickTip

To quickly change the chart type, click the Chart Type button 📊▾ on the Graph Standard toolbar.

2. In the Chart type list, click **Bar**, then in the Chart sub-type section, make sure that the **upper-left sub-type** is selected

   The selected sub-type is a Clustered Bar chart. To see how your data would look in any selected format without closing the dialog box, you can preview it.

3. Click and hold **Press and Hold to View Sample**

   A preview of the chart with your data appears in the area where the sub-types had been listed. This chart would look better if it were 3-D.

4. Release the mouse button, then click the **first sub-type in the second row**

   The box below the sub-type section shows that you have selected a 3-D bar chart with a 3-D visual effect.

5. Click **Press and Hold to View Sample**

   The preview shows a 3-D version of the column chart.

6. Release the mouse button, then click **OK**

   The chart type changes to the 3-D bar chart. Compare your screen with Figure F-7.

7. Click the **Save button** 💾 on the Graph Standard toolbar

FIGURE F-6: Chart Type dialog box

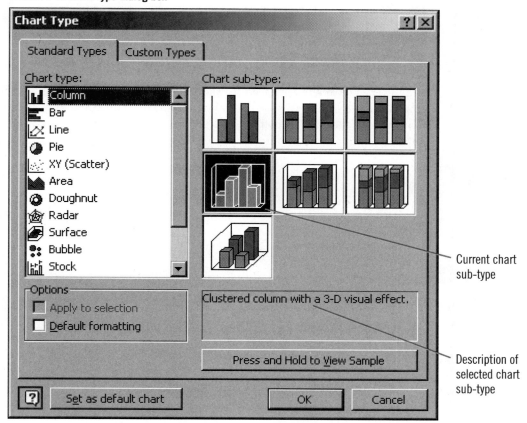

Current chart sub-type

Clustered column with a 3-D visual effect.

Description of selected chart sub-type

FIGURE F-7: Chart showing new bar chart type

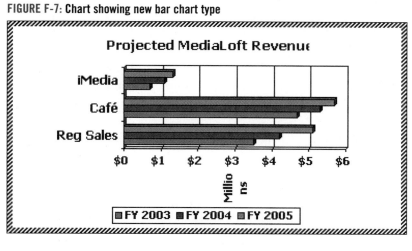

Customized chart types

There are two ways to create customized chart types: you can use PowerPoint custom types or customize your own. To use PowerPoint custom types, click the Custom Types tab in the Chart Type dialog box. You will then see more chart types, such as Floating Bars and the Area Blocks. To define a custom chart, click any chart series element (such as a bar) in the chart window, click Format on the menu bar, then click the selected series to open the Format Chart dialog box. Use the Patterns, Shape, Data Labels, or Options tabs to customize the color, shape, or appearance of the selected element. To reuse the chart type you have created, make it a type in the Chart Type dialog box by clicking the User-defined option button, clicking Add, then assigning a name to it and clicking OK. To use it later, click the name of the type you added.

Changing a Chart Display

Graph provides many advanced formatting options so that you can customize your chart to emphasize the information you think is important. For example, you can add gridlines to a chart, change the color or pattern of data markers, and format the axes. Maria wants to improve the appearance of her chart, so she makes several formatting changes.

Steps

1. **With Graph still open, click Chart on the menu bar, then click Chart Options**
   The Chart Options dialog box opens. Gridlines will help separate and clarify the data series markers.

2. **Click the Gridlines tab, and in the Category (X) axis section, click the Major gridlines check box, click the Minor gridlines check box, then click OK**
   Horizontal gridlines appear on the chart. Compare your screen to Figure F-8. Adding minor gridlines increases the number of gridlines in the chart.

3. **Click the Data Table button ⊞ on the Standard toolbar**
   Adding the data table dramatically decreases the size of the chart, so you decide to return to the previous format.

4. **Click ⊞ again**
   The chart returns to its previous format. Adding data labels to one of the data series will make the series easier to identify.

5. **Double-click one of the FY 2005 data markers in the chart**
   The Format Data Series dialog box opens.

6. **Click the Data Labels tab, click the Value check box to select it, then click OK**
   The FY 2005 values from the datasheet appear on the data markers, as shown in Figure F-9. Changing the way the numbers appear on the horizontal axis will improve the chart's appearance.

7. **Right-click one of the values on the horizontal axis, click Format Axis on the shortcut menu, click the Number tab, click the Decimal places up arrow until 1 appears, then click OK**
   After the Format Axis dialog box closes, the values on the horizontal axis display one decimal point. The labels on the vertical axis would look better if they were oriented at an angle.

8. **Right-click any of the labels on the vertical axis, click Format Axis on the shortcut menu, click the Alignment tab, drag the red diamond under the Orientation section up until the Degrees text box reads 15, then click OK**
   The labels on the vertical axis are oriented at a 15-degree angle. The Value axis title would look better if it were rotated to a horizontal position.

9. **Right-click the Millions axis label, click Format Axis Title on the shortcut menu, click the Alignment tab, drag the red diamond in the Orientation section until the Degrees text box reads 0, then click OK**

10. **Click a blank area of the slide, then save your presentation**
    Compare your screen to Figure F-10.

FIGURE F-8: Chart with new gridlines

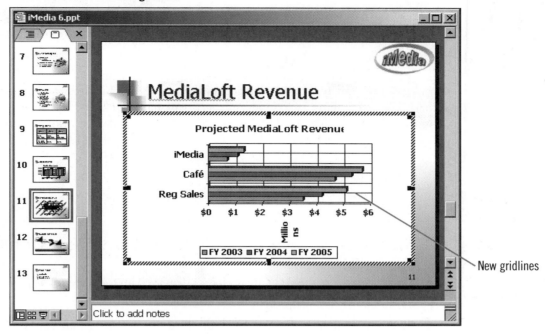

New gridlines

FIGURE F-9: Chart showing data marker labels

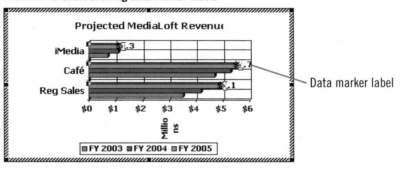

Data marker label

FIGURE F-10: Modified chart

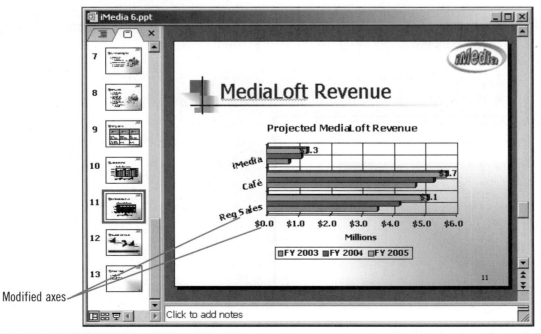

Modified axes

Working with Chart Elements

Chart elements are objects you can add and format to help highlight certain information in your chart. Chart elements include legends, arrows, shapes or lines, text objects, and chart titles. Maria decides to add a text object and an arrow to draw attention to the strong expected sales in the café in 2005.

Trouble?

If the drawing toolbar is not visible, click View on the menu bar, point to Toolbars, then click Drawing.

1. **Double-click the Graph chart object**, then click the **Text Box button** 🖳 on the Drawing toolbar
   Graph opens and the Drawing toolbar is displayed on the screen. The pointer changes to ╋ when it is positioned in the chart area.

2. **Position ╋ above the Café FY 2005 data marker, drag to create a text box, then type Over Goal**
   If the text object is not where you want it, position the pointer over its edge, then drag to reposition the object. Changing the color and size of the text would make it easier to read.

3. **Drag ⵊ over the text to select it, click the Font Size list arrow** ⟨8 ▾⟩ on the Formatting toolbar, then click **20**

Trouble?

If the text box no longer accommodates all the text, drag a sizing handle to make it larger.

4. **Click the Font Color list arrow** ⟨A ▾⟩ on the Drawing toolbar, click the Red box, then click a blank area of the chart
   Compare your screen to Figure F-11. An arrow would help connect the new text object to a data marker in the chart.

5. **Click the Arrow button** 🖋 on the Drawing toolbar, position ╋ under the word "Over," then drag an arrow to the end of the Café FY 2005 data marker
   The arrow could be more prominent.

QuickTip

To quickly change the color of the arrow, click the Line Color button 🖋 on the Drawing toolbar. To change the weight of the line, click the Line Style button ☰ on the Drawing toolbar.

6. **Click the Arrow Style button** 🖳 on the Drawing toolbar, click **More Arrows**, then click the **Color list arrow** in the Line section

7. **Click the Red box, click the Weight up arrow until 2 pt appears, then click OK**

8. **Click a blank area of the slide, then save your presentation**
   Compare your screen to Figure F-12.

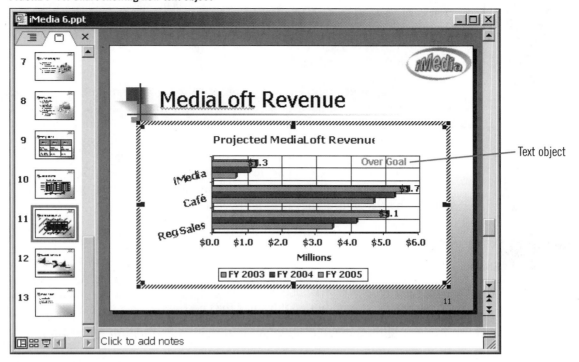

Text object

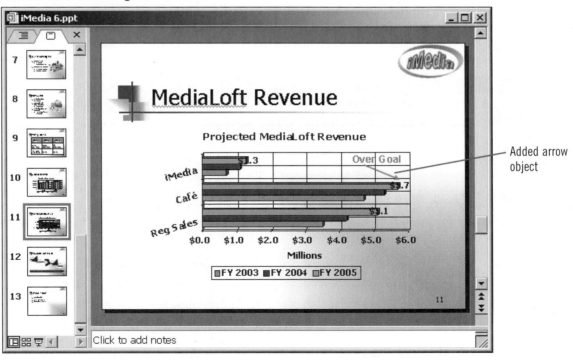

Added arrow object

Moving and sizing chart elements

To move a chart element, such as an arrow or the legend, you must first select the object to view its resizing handles, then drag the object to its new location. Make sure that the pointer is over the object's border when you drag it, not over a resizing handle. To change the size of a chart element, click the object to view its resizing handles, then drag a resizing handle.

Animating Charts and Sounds

Just as you can animate bullets and graphics on slides, you can animate chart elements. You can have bars appear by series, groups, or individually. You can choose to have the legend and grid animated. You can also control the order and timing of the animations. Sound effects, including applause, a drum roll, a typewriter, and an explosion, can accompany the chart animation. Be sure to choose sounds that are appropriate for your presentation. For example, you would not use the screeching brakes sound in a serious financial presentation. Many presentations are effective with no sound effects to distract from the speaker's message. ✎ Maria decides to animate the elements on her chart and add a sound effect.

Steps

1. **Click the chart once to select it**
   Make sure you do not double-click the chart.

2. **Click Slide Show on the menu bar, then click Custom Animation**
   The Custom Animation task pane opens.

3. **Click Add Effect in the task pane, point to Entrance, click More Effects, click Fade in the Subtle section, then click OK**
   The Fade animation effect is added to the chart, and the chart is added to the Effects list in the task pane as Chart 2. Now you can animate specific chart elements. Compare your screen to Figure F-13.

4. **Click the Chart 2 list arrow in Effects list in the task pane, then click Effect Options**
   The Fade dialog box opens.

5. **Click the Chart Animation tab, click the Group chart list arrow, then click By element in category**

6. **Click the Effect tab, click the Sound list arrow, scroll down the list, then click Push**

7. **Click OK, then watch the slide pane**
   The grid appears first, then each bar appears in each category, accompanied by the Push sound. Compare your screen to Figure F-14.

8. **Click Slide Show at the bottom of the task pane, then click the mouse button as many times as necessary to view the complete chart animation**
   Each bar appears gradually accompanied by the Push sound effect.

9. **When the animation on Slide 11 is finished, press [Esc] to return to Normal view**

10. **Click the Save button 🖫 on the Standard toolbar**

FIGURE F-13: Screen showing Custom Animation task pane

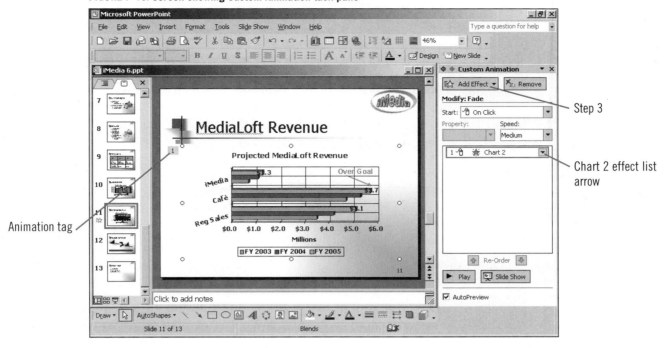

Step 3

Chart 2 effect list arrow

Animation tag

FIGURE F-14: Slide showing animated Graph chart

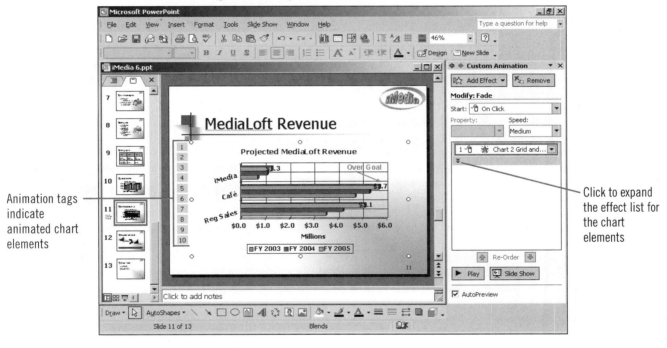

Animation tags indicate animated chart elements

Click to expand the effect list for the chart elements

CLUES TO USE

Adding voice narrations

If your computer has a sound card and a microphone, you can record a voice narration that plays with your slide show. To record a voice, click Slide Show on the menu bar, then click Record Narration. If you want the recording to be linked to the presentation, click the Link narrations in check box. If you do not select this option, the recording will be embedded in the presentation. If the Record Narration command is not available, then you do not have the necessary hardware.

Embedding an Organizational Chart

When you need to illustrate a hierarchical structure, such as the organization of a company or group, you can create and embed an organizational chart in your presentation by using the Insert Diagram or Organization Chart button on the Drawing toolbar or by changing the layout of your slide to one of the Content layouts. An organizational chart is made up of a series of connected boxes called **chart boxes** in which you can enter text, such as the names and job titles of people in your organization. ✎▬▬ Maria is satisfied with her graph and now turns her attention to creating an organizational chart showing the management structure for the iMedia group.

Steps 123 4

Trouble?

If the text you type doesn't appear as the slide title, click in the title placeholder, then type it again.

1. Go to **Slide 12**, click the **New Slide button** 🔲 on the Formatting toolbar, then type **iMedia Group**
   A new Slide 13 appears.

2. Click the **Insert Diagram or Organization Chart button** 🔯 on the Drawing toolbar
   The Diagram Gallery dialog box opens. In the Diagram Gallery dialog box, you have the option to insert one of six diagrams. See Table F-1 for information on how to use the different diagrams. The Organization Chart option is selected.

3. Click **OK**
   An organizational chart appears on the slide with the Organization Chart toolbar. See Figure F-15. The default organizational chart contains four blank chart boxes. The chart box at the top of the window is a **Manager chart box** and the three chart boxes below it are **Subordinate chart boxes**. The Manager chart box is selected and ready to accept text.

4. Type **Leilani Ho**, press **[Enter]**, then type **Manager**
   The text is entered into the text box.

5. Click the **left Subordinate chart box**, type **David Dumont**, press **[Enter]**, type **Development**, click the **middle Subordinate chart box**, type **Ann Rodriguez**, press **[Enter]**, type **Marketing**, click the **right Subordinate chart box**, type **John Wen**, press **[Enter]**, then type **Sales**
   Additional chart boxes can be added to the default organizational chart.

6. With the **John Wen chart box** still selected, click the **Insert Shape list arrow** on the Organization Chart toolbar, then click **Coworker**
   A new Coworker chart box is added to the right of the John Wen chart box.

QuickTip

Each chart box you add automatically decreases the size of all the chart boxes and their text so that the entire organizational chart will fit on the slide.

7. Click the **new chart box**, type **Cory Abrahams**, press **[Enter]**, then type **Prod. Development**

8. Click the **Ann Rodriguez chart box**, click the **Insert Shape list arrow** on the Organization Chart toolbar, then click **Subordinate**
   A new Assistant chart box appears under the Ann Rodriguez chart box.

9. Click the **new chart box,** type **Gary Robbins**, press **[Enter]**, then type **Associate**
   The chart would look better moved a little to the left on the slide.

10. Drag the chart by its border to the center of the slide, click a blank area of the slide to deselect the chart, then save your changes
    Compare your screen to Figure F-16.

FIGURE F-15: Default organization chart

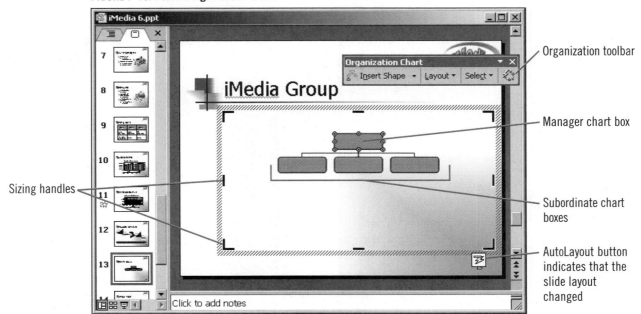

Organization toolbar

Manager chart box

Sizing handles

Subordinate chart boxes

AutoLayout button indicates that the slide layout changed

FIGURE F-16: Organization chart showing new chart boxes

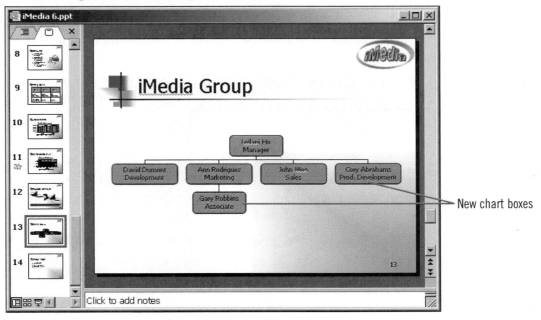

New chart boxes

TABLE F-1: Diagram Gallery dialog box

diagram icon	diagram name	diagram use
	Organization chart	Used to show hierarchical relationships
	Cycle Diagram	Used to show a process with a continuous cycle
	Radial Diagram	Used to show relationships with a core element
	Pyramid Diagram	Used to show foundational relationships
	Venn Diagram	Used to show overlap between elements
	Target Diagram	Used to show steps toward a goal

PowerPoint 2002

Modifying an Organizational Chart

After you add all the chart boxes you need for your organizational chart, you can format the chart boxes and connecting lines. Attributes of a chart box that you can format include fill color, line color, line style, font size, color, and type and shadow style. Chart boxes can also be rearranged within the organizational chart as desired. ✏️ Maria formats the chart boxes and connecting lines of her organization chart and rearranges a chart box.

Trouble?

If chart box text overlaps the edge of a chart box, click inside the chart box to expand it.

1. Click the **Leilani Ho chart box**, click the **Select button** on the Organization Chart toolbar, then click **Branch**
   All the chart boxes are selected and ready to be formatted.

2. Click the **Fill Color list arrow** 🎨▾ on the Drawing toolbar, then click the **light green color** (the first color cell from the right)
   The fill color of the chart boxes changes to light green.

3. Click the **Font list arrow** on the Formatting toolbar, scroll to the top of the list, click **Arial Black**, then click the **Shadow button** ⓢ on the Formatting toolbar
   Compare your screen to Figure F-17.

4. Click the **Shadow Style button** ▣ on the Drawing toolbar, then click **Shadow Style 4** (last style in the first row)
   A shadow is applied to each chart box. A darker shadow might make the chart boxes stand out more on the slide.

5. Click ▣, click **Shadow Settings** to open the Shadow Settings toolbar, click the **Shadow Color list arrow** 🖥▾, click the **Black color** (labeled Follow Text and Line Schemes Color), then click the **Close button** ✕ on the Shadow Settings toolbar
   Thicker connecting lines between the chart boxes would look better.

6. Click **Select** on the Organization Chart toolbar, click **All Connecting Lines**, click the **Line Style button** ▤ on the Drawing toolbar, then click **3 pt**
   The connector lines are now thicker. Gary Robbins is actually John Wen's associate.

QuickTip

Only chart boxes at the end of a branch can be moved to another position in the organizational chart.

7. Position the mouse pointer over the edge of the **Gary Robbins chart box** so that it changes to 🖑, then drag it on top of the John Wen chart box
   Compare your organizational chart to Figure F-18.

8. Drag the chart to the center of the slide, click the **Slide Show button** 🖵 to view Slide 13, then press **[Esc]** to end the slide show

9. Click the **Slide Sorter View button** 🔠
   Compare your screen to Figure F-19. Slides 11 and 13 are the only slides you modified in this unit.

10. Click the **Normal View button** 🔲, add your name as a footer to the notes and handouts, click the **Save button** 💾 on the Standard toolbar, then print the presentation as handouts (6 slides per page)

FIGURE F-17: Organization chart showing formatted chart boxes

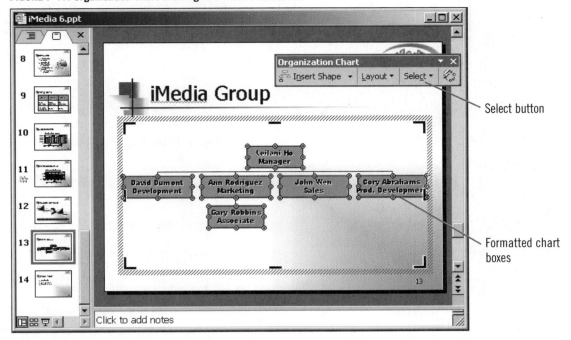

Select button

Formatted chart boxes

FIGURE F-18: Organization chart showing rearranged chart box

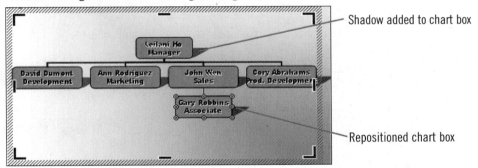

Shadow added to chart box

Repositioned chart box

FIGURE F-19: Final presentation in Slide Sorter view

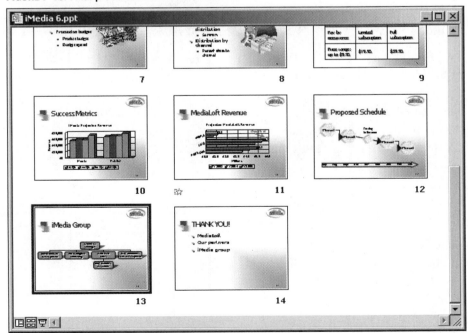

Practice

► Concepts Review

Label each of the elements of the PowerPoint window shown in Figure F-20.

FIGURE F-20

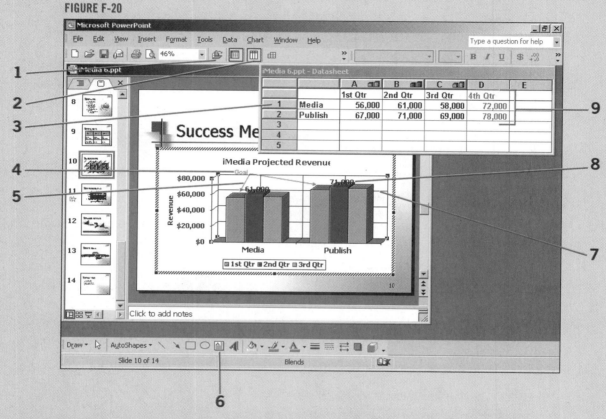

Match each of the terms with the statement that describes its function.

10. A row or column of data in a datasheet
11. A box at the edge of a datasheet, usually with a row number or column letter in it
12. A group of connected cells in a datasheet
13. Graphical representation of a data series
14. Lines that separate and clarify data series markers

a. Data series markers
b. Range
c. Data series
d. Control box
e. Gridlines

Select the best answer from the list of choices.

15. In Graph, clicking a column control box:
   a. Selects all column data markers in a chart.
   b. Selects an entire column of data in the datasheet.
   c. Switches the chart format to 3-D column.
   d. Controls the format of the datasheet.

16. **Which of the following statements about Graph charts is incorrect?**
    a. There are 2-D and 3-D chart types.
    b. You can change the format of data markers.
    c. You can format every element of a chart.
    d. The type of chart you choose does not depend on the data you have.

17. **Which of the following is incorrect about animating charts?**
    a. You can accompany chart animations with a sound.
    b. You can't control the timing of the animation.
    c. You can choose to have chart elements appear in a variety of ways.
    d. You don't need to accompany every animation with a sound.

18. **Based on what you know of organizational charts, which of the following data would best fit in an organizational chart?**
    a. A company's division structure
    b. A company's database mailing list
    c. A company's annual financial numbers
    d. Spreadsheet data

19. **To change a column's width in a datasheet, you can:**
    a. Double-click cell A1 in the datasheet.
    b. Drag the row control box up.
    c. Double-click the column control box border.
    d. Both A and C.

20. **What do chart gridlines help you do?**
    a. Gridlines help you combine data series markers.
    b. Gridlines help you separate and clarify data series markers.
    c. Gridlines help you see chart elements, such as text or lines.
    d. Gridlines help you change the chart type.

21. **Which of the following is false about organization charts?**
    a. You can create an organization chart by clicking the Insert Diagram or Organization Chart button on the Formatting toolbar.
    b. Connecting lines between chart boxes can be formatted.
    c. An assistant chart box cannot be moved.
    d. A chart box and all of its subordinate chart boxes can be moved.

► Skills Review

1. **Insert data from a file into a datasheet.**
   a. Start PowerPoint, open the presentation PPT F-3, then save it as **Royal Publishing** to the drive and location where your Project Files are stored.
   b. On Slide 3, open Microsoft Graph.
   c. Click the upper-left cell in the datasheet, and import Sheet1 of the Excel file PPT F-4 into the Graph datasheet.
   d. Exclude the Mystery row from the chart, then save the chart.

2. **Format a datasheet.**
   a. Select the range of cells from cell A1 to cell E4.
   b. Format the datasheet numbers with Currency format.
   c. Change the format of the datasheet numbers so that they have no decimal places. (*Hint*: Click the Decrease Decimal button on the Standard toolbar twice to do this quickly.)

d. Adjust the column width for all the columns to Best Fit.

e. Change the data so the series are in columns. Compare your datasheet with Figure F-21.

f. Close the datasheet.

g. Save the chart.

	A	B	C	D	E
PPT F-3.ppt - Datasheet					
2003 Fiscal Year	Victoria	Waterloo	Paddington	Euston	Liverpool
1 Fiction	$250	$230	$260	$250	$320
2 Non-Fiction	$180	$200	$240	$300	$229
3 Children's	$120	$130	$115	$120	$100
4 Mystery	$130	$150	$110	$90	$140
5					
6					
7					

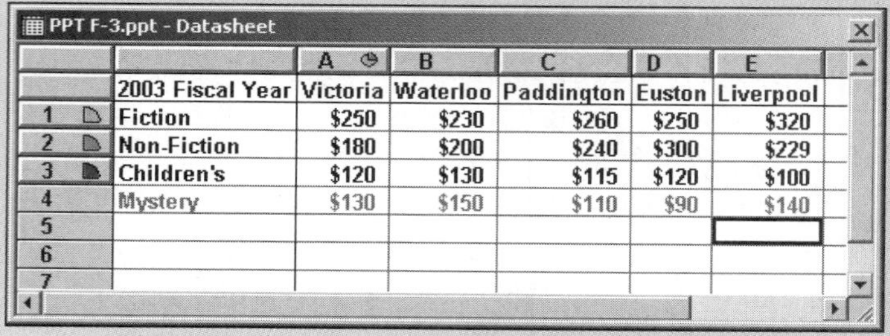

3. Change a chart's type.

a. Change the chart type to a clustered 3-D bar chart, preview it, then accept it.

b. Change the chart to a clustered 3-D column chart.

c. Save the chart.

4. Change a chart display.

a. Show major gridlines on both the x- and the z-axes.

b. Add a label to the z-axis that reads **Thousands**.

c. Open the Format Axis Title dialog box for the z-axis label and change its orientation to 90 degrees.

d. Save your changes.

5. Work with chart elements.

a. Add a text box to add a label pointing to Euston non-fiction sales.

b. Add the text **A record!** to the text box.

c. Change the point size of the text to 22 point and the font to Times New Roman.

d. Change the color of the text to blue.

e. Add a blue arrow pointing from the text box to the appropriate data point.

f. Format the arrow line as 3 point.

g. Compare your chart with Figure F-22 and adjust the text box and arrow positions as necessary.

h. Click a blank area of the slide, then save your changes.

FIGURE F-22

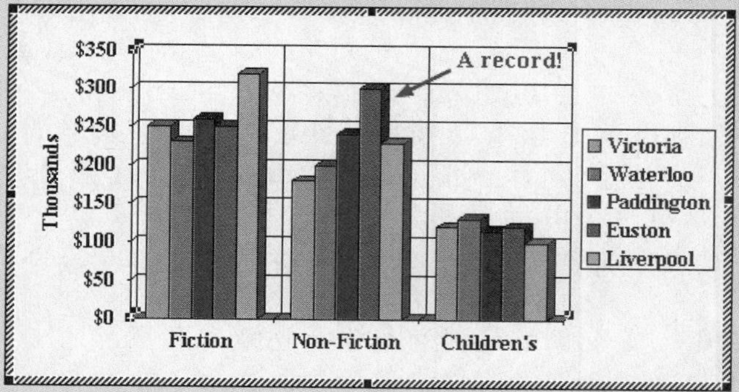

6. Animate charts and sounds.

a. Animate the chart with the Entrance Fade effect.

b. Animate the chart elements so they are introduced by series.

c. Add the Arrow sound effect to the animation.

d. In the Custom Animation task pane, click the Speed list arrow and change the speed to Fast.

e. Preview the animation.

f. Check the animation in Slide Show view, then save the presentation.

7. Embed an organizational chart.

a. Go to Slide 4.

b. Add an organization chart to the slide.

c. At the top level, type **John Edwards** as **Division Manager**.

d. In the Subordinate chart boxes, type the following names and titles:
Sarah Wiley, Distribution Manager
Robert Sarhi, Purchasing Manager
Evelyn Storey, Circulation Manager

e. Change the fill color for all the chart boxes to a light yellow color.

f. Change the line color for all the chart boxes to a dark purple color, then save your changes.

8. **Modify an organizational chart.**
   a. Add an assistant chart box to the Sarah Wiley chart box.
   b. Drag the organization chart sizing handles to make the chart as big as possible.
   c. Enter **Michael Raye** as her **Special Assistant**.
   d. Add two Subordinate boxes to the Evelyn Storey chart box, and enter the following:
      Janee Fugishi, Purchase Orders
      Lynn Perry, Financial Assistant
   e. Drag the Janee Fugishi chart box and the Lynn Perry chart box so they are under the Robert Sarhi chart box.
   f. Select the John Edwards chart box and change the font to 16 pt.
   g. Format all the other chart boxes using the formatting characteristics from the John Edwards chart box. (*Hint:* Use the Format Painter button.)
   h. Format the connecting lines to 3 pt.
   i. Go to Slide 1, then run through a slide show in Slide Show view.
   j. Add your name to the notes and handouts footer.
   k. Save your changes, print the presentation as handouts (3 slides per page), then close the presentation and exit PowerPoint.

► Independent Challenge 1

You work for Larsen Concepts, a business consulting company that helps small- and medium-sized businesses organize or restructure themselves to be more efficient and profitable. You are one of six senior consultants who works directly with clients. To prepare for an upcoming meeting with executives at ComSystems, a mobile phone communications company, you create a brief presentation outlining Larsen's typical investigative and reporting techniques, past results versus the competition, and the company's business philosophy.

The following is a sample of the type of work you perform as part of your duties at Larsen: You usually investigate a client's business practices for two weeks and analyze all relevant records. Once the initial investigation stage is complete, you submit a client recommendation report to your boss that describes the known problem areas, the consequences of the problems, the reasons for the problems, the recommended solutions, the anticipated results for each solution, the anticipated cost to the client for each solution, and Larsen's final professional recommendation. After your boss approves the client recommendation report, you prepare a full report for the client. If the client approves the plan, you develop a maintenance schedule (usually one year or less) to make sure the plan is implemented correctly.

   a. Open the file PPT F-5 from the folder where your Project Files are stored, then save it as **Larsen Presentation**.
   b. Think about the results you want to see, the information you need, and how you want to communicate the message. Sketch how you want your presentation to look.
   c. Create charts on Slides 3 and 4 using one of the charts available in the Diagram Gallery. Use the information provided to show the various stages of investigation and reporting.
   d. Create a Graph chart on Slide 5 that shows how Larsen compares with two competitors. For example, you might illustrate the satisfaction level of Larsen clients compared to its competitors' clients. Format the chart to present the information clearly.
   e. Add a concluding slide that includes a graphic.
   f. Format the text on the slides. Modify the master views to achieve the look you want.
   g. Add a template and shaded background to finish the presentation.

h. Spell check and save your presentation.

i. Add your name as a footer to the slides and handouts, print the slides of the presentation, then submit your presentation plan and printouts.

j. Close the presentation and exit PowerPoint.

▶ Independent Challenge 2

This year, you have been selected by your peers to receive a national teaching award for the educational program that you created for disabled children in your home state of Connecticut. In accepting this award, you have the opportunity to give a presentation describing your program's results since its introduction. You will give the presentation at an educator's convention in Washington, D.C.

Plan and create a slide presentation describing your results. Create your own data, but assume the following:

- Over the last four years, 3,548 children in 251 classrooms throughout Connecticut have participated in your program.
- Children enrolled in your program have shown at least a 7% improvement in skills for every year the program has been in effect.
- Children ages 4 through 12 have participated in the program.
- Money to fund the program comes from the National Education Association (NEA) and the State of Connecticut Public School Department. The money goes to each participating school district in the state.
- Funding per child is $2,867 per school year. Funding per child in a regular classroom is $3,950 per year.

a. Think about the results you want to see, the information you need to create the slide presentation, and how your message should be communicated.

b. Create a color slide presentation using a chart from the Diagram Gallery to build some of your slides. Think about how you can effectively show information in a chart.

c. Format the charts using PowerPoint's formatting features.

d. Use clip art, shapes, and a shaded background to enhance the presentation. Change the bullet and text formatting in the Master text and title placeholders to fit the subject matter.

e. Spell check and save the presentation as **Teaching Award**.

f. Add your name as a footer to the slides and handouts, then print the final slide presentation.

g. Close the presentation and exit PowerPoint.

▶ Independent Challenge 3

LabTech Industries is a large company that develops and produces technical medical equipment and machines for operating and emergency rooms throughout the United States. You are the business manager, and one of your assignments is to prepare a presentation for the stockholders on the profitability and efficiency of each division in the company.

Plan and create a slide presentation that shows all the divisions and divisional managers of the company. Also, graphically show how each division performed in relation to its previous year's performance. Create your own content, but assume the following:

- The company has seven divisions: Administration, Accounting, Sales and Marketing, Research and Development, Product Testing, Product Development, and Manufacturing.
- Three divisions increased productivity by at least 15%.
- The presentation will be given in a boardroom using a projector.

a. Think about the results you want to see, the information you need to create the slide presentation, what type of message you want to communicate, and the target audience.

b. Use Outline view to create the content of your presentation.

c. Create a Graph chart, then insert the Excel file PPT F-6 into the datasheet.

d. Create organization charts to help present the information you want to communicate.

e. Use clip art, pictures, or a shaded background to enhance the presentation, and format the content.

f. Save the presentation as **LabTech Industries** to the drive and location where your Project Files are stored.

g. Add your name as a footer to the slides and handouts, then print the final slide presentation.

h. Close the presentation and exit PowerPoint.

 # Independent Challenge 4

You are a PC game analyst for IGame Resources Inc., a computer game software research company. One of your responsibilities every quarter is to create a brief presentation that identifies the top computer games based on industry and consumer reviews. In your presentation, you include charts that help define the data you compile.

Develop your own content, but assume the following:

- Include five computer games in your presentation.
- Each game has at least two missions.
- Consumer satisfaction of each game is identified on a scale of 1.0 to 10.0.
- There are four categories of games: Adventure, Action, Driving, and Strategy.

You'll need to find the following information on the Web:

- Consumer or industry reviews of five PC computer games.
- A description of each game, including the story line of the game or mission.
- The price of each game.

a. Open a new presentation, and save it as **PC Game Review** where your Project Files are stored.

b. Add your name as the footer on all slides and handouts.

c. Connect to the Internet, then use a search engine to locate Web sites that have information on PC computer games. If your search does not produce any results, you might try the following sites: www.zdnet.com/gamespot, www.gamesdomain.com, or www.gamecenter.com.

d. Review at least two Web sites that contain information about computer games. Print the Home pages of the Web sites you use to gather data for your presentation.

e. Using PowerPoint, create an outline of your presentation. It should contain between eight and 10 slides, including a title slide.

f. Include at least one chart that identifies consumer satisfaction numbers that you develop.

g. Create a diagram or organization chart that briefly explains the story line of one of the games.

h. Create a table that lists the price of each game.

i. Enhance the presentation with clip art or other graphics, an appropriate template and/or background, or other items that improve the look of the presentation.

j. Change the master views, if necessary, to fit your presentation.

k. Spell check and save the presentation.

l. Print the slides of the presentation as handouts (4 slides per page).

m. Close the presentation and exit PowerPoint.

▶ Visual Workshop

Create two slides that look like the examples in Figures F-23 and F-24. Save the presentation as **Central Industries**. Add your name as a footer on the slides, then save and print the presentation slides.

FIGURE F-23

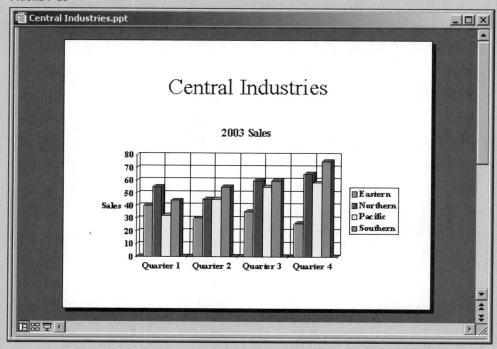

FIGURE F-24

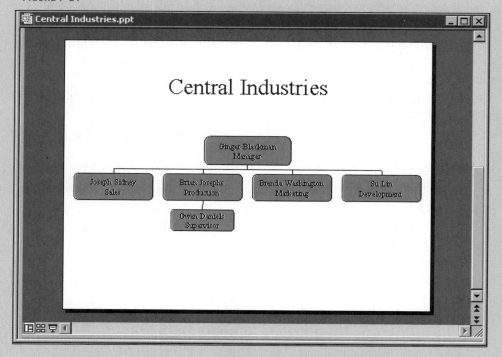

Working

with Embedded and Linked Objects and Hyperlinks

Objectives

- MOUS ► **Embed a picture**
- MOUS ► **Insert a Word table**
- MOUS ► **Embed an Excel chart**
- MOUS ► **Link an Excel worksheet**
- ► **Update a linked Excel worksheet**
- MOUS ► **Insert an animated GIF file**
- MOUS ► **Insert a sound**
- MOUS ► **Insert a hyperlink**

PowerPoint offers many ways to add graphic elements to a presentation. In this unit, you will learn how to embed and link objects. Embedded and linked objects are created in another program and then stored in or linked to the PowerPoint presentation. In this unit, Maria Abbott, MediaLoft's general sales manager, uses embedded and linked objects to create a brief presentation that outlines MediaLoft's video department. She will use the presentation in a proposal she will make to a potential new video supplier.

Embedding a Picture

You can embed more than 20 types of pictures using the Insert Picture command. Frequently, a presentation's color scheme will not match the colors in pictures, especially photographs. In order to make the picture look good in the presentation, you may need to adjust the slide's color scheme, recolor the picture, or change the presentation's template. ✐ Maria wants to embed a photograph in a slide. She will adjust the slide's color scheme to make the photograph look good.

Steps 1 2 3 4

1. Start PowerPoint, open the presentation **PPT G-1** from the drive and folder where your Project Files are located, save it as **Video Division**, click **View** on the menu bar, click **Task Pane**, click **Window** on the menu bar, then click **Arrange All**

Trouble?

If the Picture toolbar is in the way, move the toolbar to another part of the screen.

2. Click the **Slide 2 thumbnail** in the Slides tab, click the **Insert Picture button** 🖼 on the Drawing toolbar, select the file **PPT G-2** from the drive and location where your Project Files are stored, then click **Insert**

   A picture of a tropical scene appears on the slide and the Picture toolbar opens. The Automatic Layout Options button appears below the picture, which indicates that the slide layout has changed to accommodate the picture. The slide would look fine with the original slide layout.

3. Click the **Automatic Layout Options button** 🔁 on the slide, then click **Undo Automatic Layout**

   The picture moves to the middle of the slide and the size of the text in the body text box increases.

4. Resize and drag the picture to match Figure G-1

   A different slide color would provide a better contrast to the picture.

5. Click the **Slide Design button** 🗔 on the Formatting toolbar, then click the **Color Schemes link** in the Slide Design task pane

   The Slide Design task pane opens, showing the available color schemes. There are nine standard color schemes from which to choose.

6. Click each **color scheme thumbnail list arrow**, then click **Apply to Selected Slides** to preview the color schemes

   Each color scheme is applied to the presentation. The third color scheme down in the second column fits best with the picture colors.

Trouble?

If you click Apply to All Slides by mistake, click the Undo button 🔄, then repeat Step 7.

7. Click the **green color scheme list arrow** in the third row, second column, then click **Apply to Selected Slides**

   Make sure you do not click Apply to All Slides or click the color scheme box itself, which is the same as applying the scheme to all slides. The color scheme for Slide 2 changes to a green background.

8. Click a blank area of the slide, compare your screen to Figure G-2, then click the **Save button** 💾 on the Standard toolbar

FIGURE G-1: Slide showing embedded picture

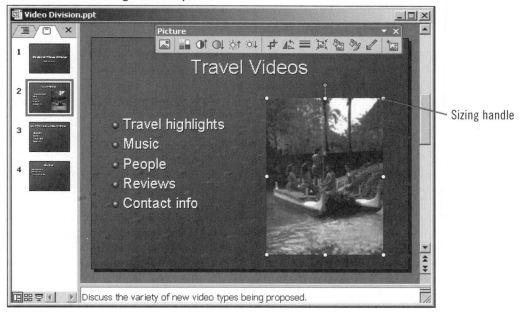

Sizing handle

FIGURE G-2: Slide showing new color scheme

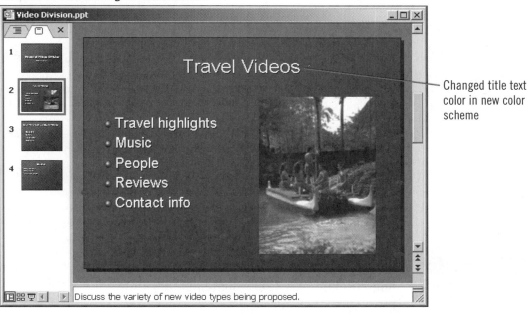

Changed title text color in new color scheme

PowerPoint 2002

CLUES TO USE

Creating a photo album

You can use PowerPoint to create a photo album using your favorite pictures. A PowerPoint photo album is a presentation set up with specific formats. To create a photo album, click Insert on the menu bar, point to Picture, then click New Photo Album. The Photo Album dialog box opens. Click File/Disk or Scanner/Camera to add pictures to the photo album. To format an existing photo album, click Format on the menu bar, then click Photo Album. You can add pictures to a photo album from your hard drive, digital camera, scanner, or Web camera. As with any presentation, you can customize the layout of a photo album by adding title text to slides, applying frames around the pictures, and applying a design template. You can also format the pictures of the photo album by adding a caption below the pictures, converting the pictures to black and white, rotating the pictures, and changing their brightness and contrast.

Inserting a
Word Table

You can easily insert a PowerPoint table in your presentation using the Insert Table button on the Standard toolbar. If you want to format a table using the Table AutoFormat command available in Microsoft Word, you can embed a Microsoft Word table in your PowerPoint slide. With an embedded Word table, you can use formatting features of both Word and PowerPoint to call attention to important information and to make the table visually appealing. Maria decides to add a new slide with a table showing the types of videos MediaLoft offers.

Steps

1. Click the **New Slide button** on the Formatting toolbar, then click the **Title Only layout** in the Slide Layout task pane
   A new Slide 3 appears.

2. Type **Largest Video Categories**, then click in a blank area of the slide

3. Click **Insert** on the menu bar, click **Object**, scroll down the Object type list box, click **Microsoft Word Document**, then click **OK**
   A blank Word document appears on the slide. The Microsoft Word menu bar and toolbars replace the PowerPoint menu bar and toolbars.

QuickTip

You can also click the Insert Table button on the Standard toolbar to insert a table.

4. Click **Table** on the menu bar, point to **Insert**, click **Table**, click the **Number of columns down arrow** in the Insert Table dialog box until **2** appears, then click **OK**
   A blank table with two rows and two columns appears on the screen. Compare your screen with Figure G-3.

5. Click **Edit** on the menu bar, click **Select All**, click the **Font Size list arrow** 12 on the Formatting toolbar, click **36**, click in the first cell in the table, enter the data shown in Figure G-4, press **[Tab]** to move from cell to cell, then click in a blank area of the slide outside the table
   After you click the slide, the PowerPoint menus and toolbars return. The table text would be easier to read if it were formatted to make it stand out from the background. Because the table is embedded, you can use Word's AutoFormat feature to do this.

QuickTip

To edit or open an embedded object in your presentation, the object's source program must be available on your computer or network.

6. Double-click the **table** to return to Word, click **Table** on the menu bar, click **Table AutoFormat**, click **Table Contemporary** in the Table styles list, click the **Heading rows check box** to deselect it, then click **Apply**
   This table is a simple list, so it doesn't need special formatting for the first row. The new table format changes the fill of the rows to two different shades of gray.

7. Click **Edit** on the menu bar, click **Select All**, click the **Center button** on the Formatting toolbar, then click the **Bold button** B on the Formatting toolbar
   The text moves to the center of the cells, increases in size, and becomes bold.

8. Click the **Line Spacing (1) list arrow** on the Formatting toolbar, click **3.0**, click the **Outside Border list arrow** on the Formatting toolbar, click the **All Borders button**, then click in a blank area of the slide
   The spacing between the rows increases and border lines are added to the table.

9. Click on the slide outside the table, then save your work
   Compare your screen to Figure G-4.

FIGURE G-3: Blank Word table on PowerPoint slide

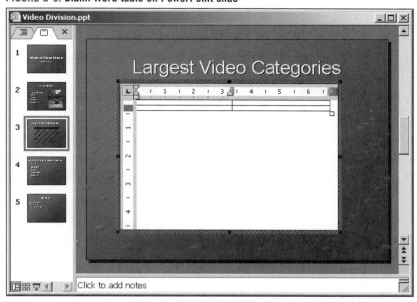

FIGURE G-4: Slide with formatted Word table

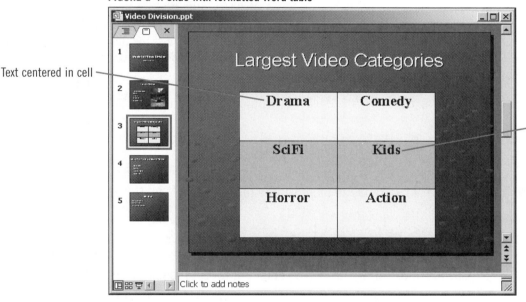

Text centered in cell

Largest Video Categories

Drama	Comedy
SciFi	Kids
Horror	Action

Table with color and format of Table Contemporary AutoFormat

Exporting a presentation

Sometimes it's helpful to use a word-processing program like Word to create detailed speaker's notes or handouts. You might also want to create a Word document based on the outline of your PowerPoint presentation. To export a presentation to Word, click File on the menu bar, point to Send to, then click Microsoft Word. The Send to Microsoft Word dialog box opens and provides you with a number of document layout options from which to choose. Select a layout, click OK, and a new Word document opens with your embedded presentation or outline, using the layout you selected. Another way to export just the text of your presentation is to save it as an outline in Rich Text format (.rtf format). You can view RTF documents in any word processing program. To do this, click File on the menu bar, click Save As, click Outline/RTF in the Save as type list box, then click Save.

Embedding an Excel Chart

When a chart is the best way to present information on a slide, you can create a chart using Microsoft Graph from within PowerPoint; however, for large amounts of data, it's easier to create a chart using a spreadsheet program like Excel. Then you can embed the chart file in your PowerPoint presentation and edit it using Excel tools. Excel is the chart file's **source program**, the program in which the file was created. PowerPoint is the **destination program**, the file into which the chart is embedded. ✐ Maria created an Excel chart showing MediaLoft's quarterly video sales. She wants to include this chart in her presentation, so she embeds it in a slide.

Steps

1. Click the **New Slide button** 🔲 on the Formatting toolbar, then click the **Title Only layout** in the Slide Layout task pane
   A new Slide 4 appears.

2. Type **Quarterly Sales** in the title placeholder

3. Click **Insert** on the menu bar, click **Object**, click the **Create from file option button** in the Insert Object dialog box, click **Browse**, locate the file **PPT G-3** in the location where your Project Files are stored, click **OK**, then click **OK** in the Insert Object dialog box
   The chart containing the video data appears on the slide. Because the chart is embedded, you can edit the worksheet using Excel formatting tools. The text labels on the chart are too small to read.

Trouble?

If the Chart toolbar appears in the middle of your screen, drag it out of the way.

4. Double-click the **chart** to open Microsoft Excel, right-click the **chart title**, click **Format Chart Title** on the shortcut menu, then click the **Font tab** in the Format Chart Title dialog box

5. Click **28** in the Size list, then click **OK**
   The chart title becomes larger.

QuickTip

After you change the first axis, you can select the next object, then press [F4] to repeat the font size increase.

6. Use the same technique to increase the text and labels on the vertical and horizontal **axes** and in the legend to **24 points**
   Compare your screen to Figure G-5.

7. Double-click the **chart background** to the right of the title, click the **Patterns tab** in the Format Chart Area dialog box, click **Fill Effects**, click the **Preset option button**, click the **Preset colors list arrow**, then scroll down and click **Gold**

8. Click the **Diagonal down option button** in the Shading styles section, click **OK**, then click **OK** in the Format Chart Area dialog box
   The chart background becomes a shaded gold color.

9. Click outside the chart to exit Excel, click a blank area of the slide to deselect the object, then save the presentation
   Compare your screen to Figure G-6.

FIGURE G-5: Embedded chart with resized text

Title text increased to 28 points

Formatted axis title

Formatted legend

Formatted axes

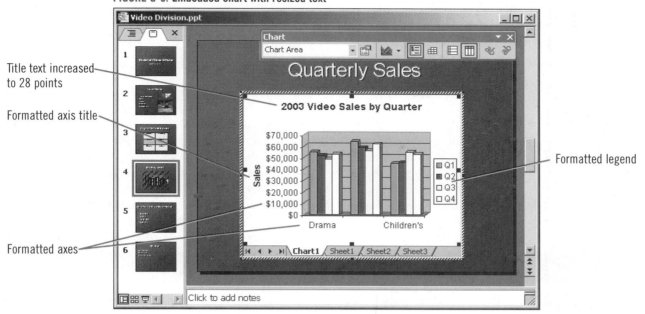

FIGURE G-6: Embedded chart with gold background

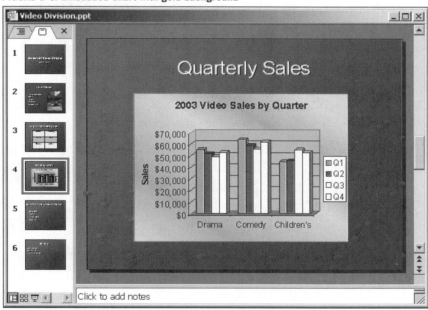

CLUES TO USE

Embedding a worksheet

You can embed all or part of an Excel worksheet into a PowerPoint slide. To embed an entire worksheet, go to the slide where you want to place the worksheet. Click Insert on the menu bar, then click Object. The Insert object dialog box opens. Click the Create from file option button, click Browse, locate and double-click the spreadsheet filename, then click OK. The worksheet is inserted into the slide. Double-click it to edit it using Excel's formatting commands as you did in this lesson. To insert only a portion of a worksheet, open the Excel workbook and copy the cells you want to include in your presentation. Leaving Excel and the source worksheet open, open the PowerPoint presentation, click Edit on the menu bar, then click Paste Special. To paste the cells as a worksheet object that you can edit in Excel, click Microsoft Excel Worksheet Object in the Paste Special dialog box.

Linking an Excel Worksheet

Another way to connect objects like Excel worksheets to your presentation is to establish a **link**, or connection, between the source file and the PowerPoint presentation. Unlike an embedded object, a linked object is stored in its source file, not on the slide, so when you link an object to a PowerPoint slide, a representation (picture) of the object, not the object itself, appears on the slide. Any changes made to the source file of a linked object are automatically reflected in the linked representation in your PowerPoint presentation. Some of the objects that you can link to PowerPoint include movies, Microsoft Excel worksheets, and PowerPoint slides from other presentations. Use linking when you want to be sure your presentation contains the latest information and when you want to include an object, such as an accounting spreadsheet, that may change over time. See Table G-1 for suggestions on when to embed an object and when to link an object. ✎ Maria needs to link an Excel worksheet to her presentation. The worksheet was created by the Accounting Department manager earlier in the year.

Steps

QuickTip

If you plan to do the steps in this unit again, be sure to make and use a copy of the Excel file Video Division Budget.

1. Click the **New Slide button** 🖻 on the Formatting toolbar, click the **Title Only layout** in the Slide Layout task pane, then type **Video Division Budget**
   A new Slide 5 appears.

2. Click **Insert** on the menu bar, click **Object**, click the **Create from file option button**, click **Browse**, locate the file **Video Division Budget** from the location where your Project Files are stored, click **OK**, then click the **Link check box** to select it
   Compare your screen to Figure G-7.

3. Click **OK** in the Insert Object dialog box
   The image of the linked worksheet appears on the slide. The worksheet would be easier to see if it were larger and had a background fill color.

4. With the worksheet still selected, drag the bottom, right sizing handle down to the right about **2"**, drag the bottom, left sizing handle down to the left about **2"**, then position the worksheet vertically in the middle of the slide
   The worksheet should be about as wide as the slide.

5. Click the **Fill Color list arrow** on the Drawing toolbar, click the **Light Blue box** (Follow Accent and Hyperlink Scheme Color), then click a blank area of the slide
   A blue background fill color appears behind the worksheet, as shown in Figure G-8.

6. Click the **Save button** 🖫 on the Standard toolbar, then click the **Close button** ☒ in the presentation title bar
   PowerPoint remains open but the Presentation window closes.

Linking objects using Paste Special

You can also link an object or selected information from another program to PowerPoint by copying and pasting. This technique is useful when you want to link part of a worksheet rather than the entire file. For example, you may want to link a worksheet from a Microsoft Excel workbook that contains both a worksheet and a chart. To link just the worksheet, open the Microsoft Excel workbook file that contains the worksheet, select the worksheet, then copy it to the Clipboard. Leaving Excel and the source worksheet open, open the PowerPoint presentation, click Edit on the menu bar, click Paste Special, click the Paste link option button, then click OK.

FIGURE G-7: Insert Object dialog box ready to link an object

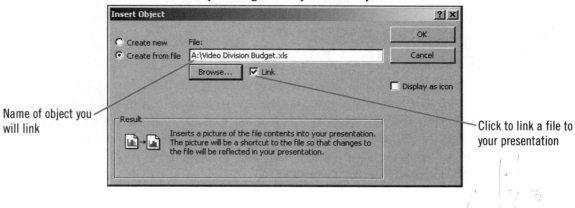

Name of object you will link

Click to link a file to your presentation

FIGURE G-8: Linked worksheet with background fill color

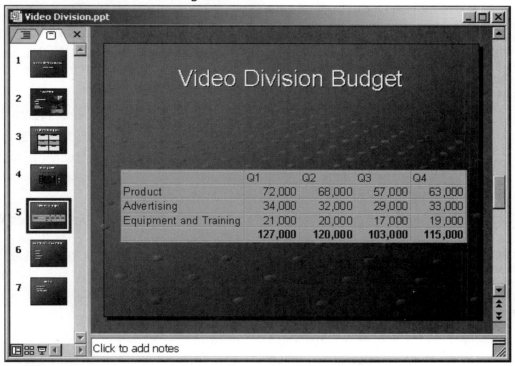

TABLE G-1: Embedding vs. Linking

situation	action
When you are the only user of an object and you want the object to be a part of your presentation	Embed
When you want to access the object in its source application, even if the original file is not available	Embed
When you want to update the object manually while working in PowerPoint	Embed
When you always want the latest information in your object	Link
When the object's source file is shared on a network or when other users have access to the file and can change it	Link
When you want to keep your presentation file size small	Link

Updating a Linked Excel Worksheet

To edit or change the information in a linked object, you must open the object's source program. For example, you must open Microsoft Word to edit a linked Word table, or you must open Microsoft Excel to edit a linked Excel worksheet. You can open the source program by double-clicking the linked object in the PowerPoint slide, as you did with embedded objects, or by starting the source program directly using any method you prefer. When you work in the source program, you can close your PowerPoint presentation or leave it open. Maria needs to update some of the data in the Excel worksheet and then update the linked object in PowerPoint. She decides to start Excel and the source file to do this.

Steps

1. Click the **Start** button on the taskbar, point to **Programs**, then click **Microsoft Excel**
   The Microsoft Excel program opens.

2. Click the **More workbooks hyperlink** in the New Workbook task pane, select the file **Video Division Budget** from the location where your Project Files are stored, then click **Open**
   The Video Division Budget worksheet opens.

3. Click cell **C2**, type **64000**, click cell **C4**, type **18000**, then press **[Enter]**
   The Q2 total is automatically recalculated and now reads 114,000 instead of 120,000.

4. Click the **Close button** ✕ in the Microsoft Excel program window, then click **Yes** to save the changes
   Microsoft Excel closes and the PowerPoint window opens.

5. Click in the PowerPoint program window to activate it, click the **Open button** 📂 on the Standard toolbar, locate the file **Video Division**, then click **Open**
   A Microsoft PowerPoint alert box opens, telling you that the Video Division presentation contains links and asking if you want to update them. See Figure G-9. This message appears whether or not you have changed the source file.

6. Click **Update Links**
   The worksheet in the presentation slide is updated.

7. Click **Window** on the menu bar, click **Arrange All**, then click the **Slide 5 thumbnail** in the Slides tab
   Compare your screen to Figure G-10. The linked Excel worksheet shows the new Q2 total, 114,000. The changes you made in Excel were automatically made in this linked copy when you updated the links.

8. Click the **Save button** 💾 on the Standard toolbar

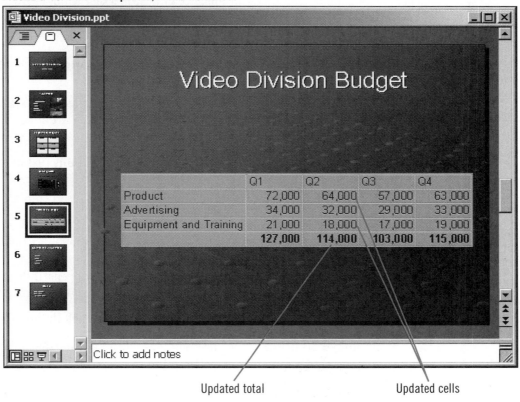

Updated total   Updated cells

Using the Links dialog box

You can use the Links dialog box to update a link, open a linked object's source program, change a linked object's source program, break a link, and determine if links are updated automatically or manually. To open the Links dialog box, click Edit on the menu bar, click Links, then click the link you want. The Links dialog box opens, as shown in Figure G-11. If the Manual option button is selected, the links in the target file will not be updated unless you select the link in this dialog box and click Update Now.

FIGURE G-11: Links dialog box

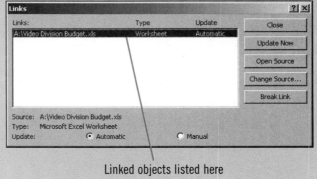

Linked objects listed here

Inserting an Animated GIF file

In your presentations, you may want to use special effects to illustrate a point or capture the attention of your audience. You can do this by inserting an animation or a movie. An **animation** contains multiple images that move or stream together when you run a slide show. Animations are stored as GIF (Graphics Interchange Format) files. PowerPoint comes with a number of animated GIFs, which are stored in the Microsoft Clip Organizer. The Clip Organizer contains various drawings, photographs, clip art, sounds, animated GIFs, and movies that you can insert into your presentation. A **movie** is live action captured in digital format by a movie camera. 🖉 Maria continues developing her presentation by embedding an animated GIF file in a slide about international videos.

Steps

1. Click the **Slide 6 thumbnail** in the Slides tab

2. Click **Insert** on the menu bar, point to **Movies and Sounds**, then click **Movie from Clip Organizer**
   The Insert Clip Art task pane opens and displays all the animated GIFs available for you to use. If you don't want to view all the animation clips in the Clip Art task pane, you can narrow the results that it displays.

3. Click **Modify** in the Insert Clip Art task pane, drag to select any text in the Search text text box, type **international**, then click **Search**
   All the clips that have an international attribute appear in the Insert Clip Art task pane. The animation clips are at the bottom of the list.

> **QuickTip**
>
> If you do not see the GIF file in Figure G-12, choose a different GIF or ask your instructor or technical support person for help.

4. Click the **down scroll arrow** until it reaches the bottom, then click the GIF file shown in Figure G-12
   The animated GIF appears on the slide and the Picture toolbar opens. If the colors of an animated GIF don't fit with the color scheme of the presentation, you can format the GIF image.

5. Click the **Automatic Layout button** 🔳 on the slide, then click **Undo Automatic Layout**

6. Resize the image so it is approximately the same height as the bulleted list, then drag the image so it's directly across from the text box

7. Click the **Color button** 🔳 on the Picture toolbar, then click **Grayscale**
   The animated GIF's colors are changed to shades of gray, which look better with the presentation's color scheme. Compare your screen with Figure G-13. The animation won't begin unless you view it in Slide Show view.

> **QuickTip**
>
> An animated GIF file will also play if you publish the presentation as a Web page and view it in a browser such as Internet Explorer or Netscape.

8. Click the **Slide Show button** 🔳, watch the animation, then press **[Esc]**

9. Click the **Save button** 🔳 on the Standard toolbar

FIGURE G-12: Clip Organizer showing animated GIF files

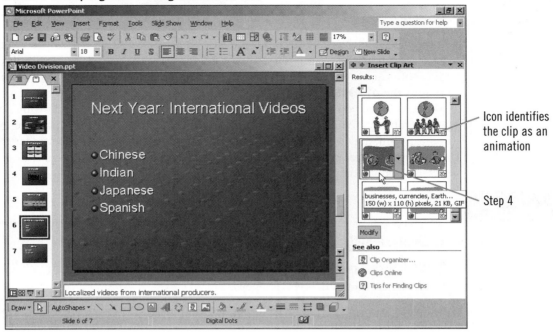

Icon identifies the clip as an animation

Step 4

FIGURE G-13: Animated GIF in slide show view

GIF image appears in Normal view but plays only in Slide Show view

CLUES TO USE

Inserting movies

You can insert movies from the Clip Organizer, the Microsoft Design Gallery Live Web site, or from disk files. To insert a movie from a disk, click Insert on the menu bar, point to Movies and Sounds, then click Movie from File. Navigate to the location of the movie you want, then insert it. If you're using the Insert Clip Art task pane, search for the file you want, then insert it. After you insert a movie, you can edit it using the Picture toolbar. You can also open the Custom Animation task pane and apply an effect to the movie. From the Custom Animation task pane, you can indicate whether to continue the slide show or to stop playing the clip.

Inserting a Sound

PowerPoint allows you to embed sounds in your presentation just as you would embed animated GIF files or movies. You can add sounds to your presentation from files on a disk, the Microsoft Clip Organizer, the Internet, or a location on a network. Use sound to enhance the message of a slide. For example, if you are creating a presentation about a raft tour of the Colorado River, you might embed a rushing water sound on a slide showing a photograph of people rafting. If you try to embed a sound that is larger than 100 KB, PowerPoint will automatically link the sound file to your presentation. You can change this setting on the General tab in the Options dialog box. Maria embeds the sound of a camera click on Slide 2 of her presentation to enhance the picture on the slide.

Steps

1. Click the **Slide 2 thumbnail** in the Slides tab

2. Click **Insert** on the menu bar, point to **Movies and Sounds**, then click **Sound from File**
   The Insert Sound dialog box opens.

3. Select the file **PPT G-4** from the location where your Project Files are stored, then click **OK**
   A dialog box opens asking if you want the sound to play automatically or if you want it to play only when you click the icon during the slide show.

Trouble?

The sound icon you see may be different from the one illustrated in Figure G-14, depending on your sound card software.

4. Click **Yes** to play the sound automatically
   A small sound icon appears on the slide, as shown in Figure G-14. The icon would be easier to see if it were larger.

5. Click **Format** on the menu bar, click **Picture**, then click the **Size tab**
   The Size tab opens in the Format Picture dialog box.

6. Double-click **100** in the Height text box in the Scale section, type **150**, then click **OK**
   The sound icon enlarges to 150% of its original size.

7. Drag the **sound icon** to the lower-right corner of the Presentation window, then click the slide background to deselect the icon
   Compare your screen to Figure G-15.

Trouble?

If you do not hear a sound, your computer may not have a sound card installed. See your instructor or technical support person for help.

8. Double-click the **sound icon**
   The sound of a camera clicking plays out of your computer's speakers.

9. Click the **Save button** 🖫 on the Standard toolbar

FIGURE G-14: Slide showing small sound icon

Sound icon

FIGURE G-15: Slide showing repositioned sound icon

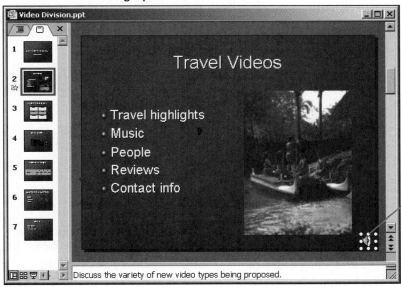

Enlarged and repositioned sound icon

CLUES TO USE

Playing music from a CD

You can play a CD audio track during your slide show. Click Insert on the menu bar, point to Movies and Sounds, then click Play CD Audio Track. The Movie and Sound Options dialog box opens. Select the beginning and ending track number and the timing options you want. See Figure G-16. When you are finished in the Movie and Sound Options dialog box, click OK. A CD icon appears on the slide. You can indicate if you want the CD to play automatically when you move to the slide or only when you click the CD icon during a slide show. The CD must be in the CD-ROM drive before you can play an audio track.

FIGURE G-16: Movie and Sound Options dialog box

Sound Options ? X

Play options

☐ Loop until stopped

☐ Rewind movie when done playing

Play CD audio track

Start: End:

Track: [1]   Track: [1]

At: [00:28]   At: [00:56]

Total playing time: 00:28
File: [CD Audio]

[OK]   [Cancel]

Inserting a Hyperlink

Often you will want to view a document that either won't fit on the slide or is too detailed for your presentation. In these cases, you can insert a **hyperlink**, a specially formatted word, phrase, graphic, or drawn object that you click during your slide show to "jump to," or display, another slide in your current presentation; another PowerPoint presentation; a Word, Excel, or Access file; or an address on the World Wide Web. Inserting a hyperlink is similar to linking because you can change the object in the source program after you click the hyperlink. ✎ Maria decides to add a hyperlink to her presentation to show a recent product review, which is in a Word document.

Steps

1. Click the **Slide 7 thumbnail** in the Slides tab

2. Drag I across **Video News** to select it, then click the **Insert Hyperlink button** 📧 on the Standard toolbar, then click **Existing File or Web Page**
   The Insert Hyperlink dialog box opens. Compare your dialog box with Figure G-17. You want to hyperlink to another file.

3. Select the file **PPT G-5** from the location where your Project Files are stored, click **OK**, then click in a blank area of the slide
   Now that you have made "Video News" a hyperlink to the file PPT G-5, the text formatting changes to a blue color, the hyperlink color for this presentation's color scheme, and is underlined. It's important to test any hyperlink you create.

4. Click the **Slide Show button** 🖵, then click the **Video News hyperlink**
   The Word document containing the review appears on the screen, as shown in Figure G-18. The Web toolbar appears below the Formatting toolbar.

5. Click the **Back button** ⬅ on the Web toolbar
   The Reviews slide reappears in Slide Show view. The hyperlink is now light purple, the color for followed hyperlinks in this color scheme, indicating that the hyperlink has been used.

6. Press **[Esc]** to end the slide show, right-click the **Word program button** on the taskbar, click **Close** on the shortcut menu, click the **Slide 1 thumbnail**, click the **Slide Sorter View button** 🔠, click in the **Zoom box** on the Standard toolbar, type **50**, then press **[Enter]**
   The Word program closes. Compare your screen to Figure G-19.

7. Run through the entire slide show, making sure you click the hyperlink on Slide 7

8. Add your name to the notes and handouts footer, click **File** on the menu bar, click **Print**, click the **Print what list arrow**, click **Notes Pages**, then click **OK**

9. Save your changes, close the presentation, then exit PowerPoint

FIGURE G-17: Insert Hyperlink dialog box

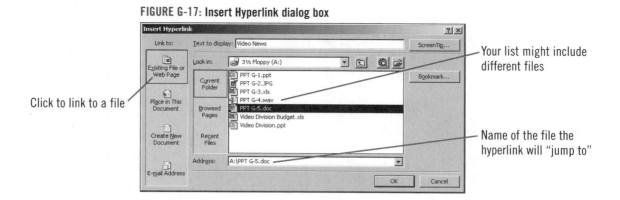

Click to link to a file

Your list might include different files

Name of the file the hyperlink will "jump to"

FIGURE G-18: Linked review in Word document

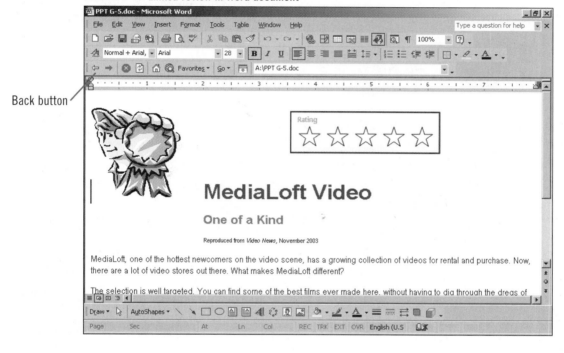

Back button

FIGURE G-19: Final presentation in Slide Sorter view

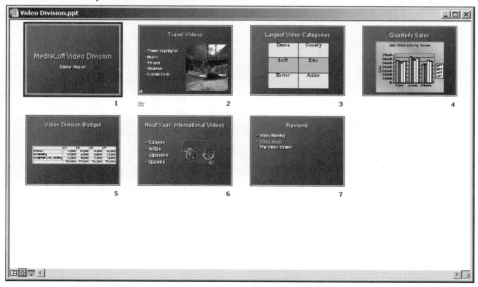

Practice

▶ Concepts Review

Label each of the elements of the PowerPoint window shown in Figure G-20.

FIGURE G-20

Match each of the terms with the statement that describes its function.

10. Photo album
11. Embedded object
12. Link
13. Source program
14. Hyperlink
15. Destination program
16. Animation
17. Movie

a. An object created in another program, then stored in PowerPoint
b. The program into which an embedded or linked object is placed
c. A presentation that displays your pictures
d. A word or object you click to view another file
e. The connection between a source file and a PowerPoint presentation
f. The program in which an embedded object is created
g. Live action captured by a movie camera
h. A multiple-imaged graphic that moves

Select the best answer from the list of choices.

18. **Which is true of a hyperlink?**
    a. Hyperlinks can only be used between two PowerPoint presentations.
    b. A hyperlink can be a word, a graphic, or a drawn object.
    c. Clicking a hyperlink closes the current file and opens a new file.
    d. Hyperlinks are used to copy a slide from one presentation to another.
19. **Which statement about embedded objects is false?**
    a. You can format embedded objects in their source program.
    b. Embedded objects are not dependent on a source file.
    c. Embedded objects are not a part of the presentation.
    d. Embedded objects increase your presentation file size more than linked objects do.
20. **Which statement about linked objects is true?**
    a. To edit a linked object, you must open its source file.
    b. A linked object is an independent object embedded directly into a slide.
    c. You can access a linked object even when the source file is not available.
    d. A linked object substantially increases the size of your presentation file.

▶ Skills Review

1. **Embed a picture.**
    a. Start PowerPoint, open the presentation PPT G-6 from the drive and folder where your Project Files are located, then save it as **Marketing 2003**.
    b. Go to Slide 4 and embed the figure PPT G-7.
    c. Resize the picture so it fits in the blank area of the slide, then use the arrow keys on the keyboard to adjust its position. Save your changes.
2. **Insert a Word table.**
    a. Insert a new slide after Slide 4 with the Title Only slide layout.
    b. Title the slide **Top Cheese Selections**.
    c. Insert a Microsoft Word table that is three columns wide and four rows tall.
    d. Select all the cells, then change the font to 28 point Arial, bold.
    e. Enter the information shown in Table G-2.
    f. Center the information in the cells and increase the line spacing in the bottom row to 2.0 using the Word Formatting toolbar.
    g. Apply the Table Grid 8 AutoFormat, with no special formatting for the last row or last column.
    h. Select the cells in the first row, then change the font to Arial Black.
    i. Exit Word, then center the table below the slide title. Save the presentation.
3. **Embed an Excel chart.**
    a. Insert a new slide after Slide 5 using the Blank slide layout.
    b. Embed the chart from the file PPT G-8.
    c. Using Excel tools, enlarge the chart title text to 26 points and the value and category axes to 14 points.
    d. Change the value axis title and legend text to 18 points and reposition the legend so it is at the bottom of the chart (*Hint*: Click the Placement tab in the Format Legend dialog box.)
    e. Resize and reposition the chart so it is centered horizontally and vertically on the slide.
    f. Save your changes.

TABLE G-2

Cow Cheese	Goat Cheese	Ewe Cheese
Abondance	Banon	Ardi-Gasna
Beaufort	Ile-D'yeu	Broccio
Camembert	Sarment	Pigouille

PowerPoint 2002

4. **Link an Excel worksheet.**
   a. Create a new slide after Slide 6 with the Title Only layout.
   b. Title the slide **Basic P & L**.
   c. Link the spreadsheet file **P & L** from the location where your Project Files are stored.
   d. Resize the object so that it fills the slide width.
   e. Reposition the object so it is centered vertically. (*Hint:* To center it more precisely, hold down [Alt] while you drag, or hold down [Ctrl] while you press the arrow keys.)
   f. Fill the spreadsheet object with light gray (the Follow Accent and Followed Hyperlink Scheme Color).
   g. Save and close the Marketing 2003 presentation.

5. **Update a linked Excel worksheet.**
   a. Start Excel and open the P & L worksheet.
   b. Replace the value in cell B4 with **95,000**.
   c. In cell D7, enter **1,350,000**.
   d. Close the Excel program after saving your changes.
   e. Open the Marketing 2003 file in PowerPoint, updating the link as you do so.
   f. Go to Slide 7 and view your changes. Save the presentation.

6. **Insert an animated GIF file.**
   a. Go to Slide 8.
   b. Insert an animated GIF file on the slide. Use the word **email** to search for an appropriate animated GIF.
   c. Resize and reposition the GIF file as necessary.
   d. Preview it in Slide Show view. Save the presentation.

7. **Insert a sound.**
   a. Go to Slide 2.
   b. Insert the sound file PPT G-9 from the location where your Project Files are stored. Set the sound to play when you click the sound icon.
   c. In the Format Picture dialog box, scale the sound icon to 150% of its original size.
   d. Drag the sound icon to the lower-right corner of the slide.
   e. Test the sound in Slide Show view. Save the presentation.

8. **Insert a hyperlink.**
   a. Go to Slide 7 in the presentation, then add a new slide with the Title and Text layout.
   b. Title the slide **Reviews**.
   c. In the first line of the main text placeholder, enter **Jeff Sanders, Web Cheese Review** and on the second line enter **Jorge Fonseca, Online Cheese Today**.
   d. Select the entire main text placeholder, and change its font size to 36 points.
   e. Resize the text placeholder to fit the text, then center it on the slide.
   f. Convert the Jeff Sanders bullet into a hyperlink to the file PPT G-10.
   g. Click in the notes pane, then type **The hyperlink links to Jeff's cheese review of the 2003 Camembert**.
   h. Run the slide show and test the hyperlink.
   i. Use the Back button to return to the presentation.
   j. End the slide show.
   k. Exit Word.
   l. Run the spellchecker, view the entire presentation in Slide Show view, and evaluate your presentation. Make any necessary changes.
   m. Add your name as a footer to notes and handouts, print the slides as Notes Pages, save and close the presentation, then exit PowerPoint.

▶ Independent Challenge 1

Quincy Engineering is a mechanical and industrial design company that specializes in designing manufacturing plants in the United States and Canada. As the company financial analyst, you need to investigate and report on a possible contract to design and build a large manufacturing plant in Belize. The board of directors wants to make sure that they can make a minimum profit on the deal. It is your job to provide a recommendation to the board.

Create your own information using the basic presentation provided and assume the following about Quincy Engineering:

- The new manufacturing plant in Belize will be 75,000 square feet in size. The projected cost for Quincy Engineering to design and build the plant in Belize is about $280.00 per square foot based on a four-phase schedule: planning and design, site acquisition and preparation, underground construction, and above-ground construction.
- Factors that helped determine Quincy Engineering's cost to build the plant include: Quincy Engineering payroll for 45 people in Belize for 24 months; materials cost; hiring two Belizean construction companies to construct the plant; and travel expenses.
- Factor in a 1.5 million dollar profit margin for Quincy Engineering above the cost of the building.

a. Open the file PPT G-11, then save it as **Belize Plant**.
b. Think about what results you want to see, what information you will need to create the slide presentation, and how your message should be communicated. In order for your presentation to be complete, it must include the following objects: (i) an embedded Word table; (ii) an embedded Excel chart; and (iii) a sound from the Clip Organizer
c. Use Microsoft Word and PowerPoint to embed objects into your presentation. Use the assumptions listed above to develop information that would be appropriate for a table.
d. Give each slide a title and add main text where appropriate.
e. Make the last slide in the presentation your recommendation to pursue the contract, based on the financial data you present.
f. Add your name as a footer to the notes and handouts, save your changes, then print the final slide presentation as handouts (2 slides per page).

▶ Independent Challenge 2

You are the director of operations at The Franklin Group, a large investment banking company in Texas. Franklin is considering merging with Redding, Inc, a smaller investment company in Arizona, to form the 10th largest financial institution in the United States. As the director of operations, you need to present some financial projections regarding the merger to a special committee formed by Franklin to study the proposed merger.

Create your own information using the basic presentation provided on your Project Disk. Assume the following facts about the merger between Franklin and Redding:

- Franklin earned a $21 million profit last year. Projected profit this year is $28 million. Projected profit next year with the merger with Redding is $34 million. Franklin's operating expenses run approximately $31 million each year. Redding's operating expenses run approximately $18 million each year.
- Redding earned $9 million in profit last year. Projected profit this year is $11 million. Projected profit next year with the merger is $19 million.
- Franklin has a 19% share of the market without Redding. Redding has a 6% share of the market without Franklin. Combined, the companies would have a 25% share of the market.
- With the merger, Franklin would need to cut $7.6 million from its annual operating costs and Redding would need to cut $2 million from its annual operating costs.

a. Open the file PPT G-12 from the drive and folder where your Project Files are located, then save it as **Merger**.

b. Think about what results you want to see, what information you will need to create the slide presentation, and how your message should be communicated. In order for your presentation to be complete, it must include the following objects: (i) an embedded Excel worksheet; (ii) a linked Excel worksheet; (iii) an embedded table, chart, or other object; and (iv) a hyperlink.

c. Use Microsoft Excel to embed a worksheet and link a worksheet to your presentation. Use the preceding assumptions to develop related information that would be appropriate for the worksheets. Use the profit and operating expense figures to create your own revenue figures for one of the worksheets. (Revenue minus operating expenses equals profit.)

d. Hyperlink to the file Redding, Inc. Choose the slide in the presentation where the hyperlink should be placed. You can use existing text or create a drawn or other object to use as the hyperlink.

e. Give each slide a title and add main text where appropriate. Create slides as necessary to make the presentation complete.

f. Add your name as a footer to the notes and the handouts, save your changes, then print the final slide presentation.

▶ Independent Challenge 3

You have just been promoted to the position of sales manager at DWImports, a U.S. company that exports goods and professional services to companies in Japan, South Korea, China, and the Philippines. One of your new responsibilities is to give a presentation at the biannual finance meeting showing how the Sales Department performed during the previous six-month period.

Plan and create a short slide presentation (six to eight slides) that illustrates the Sales Department's performance during the last six months. Identify the existing accounts (by country), then identify the new contracts acquired during the last six months. Create your own content, but assume the following:

- The majority of goods and services being exported are as follows: food products (such as rice, corn, and wheat); agriculture consulting; construction engineering; and industrial designing and engineering.
- The company gained five new accounts in China, South Korea, and the Philippines.
- The Sales Department showed a $6 million profit for the first half of the year.
- Department expenses for the first half of the year were $3.5 million.
- The presentation will be given in a boardroom using a projection machine.

a. Think about what results you want to see, what information you will need to create the slide presentation, and how your message should be communicated. In order for your presentation to be complete, it must include the following objects: (i) an embedded Word table; (ii) an embedded Excel chart; (iii) an embedded picture; and (iv) an animated GIF file or embedded movie.

b. Use the movies provided for you in PowerPoint, or if you have access to another media source, choose another appropriate movie to embed in your presentation.

c. Give each slide a title and add main text points where appropriate.

d. Add a template, background shading, or other enhancing objects to make your presentation look professional.

e. Save the presentation as **Imports** to the drive and folder where your Project Files are stored.

f. Open the Save As dialog box, click the Save As type list arrow, scroll down and click Outline/RTF, change the filename to **Imports RTF**, then click Save.

g. Add your name as a footer to the slides and notes and handouts, save your changes, then print the final slide presentation.

Independent Challenge 4

You are the business manager for LA EduCorp, a large non-profit educational organization in Los Angeles, California. One of your duties is to purchase new and used computer equipment for the organization every three years. LA EduCorp has allotted some money in the budget this year to upgrade some of the computer equipment. Your job is to prepare a brief presentation for the board of directors' next monthly meeting, which outlines the cost of purchasing new and used equipment and selling the old equipment.

Develop your own content, but assume the following:
- 15 computer systems need to be sold.
- The old computers are configured as follows: Pentium, 200 MHz, 32MB RAM, 3GB HDD, 24X CDROM with Sound and 4MB Video, 56K Modem 10/100 3Com Network Card, Windows 95.
- The 15 replacement computer systems are configured as follows: Pentium 600-800MHz, 128MB RAM, 10GB HD, 48X CD-ROM with Sound and 24MB Video, 56K Modem 10/100 3Com Network Card, Windows 98.
- Add $50.00 to the price of each purchased computer for tax and shipping.
- You are allowed to spend up to $900.00 per new computer.

You'll need to find the following information on the Web:
- The average price of the old computer systems that need to be sold.
- The prices of the new computer systems.
- Auction Web sites where the old computers can be sold.

a. Open a new presentation, and save it as **EduCorp** to the drive and folder where your Project Files are located.
b. Add your name as the footer on all slides and handouts.
c. Connect to the Internet, then use a search engine to locate Web sites that have information on used computer systems. If your search does not produce any results, you might try the following sites: www.affordablecomputers.com, www.usedcomputer.com, www.timco-computers.com
d. Think about what results you want to see, what information you will need to create the slide presentation, and how your message should be communicated. Review at least two Web sites that contain information about used computers. Print the pages of the Web sites you use to gather data for your presentation. (Remember to gather information on the old computers as well as the new computers.)
e. In order for your presentation to be complete, it must include the following objects: (i) an embedded Word table; (ii) an embedded Excel worksheet or chart; (iii) a GIF animation or movie; and (iv) a sound.
f. Use the assumptions listed above to develop worksheet and/or table information that describes the configurations and prices of the new computer systems. Categorize the new systems by their speed; for example: 600MHz, 650MHz, and 700MHz.
g. Create an Excel chart or worksheet that describes the difference between the purchase of the new systems and the sale of the old systems.
h. Create a slide that identifies different auction Web sites that you can use to sell the old computers. If your search does not produce any results, you might try the following sites: www.ebay.com, www.ubid.com, www.dealdeal.com
i. Give each slide a title and add main text where appropriate. Create slides as necessary to make the presentation complete.
j. Apply an appropriate slide design. Change the slide design colors as necessary.
k. Spell check the presentation, view the final presentation, save the final version, then print the slides as handouts.
l. Close the presentation, exit PowerPoint, and disconnect from the Internet.

PowerPoint 2002

► Visual Workshop

Create two slides that look like the examples in Figures G-23 and G-24. Save the presentation as **New Classes**. Save and print the slides. Submit the final presentation output.

FIGURE G-21

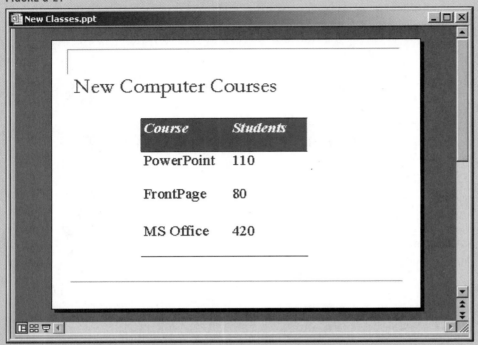

FIGURE G-22

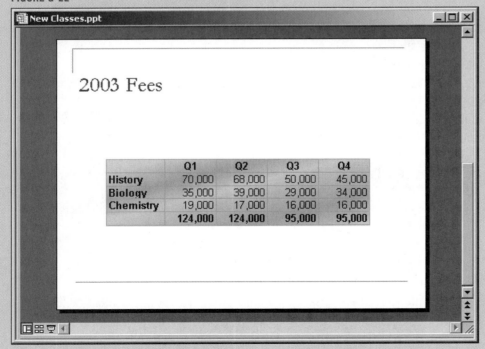

Using

Advanced Features

Objectives

- ► **Send a presentation for review**
- ► **Combine reviewed presentations**
- ► **Set up a slide show**
- ► **Create a custom show**
- ► **Use the Meeting Minder**
- ► **Rehearse slide timings**
- ► **Publish a presentation for the Web**
- ► **Broadcast a presentation**
- ► **Use the Pack and Go Wizard**

After your work on a presentation is complete, you have the option of sending the presentation over the Internet for others to review and send back to you. Reviewers can make changes to the presentation and add their own comments. Once you are finished making changes to your presentation, you need to produce the final output that you will use when you give your presentation. You can print your presentation, display it as a slide show using a computer or projector, publish it to the Web for others to view, or broadcast it live over the Web. ✎━━ Maria Abbott has finished creating the content of her presentation. She decides to send it out for review, then produce an on-screen slide show, and publish it for viewing on the World Wide Web.

Sending a Presentation for Review

When you finish creating a presentation, it is often helpful to have others look over the content for accuracy and clarity. You can use Microsoft Outlook or any other compatible 32-bit email program to send a presentation out for review. When you send a presentation for review using Outlook, a review request e-mail message is created automatically that includes an attached copy of the presentation file. Reviewers can use any version of PowerPoint to make changes and insert comments on the slides of your presentation. Outlook automatically tracks changes made by multiple reviewers, so you don't have to keep track of which reviewer made which change. Changes to a presentation sent electronically are much easier to track and combine than changes marked on printed copies of the presentation. ✐ Maria uses Outlook to send her presentation to two colleagues for their suggestions and comments.

1. Start PowerPoint, open the presentation **PPT H-1**, then save it as **Video Division Final**

2. Click **File** on the menu bar, point to **Send To**, then click **Mail Recipient (for Review)**
   A Microsoft Outlook e-mail window opens, as shown in Figure H-1. Notice that the subject line and some basic e-mail text are automatically entered in the Outlook window, and the presentation is attached.

3. Click the **To button**
   The Select Names dialog box opens. Use this dialog box to select all the people who you want to review the presentation.

4. Click your name in the list of names, click the **To button**, then click **OK**
   Your name and e-mail address appear in the To text box in the Outlook window.

5. Click in the Outlook window below the message text, then type **Please return your review this Friday by 3:00.**
   The new text appears below the original text. Compare your screen to Figure H-2.

6. Click the **Send button** 📧 on the Outlook toolbar
   Outlook sends the e-mail message with the attached presentation file (or places it in the Outlook Outbox). The Outlook window closes and you are returned to the PowerPoint presentation window. The Reviewing toolbar now appears below the Formatting toolbar, indicating that the presentation has been sent out for review.

7. Start Outlook, send the message if necessary, go to the Inbox window, then click the **Send/Receive button** 📧 on the Outlook toolbar
   The message you just sent to yourself appears in the Inbox window. You may have to wait a short time before the message appears.

8. Click the Outlook **Close button** ☒ on the title bar
   Outlook closes and the PowerPoint screen appears.

FIGURE H-1: Outlook window

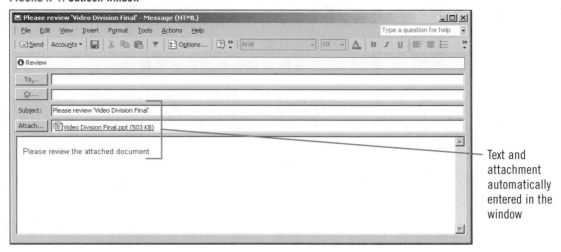

Text and attachment automatically entered in the window

FIGURE H-2: Completed Outlook window

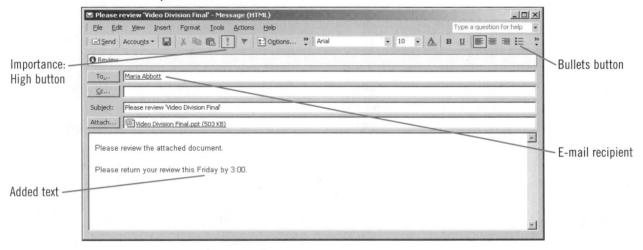

Importance: High button

Bullets button

E-mail recipient

Added text

Other ways to send or route a presentation

If you are not using Outlook as your e-mail program, you can still send a presentation out for review over the Web using another 32-bit e-mail program, as long as it is compatible with Messaging Application Programming Interface (MAPI). You can also use a Microsoft Exchange server, a network server, or a floppy disk. To send a presentation out for review using any of these methods, open the presentation, then use the Save As command to save it with a new name. In the Save As dialog box, click the Save as type list arrow, click Presentation for Review, then click Save. Open your e-mail program, create a new message, attach the presentation file to the message, then send the message.

You can also route the presentation to multiple reviewers in a specific order so they each receive the presentation after another reviewer. To route a presentation, click File on the menu bar, point to Send To, then click Routing Recipient. The Add Routing Slip dialog box opens. Click Address, then add the names of the reviewers from your e-mail address book. Select any other options in the Add Routing Slip dialog box. To send the presentation to the first reviewer, click Route; to close the dialog box without sending the presentation out for review, click Add Slip; to send the presentation out for review at a later time, click File on the menu bar, point to Send To, then click Next Routing Recipient.

Combining Reviewed Presentations

Once a reviewer has completed their review of your presentation and sends it back, you can combine the changes into your original presentation using the Compare and Merge Presentations command. You can apply individual changes, changes by slide, changes by reviewer, changes on the slide master, or changes to the entire presentation. You can continue to combine changes to your original presentation until you have applied all the changes, deleted all the changes markers, saved the presentation, or ended the review. ◢ Maria sent out the Video Division presentation to two of her colleagues. She now wants to combine the two reviewed versions with her original presentation.

Steps 1 2 3 4

1. Click **Tools** on the menu bar, then click **Compare and Merge Presentations**
   The Choose Files to Merge with Current Presentation dialog box opens.

2. Switch the Look in list to the drive and location where your Project Files are stored, click the file **PPT H-2**, press and hold **[Shift]**, click **PPT H-3**, then click **Merge**
   The two reviewed presentations are merged with your original presentation. The Revisions Pane task pane opens on the right side of the screen. It is divided into two tabs: the List tab and the Gallery tab. The List tab displays individual changes by reviewer for the current slide. The Gallery tab displays a thumbnail of the current slide and shows what the slide would look like if all the suggested changes were made. Each reviewer's changes are identified by a marker of a different color on the slide. If more than one reviewer made a change on the same object, the change is identified by a white color marker.

3. Click the **Slide 3 thumbnail**, then click the top item in the Slide changes section of the Revisions Pane
   The top item on this slide is a comment made by one of the reviewers. A description of the comment appears on the slide next to its corresponding color marker. Since this is a comment, no action on your part is required.

4. Click the next item in the Slide changes section
   See Figure H-3. Alice suggests replacing the word "Largest" in the title with the word "Primary," as shown in Figure H-3. By selecting the All changes to Title 1 check box, you will accept both changes: the word "Largest" will be deleted, and the word "Primary" will be inserted.

5. Click the **All changes to Title 1 check box** in the change description box on the slide, then click the **Next Item button** ⏩ on the Reviewing toolbar
   Slide 4 appears and a change description box with both reviewers' comments opens. The color marker is white, indicating that the marked change contains more than one reviewer's comments.

6. Click the **top check box from Anne Sarri** in the change description box, notice the change in the body text box, then click the **second check box from Anne Sarri**
   Clicking the top check box inserts some words in the body text box; clicking the next check box deletes some words that are no longer necessary. When you click the second check box, the last check box, from Alice Wegeman, also is selected, which indicates that both reviewers had made the same change. Compare your screen to Figure H-4.

7. Click the **End Review button** [End Review..] on the Reviewing toolbar, read the information in the dialog box, then click **Yes** to end the review
   The Reviewing toolbar and Revisions Pane task pane close and the color markers on the slide are deleted.

8. Save your changes, click **View** on the menu bar, click **Task Pane**, click **Window** on the menu bar, then click **Arrange All**
   Now your screen will match the rest of the figures in this book.

FIGURE H-3: Figure showing Revisions Pane

Comment color marker

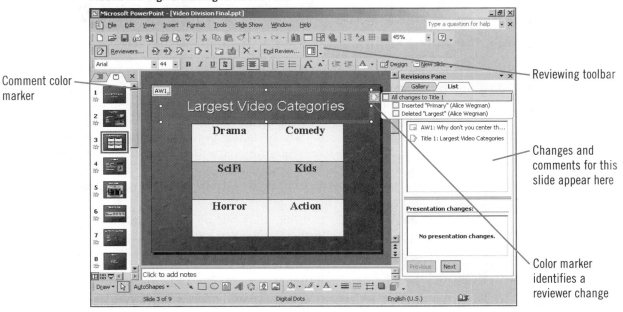

Reviewing toolbar

Changes and comments for this slide appear here

Color marker identifies a reviewer change

FIGURE H-4: Figure showing revised slide

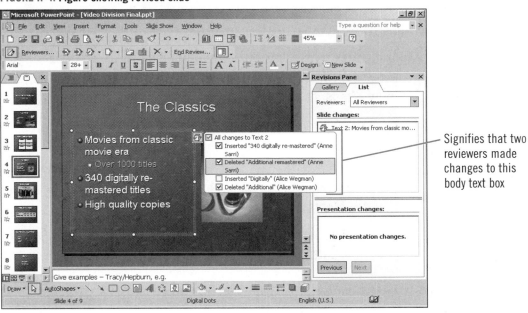

Signifies that two reviewers made changes to this body text box

CLUES TO USE

Reviewing a presentation

To evaluate a presentation someone sends for your review, simply open the presentation in PowerPoint and make your changes. The Reviewing toolbar will automatically open when you open the presentation. When you are finished making changes, save the presentation. Next, click File on the menu bar, point to Send To, then click Original Sender to send the presentation back to its original owner using Outlook. If you want to edit the message in the e-mail before you send the presentation back, you can click the Reply with Changes button on the Reviewing toolbar.

Setting Up a Slide Show

With PowerPoint, you can create a slide show that runs automatically. Viewers can then watch the slide show on a stand-alone computer, called a **kiosk,** at a convention or trade show. You can create a self-running slide show that loops, or runs, through the entire show, without users touching the computer. You can also let viewers advance the slides at their own pace by pressing the spacebar, clicking the mouse, or clicking an on-screen control button called an **action button.** A self-running slide show is also useful when you publish a presentation to the Web for others to view. ✎ Maria prepares the Video Division Final presentation so it can be used at an upcoming trade show.

Steps

1. Click **Slide Show** on the menu bar, click **Set Up Show**, then click the **Browsed at a kiosk (full screen) option button** under Show type
   The Set Up Show dialog box opens.

2. Make sure the **All option button** is selected in the Show slides section, then make sure the **Using timings, if present option button** is selected in the Advance slides section
   This will include all the slides in the presentation and have PowerPoint advance the slides at time intervals you set. Compare your Set Up Show dialog box to Figure H-5.

Trouble?

If you don't see the Slide Transition button on the Standard toolbar, click a Toolbar Options button 》 on a toolbar to locate buttons that are not visible on your toolbar.

3. Click **OK**, click the **Slide Sorter View button** ▦, then click the **Slide Transition button** 🔲 on the Slide Sorter toolbar
   The Slide Transition task pane opens.

4. In the task pane, click the **Automatically after check box** to select it in the Advance slide section, click the **Automatically after up arrow** until **00:08** appears, click **Apply to All Slides**, click **Slide Show**, view the show, let it start again, then press **[Esc]**
   PowerPoint advances the slides automatically at eight-second intervals, or faster if someone clicks the mouse or presses [Spacebar]. There may be times when you want users to advance slides by themselves. You can do this by inserting a button that is actually a hyperlink for the user to click to jump to the next slide.

5. Click **Slide Show** on the menu bar, click **Set Up Show**, in the Advance slides section, click the **Manually option button**, then click **OK**

6. Double-click **Slide 1** to view it in Normal view, click **Slide Show** on the menu bar, point to **Action Buttons**, click the **Action Button: Forward or Next button** ▷, then drag the pointer to draw a button in the lower-left corner of Slide 1
   A new action button appears on the bottom of the slide and the Action Settings dialog box opens, as shown in Figure H-6.

7. Make sure the **Hyperlink to option button** is selected, click the **Hyperlink to list arrow**, click **Next Slide** if necessary, then click **OK**
   Compare your screen to Figure H-7.

8. With the action button selected, press **[Ctrl][C]** to copy it, click the **Next Slide button** 🔽, press **[Ctrl][V]** to paste the button on Slide 2, repeat for each slide that follows, then return to **Slide 1**

QuickTip

You must be in Slide Show view to use the hyperlink buttons.

9. View the slide show, clicking the **action buttons** to move from slide to slide, press **[Esc]** to end the slide show once you've viewed it all the way through, then save your changes
   Make sure you wait for the animated objects to appear on the slides before you click the action buttons.

FIGURE H-5: Set Up Show dialog box

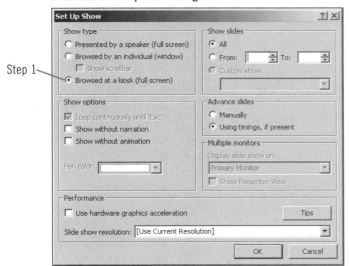

Step 1

FIGURE H-6: Action Settings dialog box

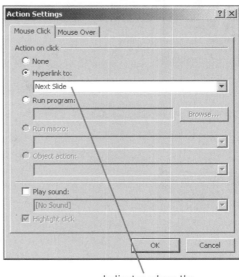

Indicates where the
hyperlink jumps to

FIGURE H-7: Slide 1 with action button to the next slide

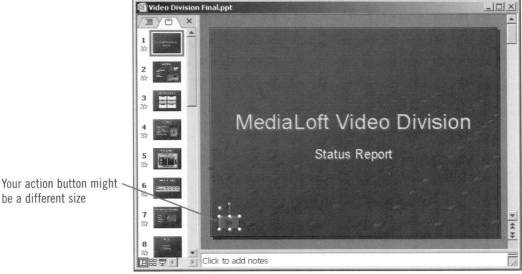

Your action button might
be a different size

Hiding a slide during a slide show

During a slide show, you can hide slides you don't want the audience to see. Hidden slides are not deleted from the presentation; they just don't appear during a slide show. The easiest way to hide a slide is to right-click the slide thumbnail in Normal view or Slide Sorter view, then click Hide Slide. When a slide is hidden, its slide number has a hide symbol—a gray box with a line through it—over it. To unhide the slide, right-click the slide thumbnail, then click Hide Slide. You can display a hidden slide during a slide show by right-clicking the slide prior to the hidden slide, pointing to By Title, then clicking the title of the hidden slide.

PowerPoint 2002

Creating a Custom Show

Often when you create a slide show, you need to create a custom version of it for a different audience or purpose. For example, you might create a 20-minute presentation about a new product to show to potential customers who will be interested in the product features and benefits. Then you could create a five-minute version of that same show for an open house for potential investors, selecting only appropriate slides from the longer show. ✐ Maria wants to use a reduced version of the slide show in a marketing presentation, so she creates a custom slide show containing only the slides relating to the video product line.

Steps

1. Click **Slide Show** on the menu bar, click **Set Up Show**, click the **Presented by a speaker (full screen) option button**, then click **OK**
   This turns off the kiosk setting.

2. Click **Slide Show** on the menu bar, click **Custom Shows**, then click **New** in the Custom Shows dialog box
   The Define Custom Show dialog box opens with the slides that are in your current presentation in the Slides in presentation list box.

> **QuickTip**
>
> If your computer has a sound card and a microphone, you can record voice narrations to play during your slide show. This can be a good choice for self-running slide shows and presentations on the Internet. On the Slide Show menu, click Voice Narrations. You can link or embed the narration.

3. Press and hold **[Ctrl]**, click **2. Travel Videos**, **4. The Classics**, **7. Next Year: International Videos**, and **8. Reviews**, then click **Add**
   The four selected slides move to the Slides in custom show list box, indicating that they will be included in the new presentation. See Figure H-8.

4. Click **4. Reviews** in the Slides in custom show list, then click the **Slide Order up arrow button** three times to move it to the top of the list
   You can arrange the slides in any order in your custom show.

5. Drag to select the existing text in the Slide show name text box, type **Marketing Presentation**, then click **OK**
   The Custom Shows dialog box lists your custom presentation. The custom show is not saved as a separate slide show on your disk even though you assigned it a new name, so to show a custom slide show, you must first open the show you used to create it. You then open the custom show from the Custom Shows dialog box.

6. Click **Show**, view the slide show, clicking the **action buttons** to move from slide to slide, then press **[Esc]** to end the custom show after you view the International Videos slide
   The slides appear in the new order: Slide 8, 2, 4, then 7. Because the slide show is not set up to loop continuously, clicking the action button on the International Videos slide doesn't do anything. You return to the presentation in Normal view. You can also run a custom show from within the presentation slide show.

> **QuickTip**
>
> If you right-click the title slide and no shortcut menu appears, you probably forgot to return the Set Up Show option to Presented by a speaker (full screen). Press [Esc], click Slide Show on the menu bar, click Set Up Show, and select that option now.

7. Press **[Ctrl][Home]**, click the **Slide Show button** 🖳, watch the text animation, right-click anywhere on the screen, point to **Go**, point to **Custom Show**, then click **Marketing Presentation**, as shown in Figure H-9

8. Use the **action buttons** to move from slide to slide in the custom show, then press **[Esc]** after viewing the International Videos slide

9. Save your changes, click **File** on the menu bar, click **Print**, click the **Custom Show option button**, make sure **Marketing Presentation** is listed in the list box, click the **Print what list arrow**, select **Handouts, 3 slides per page**, then click **OK**

FIGURE H-8: Define Custom Show dialog box

Click to add slides to
the custom show

Slide Order up arrow

FIGURE H-9: Switching to the custom slide show

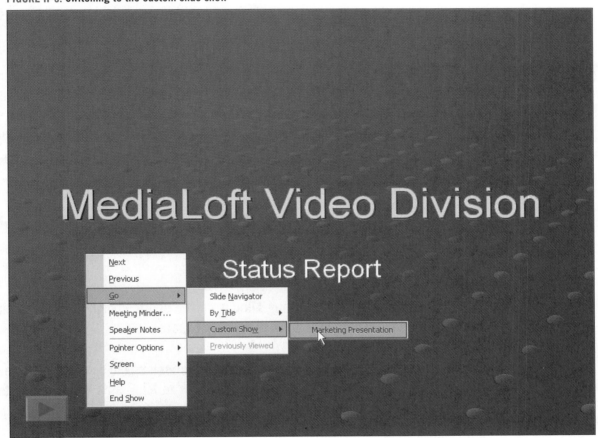

Using action buttons to hyperlink to a custom slide show

You can use action buttons to switch from the "parent" show to the custom show. Click Slide Show on the menu bar, point to Action Buttons, then choose any action button. Drag the pointer to draw a button on the slide, then, in the Action Settings dialog box, select Custom Show in the Hyperlink to list box. Select the name of the custom show to which you want to hyperlink, then click OK. When you run the show, click the hyperlink button you created to run the custom show.

PowerPoint 2002

Using the Meeting Minder

Occasionally, it's helpful to assign tasks or take notes as you present a slide show to make sure people follow up on meeting items. PowerPoint makes this task easy with the Meeting Minder. The Meeting Minder is a dialog box you use in Slide Show view to enter information related to the slides in your presentation. The action items you enter are automatically added to a new slide at the end of your presentation. You can export the action items to a Microsoft Word document to edit them or to make them part of another document. Maria practices adding action items with the Meeting Minder so she'll know how to use it when she actually runs the presentation.

QuickTip

The Assigned To text box can accept a maximum of 15 characters, including spaces.

1. Click the **Slide 5 thumbnail** in the Slides tab
   Slide 5 appears.

2. Click the **Slide Show button** 🖵, wait for the chart to appear, right-click the slide, click **Meeting Minder** on the shortcut menu, then click the **Action Items tab**
   The Meeting Minder dialog box opens.

3. Type **Compile detailed figures for Q1 Children's sales**, press **[Tab]**, type **Jodi** in the Assigned To text box, press **[Tab]**, then type **8/14/03** to replace today's date in the Due Date text box, compare your screen to Figure H-10, then click **Add**
   The action item you entered appears in the list box on the Action Items tab. If you were to enter any more action items, they would be added to this list.

4. Click **OK**
   The Meeting Minder dialog box closes and the action items are added as a new slide at the end of the presentation.

5. Right-click the slide, point to **Go** on the shortcut menu, point to **By Title**, then click **10 Action Items**
   The new Action Items slide appears with the action item you entered in the Meeting Minder. See Figure H-11.

6. Right-click the slide, click **Meeting Minder** on the shortcut menu, click the **Action Items tab**, click the item in the list, then click **Export**
   The Meeting Minder Export dialog box opens.

7. Click the **Post action items to Microsoft Outlook check box** to deselect it, make sure that the **Send meeting minutes and action items to Microsoft Word check box** is selected, then click **Export Now**
   Microsoft Word starts and opens a new Word document containing your Meeting Minder action items. See Figure H-12. Word assigns a temporary filename that begins with PPT to the document. You can edit and print this document just as you would any Word document.

8. Add your name as the first line in the document, click the **Print button** 🖨 on the Word Standard toolbar, click **File** on the menu bar, click **Save As**, save the document as **Video Division Action Items** to the location where you store your Project Files, then click the **Close button** in the Word program window
   Word saves the action items list in **Rich Text Format (RTF)**, a file format that is readable by other word processors. Your PowerPoint presentation reappears in Slide Show view.

9. Click **OK** in the Meeting Minder dialog box, click the left mouse button twice to end the slide show, then save your changes

FIGURE H-10: Meeting Minder dialog box

Action items are listed here after you click Add

Enter action items here

Enter due date here

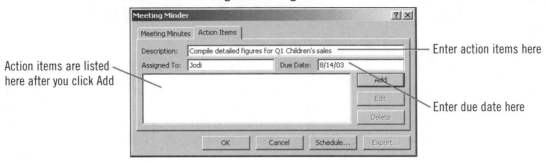

FIGURE H-11: New Action Items slide at the end of the presentation

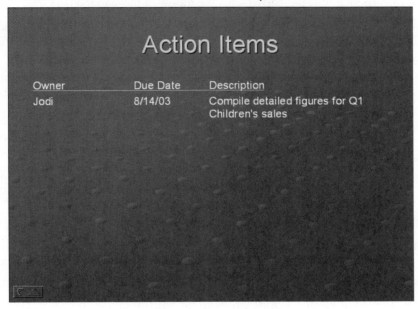

FIGURE H-12: Action items after exporting to Microsoft Word

The number in your filename will be different

Date on your screen will be the current date

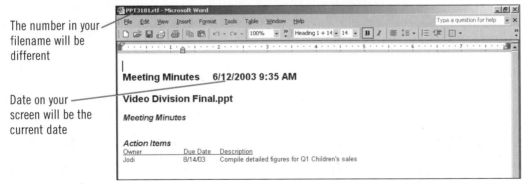

Keeping track of meeting minutes and speaker notes

You can use the Meeting Minder to keep a record of meeting minutes you type during the slide show. Right-click any slide in Slide Show view, click Meeting Minder, click the Meeting Minutes tab, then type notes in the text box. You can export the meeting minutes to Microsoft Word in the same way you export action items. You can also create speaker notes during a slide show. Right-click any slide in Slide Show view, click Speaker Notes on the shortcut menu, then type any items you want to remember. They will automatically be transferred to the Speaker Notes section of that slide.

Rehearsing Slide Timings

Whether you are creating a self-running slide show or you're planning to talk about the slides as they appear, you should rehearse the **slide timings**, the amount of time each slide stays on the screen. If you assign slide timings to your slides without actually running through the presentation, you will probably discover that the timings do not allow enough time for each slide or point in your presentation. To set accurate slide timings, use the PowerPoint Rehearse Timings feature. As you run through your slide show, the Rehearsal toolbar shows you how long the slide stays on the screen. When enough time has passed, click the mouse to move to the next slide. ✐ Maria rehearses the slide timings.

Steps

1. Click the **Slide Sorter View button** 🔠, then click **Slide 1**
Before you continue through the steps of the lesson, you may first want to read the steps and comments in this lesson so you are aware of what happens during a slide show rehearsal.

2. Click the **Rehearse Timings button** 🖭 on the Slide Sorter toolbar
Slide Show view opens, and Slide 1 appears. The Rehearsal toolbar appears in the upper-left corner of the screen, as shown in Figure H-13.

> **Trouble?**
>
> Make sure you wait until the animations are finished on each slide before clicking the Next button.

3. When you feel an appropriate amount of time has passed for the presenter to speak and for the audience to view the slide, click the **Next button** ➡ on the Rehearsal toolbar or click your mouse anywhere on the screen
Slide 2 appears.

4. Click ➡ at an appropriate interval after Slide 2 appears, then click ➡ after viewing Slide 3

> **QuickTip**
>
> If too much time has elapsed, click the Repeat button 🔄 on the Rehearsal toolbar to restart the timer for that slide. You can also set the time for each slide by typing it in the Elapsed Time text box.

5. Continue setting timings for the rest of the slides in the presentation
Be sure to leave enough time to present the contents of each slide thoroughly. At the end of the slide rehearsal, a Microsoft PowerPoint message box opens asking if you want to save the slide timings. If you save the timings, the next time you run the slide show, the slides will appear automatically at the intervals you specified during the rehearsal.

6. Click **Yes** to save the timings
Slide Sorter view appears showing the new slide timings, as shown in Figure H-14. Your timings will be different. When you run the slide show, it will run by itself, using the timings you rehearsed. The rehearsed timings override any previous timings you set.

> **QuickTip**
>
> To move to the next slide before your rehearsed slide timing has elapsed, click the slide to advance to the next slide.

7. Click the **Slide Show button** 🖥, then view the presentation with your timings

8. Save your changes, click **File** on the menu bar, click **Print**, click the **All option button**, click the **Print what list arrow**, click **Handouts, 4 slides per page**, click the Include comment pages check box, then click **OK**
The presentation is printed, including the comment made by a reviewer on Slide 3.

FIGURE H-13: **Rehearsal toolbar in Slide Show view**

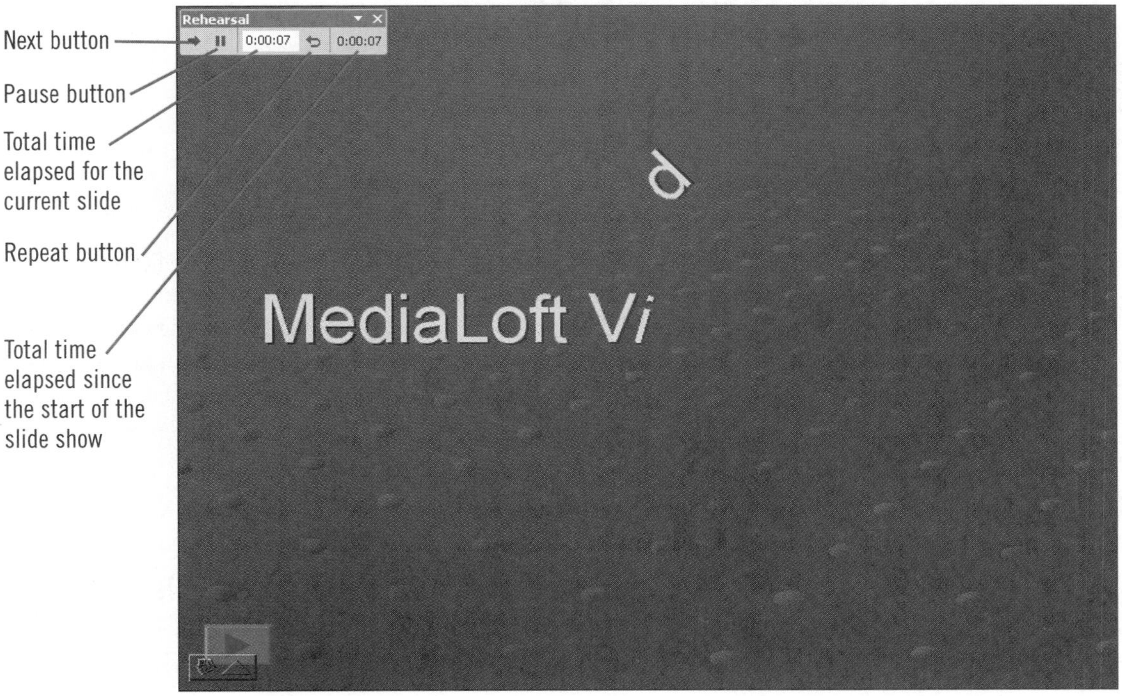

Next button

Pause button

Total time elapsed for the current slide

Repeat button

Total time elapsed since the start of the slide show

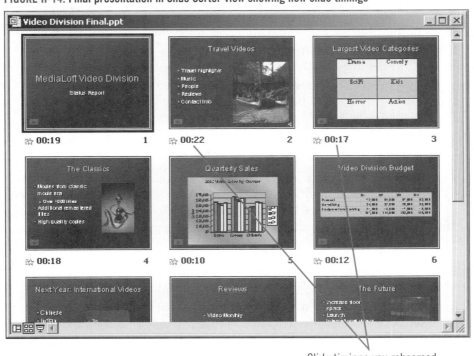

FIGURE H-14: **Final presentation in Slide Sorter view showing new slide timings**

Slide timings you rehearsed (your times will be different)

Publishing a Presentation for the Web

You can use PowerPoint to create presentations for viewing on the Web by saving the file in Hypertext Markup Language (HTML) format. To save the entire file in its current version, click Save as Web Page from the File menu, then click Save in the dialog box that opens. Others can then view (but not change) the presentation over the Web. If you want to customize the version that you are saving as a Web page (for example, if you wanted to save only the custom show, or if you wanted to make adjustments to how the presentation will look as a Web page), use the Publish command. ✎ Maria wants to create a version of her Video Division Final presentation that can be viewed on the MediaLoft intranet page. She does not want to include the financial information on Slides 5 and 6, so she uses the Publish feature to publish the custom show she created earlier.

Steps

1. Click **File** on the menu bar, click **Save as Web Page**, click the **Save in list arrow**, then select the drive and location where your Project Files are stored
The Save As dialog box opens.

2. Make sure the filename in the File name text box is selected, then type **videofnl**

3. Click **Publish**
The Publish as Web Page dialog box opens.

4. Click the **Custom Show option button** in the Publish what? section, then click the **Display speaker notes check box** to deselect it

5. In the Browser support section, click the **All browsers listed above (creates larger files) option button**
You want to make sure most browsers can view the HTML file you publish. At the bottom of the dialog box, notice that the default filename for the HTML file you are creating is the same as the presentation filename, and that it will be saved to the same folder in which the presentation is stored. Compare your screen to Figure H-15.

6. Click the **Open published Web page in browser check box** to select it, then click **Publish**
PowerPoint creates a copy of your presentation in HTML format and opens the published presentation in your default Internet browser similar to Figure H-16, which shows the presentation in Internet Explorer 5. Your original presentation remains open on the screen. There is also a folder named videofnl_files that contains necessary supporting files for the HTML file. The list of slide titles on the left are hyperlinks to each slide.

7. Click the **Previous Slide** ⊲ and **Next Slide** ⊳ buttons at the bottom of the screen or the **slide title hyperlinks** on the left side of the screen to view the presentation slides
Because each slide in this presentation has an action button, you can also click them to advance the slides.

8. Close your browser window, save the PowerPoint presentation, then close the presentation

FIGURE H-15: Publish as Web Page dialog box

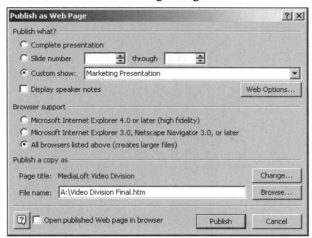

FIGURE H-16: Custom show from Video Division presentation in Internet Explorer

Browser menu and toolbars

Slide titles appear as hyperlinks in the browser

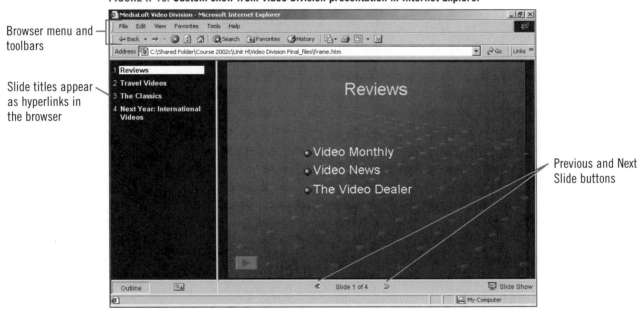

Previous and Next Slide buttons

Online meetings

If you are on a network, you can use Windows NetMeeting and PowerPoint to host or participate in meetings over an intranet or the Web. As the host of a meeting, you can share a presentation in real time with others who may be located in another office in your building or across the country. If you are the host of a meeting, you are required to have NetMeeting (a program automatically installed with Office), the shared document, and its application installed on your computer. As a participant in a meeting, all you are required to have installed on your computer is NetMeeting. As the host, you can schedule a meeting by clicking Tools on the menu bar, pointing to Online Collaboration, then clicking Schedule Meeting. Follow the steps in the dialog boxes to send an e-mail message to the person you are inviting to the meeting. To start an unscheduled online meeting from within the presentation you want to share, click Tools on the menu bar, point to Online Collaboration, then click Meet Now. Follow the steps in the dialog boxes to call participants to the meeting. If the participants accept your meeting invitation, the Online Meeting toolbar opens and the meeting begins.

Broadcasting a Presentation

PowerPoint 2002

You can use PowerPoint as a communication tool to broadcast the presentation over an intranet or the Web. You can start an unscheduled broadcast at any time, or use NetMeeting to schedule a broadcast to take place at a specific date and time. If you want your presentation broadcast available for on-demand viewing, you can record and save it to a network server where others can access the broadcast and replay it at their convenience. ✎ In this lesson, Maria learns the basics of broadcasting a presentation.

► Set up a presentation broadcast

Using PowerPoint's broadcasting feature, you can set up a presentation broadcast for a small group of up to 10 computers that are all on the same intranet or have access to the Web. As the presenter, you will need PowerPoint 2002, Microsoft Internet Explorer 5.1 or later, Microsoft Outlook 2002, or another e-mail program, a shared computer or server, and a connected video camera and microphone if you want to broadcast live video and audio. To broadcast a presentation to more than 10 computers at one time, you'll need to have access to a Windows Media Server or a third-party Windows Media Server provider.

► Schedule a presentation broadcast

To give the members of your audience plenty of time to prepare for a presentation broadcast, you can schedule the broadcast for a specific date and time. To schedule a broadcast, open the presentation that you want to broadcast, click **Slide Show** on the menu bar, point to **Online Broadcast**, then click **Schedule a Live Broadcast**. In the Schedule Presentation Broadcast dialog box, click **Settings** to open the Broadcast Settings dialog box. Indicate your audio, video, and display preferences. Use the File Location section to enter your server or shared computer information. See Figure H-17. If you will be using a Windows Media Server or including audience feedback, click the **Advanced tab**, then enter the necessary information. Click **OK**, then click **Schedule**. A dialog box similar to an e-mail message box opens. Add participants' e-mail addresses to the To text box, change other settings in the dialog box as necessary, then click the Send button on the toolbar.

► Begin a presentation broadcast

When you are ready to begin your presentation broadcast, you start by clicking **Slide Show** on the menu bar, pointing to **Online Broadcast**, then clicking **Start Live Broadcast Now**. If Outlook is your e-mail program, a message dialog box opens telling you that a program is trying to access your e-mail addresses; click **Yes** to continue. The Live Presentation Broadcast dialog box opens and lists the available presentations ready for broadcast. Select the **presentation** you want to broadcast, then click **Broadcast**.

- If the broadcast has been previously scheduled and you are using a microphone or camera in your broadcast, the Broadcast Presentation dialog box opens. Complete the testing of the equipment, then click Start. The presentation broadcast begins.

- If the broadcast is unscheduled, the Live Presentation Broadcast dialog box opens similar to Figure H-18. Click Settings, select the appropriate preferences for this broadcast, then click OK. Click Invite Audience and let the people you want to attend know that you are broadcasting. When you are ready to start the broadcast, click Start. If you are using audio and video, complete the testing of the equipment, then click Start.

► View a presentation broadcast

The easiest way to participate in an online broadcast is to open the e-mail message that contains the broadcast invitation and click the URL for the broadcast. The lobby page of the online broadcast appears in your browser. At the scheduled broadcast time, the presentation appears on your screen. During the meeting, you are able to send e-mail messages to the presenter. Figure H-19 shows how your screen might look if you were participating in an online broadcast.

FIGURE H-17: Broadcast Settings dialog box

Indicate your display preferences
in this section

Enter server or shared file
location here

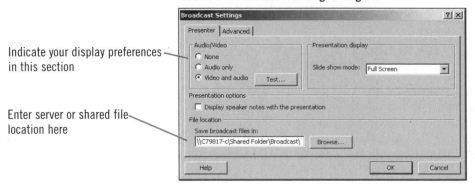

FIGURE H-18: Live Presentation Broadcast dialog box

Click to open the
Broadcast Settings
dialog box

FIGURE H-19: Presentation broadcast in Internet Explorer

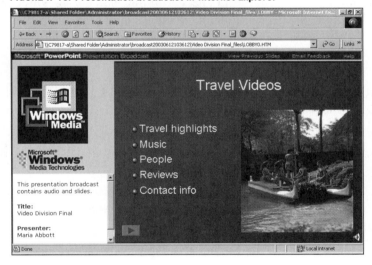

Record and save a broadcast

If you don't want to broadcast your presentation live, you can record it and save it to a network server where others can access it at any time. Open the presentation you want to broadcast, click Slide Show on the menu bar, point to Online Broadcast, then click Record and Save a Broadcast. The Record Presentation Broadcast dialog box opens. Change the information as necessary. Click Settings, change any of the video, audio, and display preferences, then identify the server or shared computer where the broadcast files will be stored. Click Record, complete the equipment testing, then click Start. Record your broadcast. When you want others to view the recorded broadcast, you will need to send an e-mail and identify the link to the starting page of the broadcast. To view the broadcast, the audience member clicks Replay Broadcast on the start page of the presentation.

Using the Pack and Go Wizard

Occasionally you need to present your slide show using another computer. To transport everything (including your presentation, embedded objects, linked objects, and fonts) to the new computer, you use the Pack and Go Wizard. The Pack and Go Wizard compresses and packages all the necessary files that you'll need to take a presentation on the road. You can also package the PowerPoint Viewer with the presentation. **PowerPoint Viewer** is a program that allows you to view a slide show even if PowerPoint is not installed on the computer. ✎ Maria packages the Video Division Final presentation using the Pack and Go Wizard so she can present it at an off-site meeting at a conference center.

Steps

Trouble?

If you decide to place the PackNGo folder in a different location, make sure the folders in the path name have a maximum of eight characters and contain no spaces.

1. Open the file **Video Division Offsite**, click **File** on the menu bar, click **Save As**, click the **Save in list arrow**, navigate to the folder where your Project Files are stored, then click the **Create New Folder button** 🗁 in the dialog box toolbar
   The New Folder dialog box opens.

2. Type **PackNGo** in the Name text box, then click **OK**
   The Save in list box changes to the new PackNGo folder. You will save your packaged presentation in this new folder.

3. Click the **Save as type list arrow**, then click **PowerPoint 97-2002 & 95 Presentation**
   Now save the file with a new name.

4. Change the filename in the File name list box to **Video Division Offsite Packed Version**, click **Save**, then click **Yes** in the warning box
   If your original presentation is on your hard disk, you can place the packaged version directly on a floppy disk. If the presentation is too big for one disk, PowerPoint lets you save across multiple floppy disks.

5. Click **File** on the menu bar, click **Pack and Go**, read the screen, then click **Next**
   The Pick files to pack screen opens, as shown in Figure H-20. You indicate here which presentation you would like to package.

6. Make sure the **Active presentation check box** is selected, then click **Next**
   The Choose destination screen opens.

7. Click the **Choose destination option button**, click **Browse**, locate and click the **PackNGo folder** you created, then click **Select**
   See Figure H-21.

8. Click **Next,** click the **Embed TrueType fonts check box** to select it, then click **Next**
   The Links screen opens. There aren't any links in this version of the presentation. The Viewer screen opens. To package the PowerPoint Viewer with your presentation, it needs to be installed on your computer. If the PowerPoint Viewer is not installed on your computer, the Viewer screen displays information on how to download and install the latest PowerPoint Viewer from the Microsoft Office Web site.

Trouble?

If you are working on a network and you get a message telling you that PackNGo is not installed, ask your instructor or technical support person for help.

9. Make sure the **Don't include the Viewer option button** is selected, click **Next**, read the Finish screen, then click **Finish**
   The Pack and Go Wizard packages the Video Division Offsite presentation. Now you can show this presentation on any computer that has PowerPoint installed.

10. Close the presentation, exit PowerPoint, then delete the PackNGo folder and its contents from the hard drive

FIGURE H-20: Pick files to pack screen in the Pack and Go Wizard

FIGURE H-21: Choose destination screen in the Pack and Go Wizard

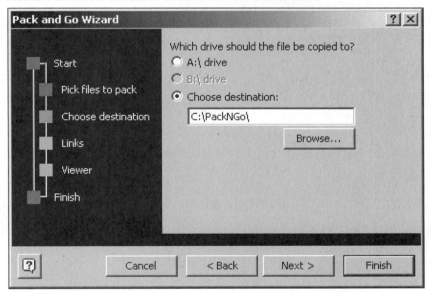

Using the Microsoft PowerPoint Viewer

The Microsoft PowerPoint Viewer is a program used to show a presentation on a computer that doesn't have PowerPoint installed. The PowerPoint Viewer is a free program distributed by Microsoft from the Office Web site. You can include the PowerPoint Viewer with your presentation by choosing the Viewer for Microsoft Windows in the Pack and Go Wizard. To view a presentation slide show using the PowerPoint Viewer, open the PowerPoint Viewer dialog box by double-clicking the Ppview32 icon. From the Microsoft PowerPoint Viewer dialog box, you can run a slide show, set Viewer options, and print a presentation. To show a packaged presentation using the PowerPoint Viewer, you must first unpackage the presentation. Locate the folder that contains the packaged presentation, then double-click the pngsetup icon. Extract the presentation to a folder. A message dialog box appears asking if you want to run a slide show; click Yes.

Practice

► Concepts Review

Label each of the elements of the PowerPoint window shown in Figure H-22.

FIGURE H-22

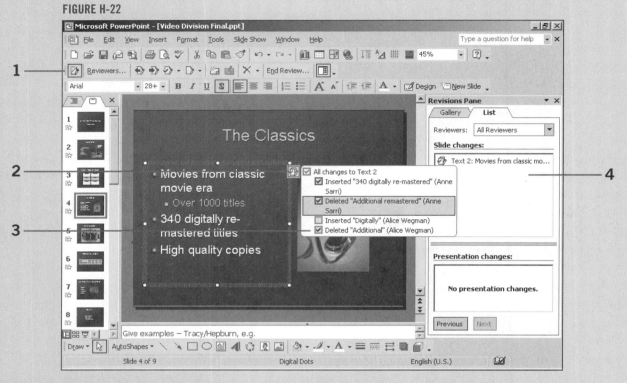

Match each of the terms with the statement that describes its function.

5. A presentation created from selected slides in a presentation
6. An on-screen control button
7. A stand-alone computer that runs a slide show
8. A dialog box that lets you keep track of meeting minutes and action items during a slide show
9. A feature that packages a presentation to take it to another computer

a. Action button
b. Kiosk
c. Custom show
d. Pack and Go Wizard
e. Meeting Minder

Select the best answer from the list of choices.

10. Which method could you use to send a presentation out for review?
    a. Microsoft Outlook
    b. Any 32-bit e-mail program compatible with MAPI
    c. A floppy disk
    d. Any of the above answers
11. Which of the following statements is true about rehearsing your slide timings?
    a. Rehearsing the slides in your presentation gives each slide the same slide timing.
    b. During a rehearsal, you have no way of knowing how long the slide stays on the screen.
    c. If you give your slides random slide timings, you may not have enough time to adequately view each slide.
    d. If you rehearse your presentation, someone on another computer can set the slide timings.

▶ Skills Review

1. Send a presentation for review.
   a. Open the presentation PPT H-4 and save it as **KC Series Proposal**.
   b. Send the presentation to yourself for review.
   c. Open Outlook, then make sure the e-mail message was received, then close Outlook.

2. Combine reviewed presentations.
   a. Compare and merge the presentation PPT H-5 to KC Series Proposal.
   b. Read but do not accept any comments, then accept all other suggested changes from the reviewer.
   c. End the review, then save your changes.

3. Set up a slide show.
   a. Set up a slide show that will be browsed at a kiosk, using slide timings.
   b. Set the slides to appear every three seconds.
   c. Run the slide show all the way through once, then stop it.
   d. Set the slide show to run manually, presented by a speaker.
   e. Put a Forward or Next action button, linked to the next slide, in the lower-right corner of Slide 1.
   f. Copy the action button, then paste it onto all of the slides except the last one.
   g. Move to Slide 2 and place an Action Button: Back or Previous in the lower-left corner. Have it link to the previous slide. Resize the button so it is the same size as the button you created in Step e, and place it at the bottom of the slide, approximately one inch from the left side.
   h. Copy the Back button, then paste it on all of the slides except the first one.
   i. Run through the slide show from Slide 1 using the action buttons you inserted. Move forward and backward through the presentation, watching the animation effects as they appear.
   j. When you have finished viewing the slide show, save your changes.

4. Create a custom show.
   a. Create a custom show called **New Series Format** which includes Slides 3, 4, 5, 6, and 7.
   b. Move the two performance slides above the lecture slides.
   c. View the show from within the Custom Shows dialog box, using the action buttons to move among the slides and waiting for the graphics animations. Press [Esc] to end the slide show after viewing the Financing Lectures slide.
   d. Move to Slide 1, begin the slide show, then, when Slide 1 appears, go to the Custom Show.
   e. View the custom slide show, then return to slide view and save your changes.

5. Use the Meeting Minder.
   a. Run the slide show beginning at Slide 2, then open the Meeting Minder.
   b. Display the Meeting Minutes tab and enter the following items, pressing [Enter] after each one:
   Work with community liaison committee.
   Do research on literary/cultural profile.
   c. Display the Action Items tab.
   d. Enter an action item with the description **1. Speak to Marketing for their ideas**. Assign the task to yourself, then change the Due Date to one week from today's date.
   e. Add the note to the Action Items list, click OK, then click [Esc].
   f. Add a Forward or Next action button to Slide 9, and a Back or Previous action button to Slide 10.
   g. In Slide Show view, go through the presentation until the Action Items slide appears.
   h. Open the Meeting Minder, then export the meeting minutes and action items to Word. (Do not post the action items to Outlook.)
   i. Add your name as the first line of the Word document. Save the Microsoft Word document as **ML Action**, print the document, then exit Word.
   j. Close the Meeting Minder dialog box and end the slide show.

6. **Rehearse slide timings.**
   a. Open the Rehearsal toolbar, set new slide timings, then save your new timings and review them.
   b. Add your name as a footer on notes and handouts, then save your changes.
   c. Print your New Series Format custom show without animations as handouts, 6 slides per page.
   d. Print all the slides in the presentation as handouts, 6 slides per page.

7. **Publish a presentation for the Web.**
   a. Publish the entire KC Series Proposal presentation for the World Wide Web as **kcpropsl**. Make the page title "Kansas City Series Proposal." Do not include speaker notes, and make it viewable using all browsers listed.
   b. Open the HTML file in your browser and navigate through the presentation.
   c. Close your browser, then close the presentation and PowerPoint.

8. **Use the Pack and Go Wizard.**
   a. Create a new folder on your hard drive and name it **PackNGo2**.
   b. Save the presentation in the PackNGo2 folder you created, naming it **KC Series Proposal Packed**.
   c. Open the Pack and Go Wizard and specify that you want to pack the active presentation.
   d. For the destination, navigate to the PackNGo2 folder on your hard drive.
   e. Indicate that you want to Embed TrueType Fonts, then don't include the Viewer for Microsoft Windows.
   f. Close the KC Series Proposal presentation, then delete the PackNGo2 folder.

▶ Independent Challenge 1

You work for Pacific Tours, an international tour company that provides specialty tours to destinations in the Pacific Ocean region. You have to develop presentations that the sales force can use to highlight different tours at conferences and meetings. In this challenge, you will use some of PowerPoint's advanced slide show features such as slide builds and interactive settings to finish the presentation you started. Create at least two additional slides for the basic presentation provided on your Project Disk using your own information. Assume that Pacific Tours has a special (20% off regular price) on tours to Bora Bora and Tahiti during the spring of 2004. Also assume that Pacific Tours best-selling tour packages are to the major islands of the Pacific: the Philippines, Japan, Australia, and New Zealand.

   a. Open the file PPT H-6, then save it as **South Pacific** to the drive and folder where your Project Files are located.
   b. Merge the file PPT H-7 to the South Pacific file. Accept all the suggested changes.
   c. Use the assumptions provided to help you develop additional content for your presentation. Use pictures, movies, and sounds provided on the Office CD-ROM or from other media sources to complete your presentation.
   d. Animate the entire chart object so that it dissolves in and have an appropriate sound effect play as it appears.
   e. Create a custom version of the show that can be shown at a trade show kiosk.
   f. Rehearse slide timings.
   g. Use the Meeting Minder to create action items that could result from your presentation. Export the minutes and action items to Word. Add your name as the first line in the document. Save the document as **SP Action Items**, then print it.
   h. Add your name as a footer on all notes and handouts. Print the final slide presentation and all related documents in the format of your choice.

▶ Independent Challenge 2

You work for WorldWide Travel Services, a travel service company. WorldWide Travel is a subsidiary of Globus Inc. Every year in October, WorldWide Travel needs to report to Globus Inc on the past year's activity. Create your own information using the basic presentation provided in the Project File. Assume the following:
   • WorldWide purchased major routes from Canada to Asia and the Far East from Canadian AirTours.
   • WorldWide's operating expenses run $8 million per quarter.

- Twelve new tour packages to Eastern Europe were created this year. Two of the new tours are The Great Wall Tour and The Trans-Siberian Rail Tour.
- WorldWide hired 35 new employees during the year.

a. Open the file PPT H-8, then save it as **WorldWide**.

b. Use the assumptions provided to help you develop additional content for your presentation. Use pictures, movies, or sounds provided on the Office CD-ROM or from other media sources to complete your presentation.

c. Animate the chart object so it enters from the bottom and have an appropriate sound effect play as it appears.

d. Rehearse slide timings.

e. Create a custom version of your show to run continuously at a conference kiosk, using the timings that you rehearsed.

f. Create a custom version of the show for a specific audience of your choice.

g. Publish the presentation in HTML format, save it as **wrldwide**, then preview it in your browser.

h. Print the final slide presentation and all related documents in the format of your choice.

► Independent Challenge 3

You are the assistant director of operations at Pacific Fleet Inc, an international marine shipping company based in San Francisco, California. Pacific Fleet handles 65% of all the trade between Asia, the Middle East, and the West Coast of the United States. You need to give a quarterly presentation to the company's operations committee which outlines the type and amount of trade Pacific Fleet handled during the previous quarter. Plan and create a 10- to 15-slide presentation that details the type of goods Pacific Fleet carried, how much was carried, which companies (foreign and domestic) purchased goods, which companies (foreign and domestic) sold goods, and how much revenue Pacific Fleet earned. You also need to identify the time it took to deliver the goods to their destinations and the delivery cost. Create your own content, but assume the following:

- Pacific Fleet hauled cars and trucks from Tokyo to San Francisco during the last quarter. A car carrier ship can hold 184 cars or 166 pickup trucks.
- Pacific Fleet hauled large tractor equipment and parts made by Caterpillar Tractor and John Deere Tractor from the United States. One ship went to Brazil and one went to Kuwait.
- Typical household goods carried by Pacific Fleet include electronic equipment, appliances, toys, and furniture.
- The cost of hauling goods by ship is $3,380 per ton. Pacific Fleet owns five cargo ships that can operate simultaneously. All five ships were in operation during the last quarter.
- Pacific Fleet hauled a total of 980,000 tons during the last quarter.

a. Create a new presentation, then save it as **Pacific Report Q1**.

b. Use clip art or shapes to enhance your presentation.

c. Use the assumptions provided to help you develop the content for your presentation. Use movies and sounds provided on the Office CD-ROM or from other media sources to complete your presentation.

d. Use Word and Excel to embed or link objects into your presentation. Use the preceding assumptions to develop related information that would be appropriate for a table or worksheet.

e. Set transitions and animations, and rehearse slide timings.

f. Publish your presentation in HTML format, then preview the new version using your browser.

g. Review the lesson on broadcasting, then broadcast your presentation.

h. Print the final slide presentation and all related documents in the format of your choice.

Independent Challenge 4

You are the sales manager for Music International, an international music distributor of South American music located in Brasilia, Brazil. This year, a large music festival, which showcases different musical groups and styles from all over Central and South America. This year, the festival is being held in Brasilia, and your boss wants you to create a presentation that highlights the variety of musical groups and styles distributed by Music International. There is wide international appeal for South and Central American music, especially in Europe and Asia. The music festival attracts thousands of artists, presenters, recording company representatives, promoters, and fans every year.

a. Open a new presentation, and save it as **Music Pres**.

b. Add your name as the footer on all slides and handouts.

c. Connect to the Internet, then use a search engine to locate Web sites that have information on South American music. You'll need to find the names of at least five South American musical groups. If your search does not produce any results, you might try the following site: www.half.com.

d. Think about what results you want to see, what information you need to create the slide presentation, and how your message should be communicated. Print the pages of the Web sites you use to gather data for your presentation.

e. In order for your presentation to be complete, it must include the following objects: (i) an embedded Word table; (ii) a GIF animation or movie; and (iii) a sound.

f. Title each slide and add main text where appropriate. Create more slides to make the presentation complete.

g. Apply an appropriate slide design. Change the slide design colors as necessary.

h. Create a custom show that focuses on the interest in South American music in Europe and Asia.

i. Spell check the presentation, view the final presentation, save the final version, then print the slides and handouts.

j. Publish the presentation for the Web as **music**, then view the presentation using your Internet browser.

k. Close the presentation, exit PowerPoint, then disconnect from the Internet.

► Visual Workshop

Create the slide shown in Figure H-23. Save the presentation as **Sierra Tours**. The clip art is in the Clip Organizer. Set transitions, animations, and slide timings. Insert forward and backward action buttons for this slide. Create a title slide and a third slide with appropriate information. Print the presentation as handouts, 3 slides per page.

FIGURE H-23

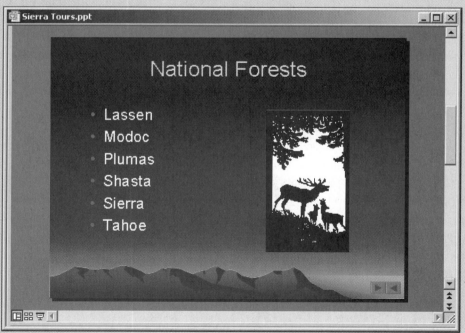

Project Files List

Read the following information carefully!

It is very important to organize and keep track of the files you need for this book.

1. Find out from your instructor the location of the Project Files you need and the location where you will store your files.

- To complete many of the units in this book, you need to use Project Files. Your instructor will either provide you with a copy of the Project Files or ask you to make your own copy.

- If you need to make a copy of the Project Files, you will need to copy a set of files from a file server, stand-alone computer, or the Web to the drive and folder where you will be storing your Project Files.

- Your instructor will tell you which computer, drive letter, and folders contain the files you need, and where you will store your files.

- You can also download the files by going to www.course.com. See the inside back cover of the book for instructions on how to download your files.

2. Copy and organize your Project Files.

Floppy disk users

- If you are using floppy disks to store your Project Files, the list on the following pages shows which files you'll need to copy onto your disk(s).

- Unless noted in the Project Files List, you will need one formatted, high-density disk for each unit. For each unit you are assigned, copy the files listed in the **Project File Supplied column** onto one disk.

- Make sure you label each disk clearly with the unit name (e.g., PowerPoint Unit A).

- When working through the unit, save all your files to this disk.

Users storing files in other locations

- If you are using a zip drive, network folder, hard drive, or other storage device, use the Project Files List to organize your files.

- Create a subfolder for each unit in the location where you are storing your files, and name it according to the unit title (e.g., PowerPoint Unit A).

- For each unit you are assigned, copy the files listed in the **Project File Supplied column** into that unit's folder.

- Store the files you modify or create for each unit in the unit folder.

3. Find and keep track of your Project Files and completed files.

- Use the **Project File Supplied column** to make sure you have the files you need before starting the unit or exercise indicated in the **Unit and Location column**.

- Use the **Student Saves File As column** to find out the filename you use when saving your changes to a Project File that was provided.

- Use the **Student Creates File column** to find out the filename you use when saving a file you create new for the exercise.

Unit and Location	Project File Supplied	Student Saves File As	Student Creates File
PowerPoint Unit A			
Lessons			New Ad Campaign.ppt
Skills Review			Practice.ppt
Independent Challenge 1	(No files provided or created)		
Independent Challenge 2			ArtWorks.ppt
Independent Challenge 3			Sales Trainging.ppt
Independent Challenge 4			PowerPoint Productivity Tips.doc
Visual Workshop			Phase 3A.ppt
PowerPoint Unit B			
Lessons			iMedia1.ppt
Skills Review			RouterJet Testing.ppt
Independent Challenge 1			Harvest Proposal.ppt
Independent Challenge 2			Class 1.ppt
Independent Challenge 3			Training Class.ppt
Independent Challenge 4			Presentation Tips.ppt
Visual Workshop			Sales Project.ppt
PowerPoint Unit C			
Lessons	PPT C-1.ppt	iMedia2.ppt	
	PPT C-2.doc		
Skills Review	PPT C-3.ppt	Cafe Report.ppt	
	PPT C-4.doc		
Independent Challenge 1			Arranging Objects.doc
Independent Challenge 2	PPT C-5.ppt		Title Meeting 9-23-03.ppt
	PPT C-6.doc		
Independent Challenge 3			Software Learning.ppt
Independent Challenge 4			401K Plans.ppt
Visual Workshop			SASLtd.ppt
PowerPoint Unit D			
Lessons	PPT D-1.ppt	IMedia3.ppt	
	PPT D-2.tif		
Skills Review	PPT D-3.ppt	CD Product Report.ppt	
	PPT D-4.bmp		
Independent Challenge 1	PPT D-5.ppt	Fund Seminar.ppt	
Independent Challenge 2			Student Employment.ppt
Independent Challenge 3			JM Design.ppt
Independent Challenge 4	PPT D-6.ppt	Retirement Presentation.ppt	
Visual Workshop			Costs.ppt

Unit and Location	Project File Supplied	Student Saves File As	Student Creates File
PowerPoint Unit E			
Lessons	PPT E-1.ppt	iMedia5.ppt	
	PPT E-2.tif		
			iMedia Template.pot
Skills Review	PPT E-3.ppt	Book Presentation.pot	
			MediaLoft Template.pot
Independent Challenge 1	PPT E-4.ppt	Premier.ppt	
			Catering 1.pot
Independent Challenge 2	PPT E-5.ppt	Splat.ppt	
Independent Challenge 3			Games.ppt
Independent Challenge 4			Bandwidth.ppt
Visual Workshop			New Products.ppt
PowerPoint Unit F			
Lessons	PPT F-1.ppt	iMedia 6.ppt	
	PPT F-2.xls		
Skills Review	PPT F-3.ppt	Royal Publishing.ppt	
	PPT F-4.xls		
Independent Challenge 1	PPT F-5.ppt	Larsen Presentation.ppt	
Independent Challenge 2			Teaching Award.ppt
Independent Challenge 3			LabTech Industries.ppt
	PPT F-6.xls		
Independent Challenge 4			PC Game Review.ppt
Visual Workshop			Central.ppt
PowerPoint Unit G*			
DISK 1 Lessons	PPT G-1.ppt	Video Division.ppt	
	PPT G-2.jpg		
	PPT G-3.xls		
	Video Division Budget.xls		
	PPT G-4.wav		
	PPT G-5.doc		
DISK 2 Skills Review	PPT G-6.ppt	Marketing 2003.ppt	
	PPT G-7.jpg		
	PPT G-8.xls		
	P & L.xls		
	PPT G-9.wav		
	PPT G-10.doc		
DISK 3 Independent Challenge 1	PPT G-11.ppt	Belize Plant.ppt	

Unit and Location	Project File Supplied	Student Saves File As	Student Creates File
DISK 4 Independent Challenge 2	PPT G-12.ppt	Merger.ppt	
	Redding, Inc.ppt		
DISK 5 Independent Challenge 3			Imports.ppt
			Imports RTF.rtf
DISK 6 Independent Challenge 4			EduCorp.ppt
DISK 7 Visual Workshop			New Classes.ppt

*Because the files created in this unit can be very large, depending on the elements you insert into each presentation, you will need to organize the files onto 7 floppy disks if you are completing all the exercises. Copy the files as outlined above, and label each disk clearly (e.g., PowerPoint Unit G Disk 1).

PowerPoint Unit H*

HARD DISK and DISKS 1 and 2

Unit and Location	Project File Supplied	Student Saves File As	Student Creates File
DISK 1 Lessons	PPT H-1.ppt	Video Division Final.ppt	
	PPT H-2.ppt		
	PPT H-3.ppt		
DISK 2			Video Division Action Items.doc
			Videofnl.htm
DISK 1	Video Division Offsite.ppt	Video Division Offsite Packed Version.ppt	
DISK 3 Skills Review	PPT H-4.ppt	KC Series Proposal.ppt	
	PPT H-5.ppt		
			ML Action.doc
			Kcpropsl.htm
			KC Series Proposal Packed Version.ppt
DISK 4 Independent Challenge 1	PPT H-6.ppt	South Pacific.ppt	
	PPT H-7.ppt		
			SP Action Items.doc
Independent Challenge 2	PPT H-8.ppt	WorldWide.ppt	
			Wrldweb.htm
Independent Challenge 3			Pacific Report Q1.ppt
			pacrepq1.htm
Independent Challenge 4			Music Pres.ppt
			musicweb.htm
Visual Workshop			Sierra Tours.ppt

*Because the project files used in the lessons are very large, you will need to have access to a hard disk to complete the lessons. The final solution files for the lessons, except for the HTML file and its associated folder, can then be copied onto a floppy disk (Disk 1). The HTML file and its associated folder also can be copied onto a floppy disk (Disk 2). If you complete all of the exercises, you will need to organize these files onto separate floppy disks as well. Copy the files as outlined above, and label each disk clearly (e.g., PowerPoint Unit H Disk 1).

Microsoft PowerPoint 2002
MOUS Certification Objectives

Below is a list of the Microsoft Office User Specialist program objectives for the Comprehensive PowerPoint 2002 skills, showing where each MOUS objective is covered in the Lessons and Practice. For more information on which Illustrated titles meet MOUS certification, please see the inside cover of this book.

MOUS standardized coding number	Activity	Lesson page where skill is covered	Location in lesson where skill is covered	Practice
PP2002-1	**Creating Presentations**			
PP2002-1-1	Create presentations (manually and using automated tools)	POWERPOINT A-8	Steps 1-9	Skills Review Independent Challenges 2, 3 Visual Workshop
		POWERPOINT B-3	Clues to Use	Skills Review
		POWERPOINT B-4	Steps 1-10	Independent Challenges 1-4
		POWERPOINT B-12	Steps 1-5 QuickTip Step 2	Visual Workshop
		POWERPOINT B-13	Clues to Use	
		POWERPOINT E-16	Steps 4-8	Skills Review Independent Challenge 1
PP2002-1-2	Add slides to and delete slides from presentations	POWERPOINT B-6 POWERPOINT B-8	Steps 1-3 Steps 2-6	Skills Review Independent Challenges 1-4 Visual Workshop
		POWERPOINT C-14	Step 6	Skills Review Independent Challenges 2-4
		POWERPOINT E-16	Step 7	Skills Review Independent Challenge 1
PP2002-1-3	Modify headers and footers in the Slide Master	POWERPOINT B-10	Steps 1-9	Skills Review Independent Challenges 1-4 Visual Workshop
		POWERPOINT E-2	Step 4 and bulleted list	
PP2002-2	**Inserting and Modifying Text**			
PP2002-2-1	Import text from Word	POWERPOINT C-14	Steps 1-3	Skills Review Independent Challenge 2
PP2002-2-2	Insert, format, and modify text	POWERPOINT B-4 POWERPOINT B-6 POWERPOINT B-8 POWERPOINT B-14	Steps 2-9 Steps 4-9 Steps 3-6 Steps 1-4	Skills Review Independent Challenges 1-4 Visual Workshop
		POWERPOINT C-10 POWERPOINT C-12	Steps 2-8 Steps 1-10	Skills Review Independent Challenges 2-4 Visual Workshop
PP2002-3	**Inserting and Modifying Visual Elements**			
PP2002-3-1	Add tables, charts, clip art, and bitmap images to slides	POWERPOINT D-2	Steps 3-5 Clues to Use	Skills Review Independent Challenges 1-4
		POWERPOINT D-4	Steps 1-9 Clues to Use	Visual Workshop
		POWERPOINT D-6 POWERPOINT D-12	Steps 2-3 Steps 1-4	
		POWERPOINT G-2	Step 2-7	Skills Review

MOUS standardized coding number	Activity	Lesson page where skill is covered	Location in lesson where skill is covered	Practice
PP2002-3-2	Customize slide backgrounds	POWERPOINT C-16	Steps 1-8	Skills Review Independent Challenges 2-4
		POWERPOINT D-4	Steps 2-3 Clues to Use	Skills Review Independent Challenge 2
		POWERPOINT E-16	Steps 2-3	
PP2002-3-3	Add OfficeArt elements to slides	POWERPOINT C-4 POWERPOINT C-6	Steps 4-8 Steps 1-9	Skills Review Independent Challenges 2-4 Visual Workshop
		POWERPOINT E-10 POWERPOINT E-12	Steps 1-9 Clues to Use Steps 1-8	Skills Review Independent Challenges 1-4 Visual Workshop
		POWERPOINT F-10 POWERPOINT F-14 POWERPOINT F-16	Steps 6-8 Steps 2-10 Steps 1-8	Skills Review Independent Challenges 1, 3, 4 Visual Workshop
PP2002-3-4	Apply custom formats to tables	POWERPOINT D-12	Steps 5-9	Skills Review Independent Challenges 1, 3, 4
		POWERPOINT G-4	Steps 3-8	Skills Review Independent Challenges 1-4 Visual Workshop
PP2002-4	**Modifying Presentation Formats**			
PP2002-4-1	Apply formats to presentations	POWERPOINT B-6 POWERPOINT B-7 POWERPOINT B-12	Steps 2-3 Table Steps 1-5 QuickTip Step 5	Skills Review Independent Challenge 1-4 Visual Workshop
		POWERPOINT C-4	Steps 2-3	Skills Review Independent Challenges 2, 4
		POWERPOINT D-4 POWERPOINT D-6	Step 3-4 Steps 1-2	Skills Review Independent Challenges 1-4
		POWERPOINT E-2 POWERPOINT E-6 POWERPOINT E-8 POWERPOINT E-13 POWERPOINT E-14	Step 3-4 Clues to Use Steps 2-9 Clues to Use Step 6	Skills Review Independent Challenges 1, 4
PP2002-4-2	Apply animation schemes	POWERPOINT D-18	Steps 1-7	Skills Review Independent Challenges 1-3
		POWERPOINT F-12	Steps 1-9	Skills Review
PP2002-4-3	Apply slide transitions	POWERPOINT D-16	Steps 1-6	Skills Review Independent Challenges 1-3
PP2002-4-4	Customize slide formats	POWERPOINT B-6 POWERPOINT B-7 POWERPOINT B-12	Steps 2-3 Table Steps 1-5	Skills Review Independent Challenges 1-4 Visual Workshop
		POWERPOINT C-4	Steps 2-3	Skills Review Independent Challenges 2, 4
		POWERPOINT D-4 POWERPOINT D-6	Steps 3-4 Steps 1-2	Skills Review Independent Challenges 1-4
		POWERPOINT E-2 POWERPOINT E-4 POWERPOINT E-6 POWERPOINT E-8 POWERPOINT E-13 POWERPOINT E-14	Step 3 Steps 2-7 Clues to Use Steps 2-9 Clues to Use Step 6	Skills Review Independent Challenges 1-4

MOUS standardized coding number	Activity	Lesson page where skill is covered	Location in lesson where skill is covered	Practice
PP2002-4-5	Customize slide templates	POWERPOINT B-12	Steps 1-5 QuickTip Step 2 Clues to Use	Skills Review Independent Challenge 1 Visual Workshop
		POWERPOINT C-16	Steps 1-8	Skills Review Independent Challenge 2-4
		POWERPOINT E-16	Steps 1-8	Skills Review Independent Challenge 1
PP2002-4-6	Manage a Slide Master	POWERPOINT E-2	Steps 3-4 QuickTip Step 4	Independent Challenge 1
PP2002-4-7	Rehearse timing	POWERPOINT H-12	Steps 1-7	Skills Review Independent Challenge 1, 2, 3
PP2002-4-8	Rearrange slides	POWERPOINT B-8 POWERPOINT B-16	Steps 8-9 Steps 2-3	Skills Review Independent Challenges 1-4
		POWERPOINT H-8	Step 4	Skills Review Independent Challenges 1, 2
PP2002-4-9	Modify slide layout	POWERPOINT B-6 POWERPOINT B-7	Steps 2-3 Table	Skills Review Independent Challenges 1-4 Visual Workshop
		POWERPOINT C-4	Steps 2-3	
		POWERPOINT D-4 POWERPOINT D-6	Steps 3-4 Steps 1-2	Skills Review Independent Challenges 1-4
		POWERPOINT E-6 POWERPOINT E-8 POWERPOINT E-14	Clues to Use Steps 2-9 Step 6	Independent Challenges 1, 4
PP2002-4-10	Add links to a presentation	POWERPOINT G-16	Steps 2-6	Skills Review Independent Challenge 2
PP2002-5	**Printing Presentations**			
PP2002-5-1	Preview and print slides, outlines, handouts, and speaker notes	POWERPOINT A-16	Steps 1-7	Skills Review Independent Challenge 2, 3 Visual Workshop
		POWERPOINT B-11 POWERPOINT B-14	Clues to Use Step 5 QuickTip	Skills Review
		POWERPOINT G-16	Step 8	Skills Review
		POWERPOINT H-4	Step 9	Skills Review
PP2002-6	**Working with Data from Other Sources**			
PP2002-6-1	Import Excel charts to slides	POWERPOINT G-6 POWERPOINT G-7 POWERPOINT G-8	Steps 1-9 Clues to Use Steps 1-5 Table Clues to Use	Skills Review Independent Challenges 1-4
PP2002-6-2	Add sound and video to slides	POWERPOINT D-16	Step 5	Independent Challenges 1-3
		POWERPOINT G-12 POWERPOINT G-13 POWERPOINT G-14 POWERPOINT G-15	Steps 2-7 Clues to Use Steps 2-8 Clues to Use	Skills Review Independent Challenges 1, 3
PP2002-6-3	Insert Word tables on slides	POWERPOINT G-4	Steps 3-9	Skills Review Independent Challenges 1-4 Visual Workshop
PP2002-6-4	Export a presentation as an outline	POWERPOINT G-5	Clues to Use	Independent Challenge 3

MOUS standardized coding number	Activity	Lesson page where skill is covered	Location in lesson where skill is covered	Practice
PP2002-7	**Managing and Delivering Presentations**			
PP2002-7-1	Set up slide shows	POWERPOINT H-6 POWERPOINT H-8	Steps 1-10 Steps 1-8	Skills Review Independent Challenges 1, 2, 4
PP2002-7-2	Deliver presentations	POWERPOINT A-10	Steps 6-7	Skills Review Independent Challenge 2
		POWERPOINT B-16	Steps 1-4 Details	Skills Review Independent Challenges 1-4
		POWERPOINT D-14 POWERPOINT D-16 POWERPOINT D-18	Steps 1-9 Steps 1-6 Steps 1-7	Skills Review Independent Challenges 1-4
		POWERPOINT H-6 POWERPOINT H-8 POWERPOINT H-12	Steps 1-10 Steps 1-8 Steps 1-7 QuickTip Step 7	Skills Review Independent Challenges 1-4
PP2002-7-3	Manage files and folders for presentations	POWERPOINT H-18	Steps 1-2	Skills Review
PP2002-7-4	Work with embedded fonts	POWERPOINT A-13	Clues to Use	Skills Review
		POWERPOINT H-18	Steps 1-9	Skills Review
PP2002-7-5	Publish presentations to the Web	POWERPOINT H-14	Steps 1-2 QuickTip Step 1	Skills Review Independent Challenge 2-4
PP2002-7-6	Use Pack and Go	POWERPOINT H-18	Steps 1-9	Skills Review
PP2002-8	**Workgroup Collaboration**			
PP2002-8-1	Set up a review cycle	POWERPOINT H-2	Steps 2-8 Clues to Use	Skills Review
PP2002-8-2	Review presentation comments	POWERPOINT H-4	Steps 1-7	Skills Review Independent Challenge 1
PP2002-8-3	Schedule and deliver presentation broadcasts	POWERPOINT H-16	Details 1-4	Independent Challenge 3
PP2002-8-4	Publish presentations to the Web	POWERPOINT H-14 POWERPOINT H-16	Steps 1-6 QuickTip Step 1 Details 1-2	Skills Review Independent Challenge 2-4

Glossary

Action button An object on a screen that you click to perform an activity, such as advancing to the next slide.

Active cell A selected cell in a Graph datasheet or an Excel worksheet.

Adjustment handle A small yellow diamond that changes the appearance of an object's most prominent feature.

Align To place objects' edges or centers on the same plane.

Animation A graphic such as a .gif (Graphics Interchange Format) file that moves (like a cartoon) when you run the slide show.

Animation scheme A set of predefined visual effects for a slide transition, title text, and bullet text of the slides in a PowerPoint presentation.

Annotate A freehand drawing on the screen made by using the Annotation tool. You can annotate only in Slide Show view.

AutoContent Wizard A wizard that helps you get a presentation started by supplying a sample outline and a design template.

Background The area behind the text and graphics on a slide.

Body text Subpoints or bullet points on a slide under the slide title.

.bmp The abbreviation for the bitmap graphics file format.

Bullet A small graphic symbol, usually a round or square dot, often used to identify items in a list.

Cell The intersection of a column and row in a worksheet, datasheet, or table.

Chart A graphical representation of information from a datasheet or worksheet. Types include 2-D and 3-D column, bar, pie, area, and line charts.

Chart boxes In Organization Chart, the placeholders for text. The placeholders can contain names and positions in an organization's structure.

Clip art Predesigned graphic images you can insert in any document or presentation to enhance its appearance.

Clip Organizer A library of art, pictures, sounds, video clips, and animations that all Office applications share.

Clipboard task pane A task pane that shows the contents of the Office Clipboard; contains options for copying and pasting items to and from the Office Clipboard.

Color scheme The eight coordinated colors that make up a PowerPoint presentation; a color scheme assigns colors for text, lines, objects, and background. You can change the color scheme on any presentation at any time.

Column heading Gray boxes along the top of a datasheet.

Control boxes Gray boxes along the top of a datasheet that contain the row and column identifiers.

Crop To hide part of a picture or object using the Cropping tool.

Data label Information that identifies the data in a column or row in a datasheet.

Data series A column or row in a datasheet that is converted into a graphic and shown as a chart.

Data series marker A graphical representation of a data series, such as a bar or column.

Datasheet The component of a chart that contains the numerical data displayed in a chart.

Design templates Predesigned slide designs with formatting and color schemes that you can apply to an open presentation.

Destination program The program a file or object is embedded into.

Dialog box A window that opens when a program needs more information to carry out a command.

Drawing toolbar A toolbar that contains buttons that let you create lines, shapes, and special effects.

Embedded object An object that is created in one application and copied to another. Embedded objects remain connected to the original program file in which they were created for easy editing.

File format A file type, such as .wmf or .gif.

Folder A subdivision of a disk that works like a filing system to help you organize files.

Formatting toolbar A toolbar that contains buttons for the most frequently used formatting commands.

.gif The abbreviation for the graphics interchange format.

Grid Evenly spaced horizontal and vertical lines that appear on a slide when it is being created but not when it is shown or printed.

Group To combine multiple objects into one object.

Handout master The master view for printing handouts.

Hanging indent The first line of a paragraph begins to the left of all subsequent lines of text.

Hyperlink An object or link (a filename, word, phrase, or graphic) that, when clicked, "jumps to" another location in the current file or opens another PowerPoint presentation, a Word, Excel, or Access file, or an address on the World Wide Web.

Indent levels Text levels in the master text placeholder. Each level is indented a certain amount from the left margin, and you control their placement by dragging indent markers on the ruler.

Indent markers Small triangles on the horizontal ruler that indicate the indent settings for the selected text.

Insertion point A blinking vertical line that indicates where text appears in a text placeholder in PowerPoint.

Kiosk A freestanding computer used to display information, usually in a public area.

Leading The spacing between lines of text in a text object.

Link A "live" connection between a source file and its representation in a target file; when one is updated, the other is updated automatically. Can also refer to a hyperlink (see also *Hyperlink*).

Main text placeholder A reserved box on a slide for the main text points.

Master text placeholder The placeholder on the Slide Master that controls the formatting and placement of the Main text placeholder on each slide. If you modify the Master text placeholder, each Main text placeholder is affected in the entire presentation.

Master title placeholder The placeholder on the Slide Master that controls the formatting and placement of the Title placeholder on each slide. If you modify the Master title placeholder, each Title placeholder is affected in the entire presentation.

Master view A specific view in a presentation that stores information about font styles, text placeholders, and color scheme. There are three master views: Slide Master view, Handout Master view, and Notes Master view.

Menu bar The bar beneath the title bar that contains menus from which you choose program commands.

Microsoft Graph The program that creates a datasheet and chart to graphically depict numerical information.

Movie Live action captured in digital format.

Normal view A presentation view that divides the presentation window into Outline, Slide, and Notes panes.

Notes master The master view for Notes Page view.

Notes Page view A presentation view that displays a reduced image of the current slide above a large text box where you can type notes.

Notes pane The area in Normal view that shows speaker notes for the current slide; also in Notes Page view, the area below the slide image that contains speaker notes.

Object An item you place or draw on a slide that can be manipulated. Objects are drawn lines and shapes, text, clip art, imported pictures, and embedded objects.

Office Assistant An animated character that appears to offer tips, answer questions, and provide access to the program's Help system.

Organization chart A diagram of connected boxes that shows reporting structure in a company or organization.

Outline tab The area in Normal view that displays your presentation text in the form of an outline, without graphics.

Pane A section of the PowerPoint window, such as the Slide or Notes pane.

Photo album A type of presentation that displays photographs.

Placeholder A dashed line box where you place text or objects.

PowerPoint Viewer A special program designed to run a PowerPoint slide show on any compatible computer that does not have PowerPoint installed.

PowerPoint window A window that contains the running PowerPoint application. The PowerPoint window includes the PowerPoint menus, toolbars, and Presentation window.

Presentation software A software program used to organize and present information.

Presentation window The area where you work and view your presentation. You type text and work with objects in the Presentation window.

Publish To save a version of a presentation in HTML format. You can save the HTML files to a disk or save them directly to an intranet or Web server.

Range A continuous group of cells.

Rotate handle A green circular handle at the top of a selected object that you can drag to, rotate the selected object upside-down, sideways, or to any angle in between.

Row heading The gray box containing the row number to the left of the row.

Scale To change the size of a graphic to a specific percentage of its original size.

Scroll To use the scroll bars or arrow keys to display different parts of a document.

Selection box A slanted line border that appears around a text object or placeholder, indicating that it is ready to accept text.

Sizing handles The small circles that appear around a selected object. Dragging a handle resizes the object.

Slide indicator box A small box that appears when you drag the vertical scroll box in Slide and Notes Page view identifying which slide you are on.

Slide layout This determines how all of the elements on a slide are arranged, including text and content placeholders.

Slide Master A template for all slides in a presentation except the title slides. Text and design elements you place on the slide master appear on every slide of the presentation. See also *Title Master, Notes Master,* and *Handout Master*.

Slide-master title pair The title master and the slide master slides in Slide Master view.

Slide pane The area of Normal view that contains the current slide.

Slide Show view A view that shows a presentation as an electronic slide show.

Slide Sorter view A view that displays a thumbnail of all slides in the order in which they appear in your presentation; used to rearrange slides and add special effects.

Slides tab The area in Normal View that displays the slides of your presentation as small thumbnails.

Slide timings The amount of time a slide is visible on the screen during a slide show. You can assign specific slide timings to each slide, or use the PowerPoint Rehearse Timings feature to simulate the amount of time you will need to display each slide in a slide show.

Slide transition The special effect that moves one slide off the screen and the next slide on the screen during a slide show. Each slide can have its own transition effect.

Source program The program in which a file was created.

Standard toolbar The toolbar containing the buttons that perform some of the most frequently used commands.

Status bar The bar at the bottom of the PowerPoint window that contains messages about what you are doing and seeing in PowerPoint, such as the current slide number or a description of a command or button.

Task pane A separate pane available in all the PowerPoint views except Slide Show view that contains sets of hyperlinks for commonly used commands.

Text anchor The location in a text object that determines the location of the text within the placeholder.

Text label A text box you create using the Text Box button, where the text does not automatically wrap inside the box.

Text box Any text you create using the Text Box button. A word processing box and a text label are both examples of a text box.

Text placeholder A box with a dashed-line border and text that you replace with your own text.

Thumbnail A small image of a slide. Thumbnails are found on the Slides tab and in Slide Sorter view.

Timing See *slide timings*.

Title The first line or heading on a slide.

Title bar The bar at the top of the program window that indicates the program name and the name of the current file.

Title Master A template for all title slides in a presentation. Text and design elements you place on the Title Master appear on all slides in the presentation that use the title slide layout.

Title placeholder A box on a slide reserved for the title of a presentation or slide.

Title slide The first slide in your presentation.

Toggle button A button that turns a feature on and off.

View A way of displaying a presentation, such as Normal view, Notes Page view, Slide Sorter view, and Slide Show view.

View buttons The buttons at the bottom of the Outline tab and the Slides tab that you click to switch among views.

Window A rectangular area of the screen where you view and work on the open file.

Wizard An interactive set of dialog boxes that guides you through a task.

Index

Index

Index

templates
    creating, POWERPOINT E-16–17
    design, POWERPOINT B-1,
        POWERPOINT B-12–13
    multiple, applying simultaneously,
        POWERPOINT B-12
    from other presentations, applying,
        POWERPOINT E-5
    from Web servers, POWERPOINT B-3
text
    adjusting text objects, POWERPOINT E-8–9
    arranging, POWERPOINT C-10,
        POWERPOINT C-11
    body, POWERPOINT B-6
    entering. *See* entering text
    formatting. *See* formatting text
    importing form Microsoft Word,
        POWERPOINT C-14–15
    moving, POWERPOINT C-10,
        POWERPOINT E-8, POWERPOINT E-9
    preventing wrapping, POWERPOINT C-10
    replacing, POWERPOINT C-13
text anchor feature, POWERPOINT E-8–9
text boxes, size, POWERPOINT F-12
text placeholders, POWERPOINT B-4,
    POWERPOINT B-5

3-D style(s), POWERPOINT E-12,
    POWERPOINT E-13
3-D Style button, POWERPOINT C-7
thumbnails, POWERPOINT A-6
timing, slide shows, POWERPOINT D-16,
    POWERPOINT D-17
title bar, POWERPOINT A-6, POWERPOINT A-7
title placeholders, POWERPOINT B-4,
    POWERPOINT B-5
toolbar(s), POWERPOINT A-6, POWERPOINT A-7.
    See also specific toolbars
Toolbar Options button, POWERPOINT D-10
transitions, slide shows, POWERPOINT D-16,
    POWERPOINT D-17
transparencies. *See* overhead transparencies

▶ U

Unapply button, POWERPOINT H-4
Undo button, POWERPOINT B-8
undoing changes, POWERPOINT H-4
updating, linked worksheets,
    POWERPOINT G-10–11

▶ V

Venn diagrams, POWERPOINT F-15
view buttons, POWERPOINT A-6,
    POWERPOINT A-7
viewing presentations, POWERPOINT A-10–11
    black and white, POWERPOINT A-17
    grayscale, POWERPOINT A-17
    presentation broadcasts, POWERPOINT H-16
voice narrations
    charts, POWERPOINT F-13
    slide shows, POWERPOINT H-8

▶ W

Web
    hosting online meetings, POWERPOINT H-15
    publishing presentations for,
        POWERPOINT H-14–15
Web presentations, POWERPOINT A-3
Web servers, templates, POWERPOINT B-3
Word tables, inserting in presentations,
    POWERPOINT G-4–5

▶ X

XY charts, POWERPOINT D-7